Marvin Richardson Vincent

The Covenant of Peace

Marvin Richardson Vincent

The Covenant of Peace

ISBN/EAN: 9783337225674

Printed in Europe, USA, Canada, Australia, Japan

Cover: Foto ©Lupo / pixelio.de

More available books at **www.hansebooks.com**

THE
COVENANT OF PEACE.

BY

MARVIN R. VINCENT, D.D.,

Author of
"GATES INTO THE PSALM COUNTRY," ETC.

EDWARD O. JENKINS' SONS,
PRINTERS AND STEREOTYPERS,
20 *North William Street, New York.*

INTRODUCTORY.

THIS volume, which is published by special request, is addressed principally to Christian believers. It does not discuss disputed questions in theology, or issues between science and religion, nor is it an attempt to re-state the truths of the Gospel in the terms of modern science. It endeavors to deal, in a direct and practical fashion, with certain hard, painful, and puzzling phases of Christian experience, and with certain mischievous mistakes in popular Christian conceptions of duty and of privilege. It is for the tempted, the unsuccessful, the discouraged, and the weary: for souls fighting for life and victory under the burden of infirmity and the sting of sorrow. The sermons are the outgrowth of a pastor's experience. They are printed substantially as they were delivered, without any attempt to eliminate their colloquialisms, or to convert them into finished specimens of sermon-rhetoric.

CONTENTS.

	PAGE
I.—The Mountains and God's Kindness,	1
II.—The Seed of Light,	18
III.—The Promise of Godliness for the Present Life,	33
IV.—From Beyond Jordan,	50
V.—Creating and Carrying,	66
VI.—The Refuge from Talk,	81
VII.—Strength in Weakness,	96
VIII.—Between Sowing and Harvest,	111
IX.—The Eternal Guide,	126
X.—Knowing by Doing,	143
XI.—God Greater than our Heart,	160
XII.—Sonship the Foreshadowing of Heaven,	175
XIII.—The God of the Unsuccessful,	191
XIV.—Maiming and Life,	206
XV.—Detaching,	219
XVI.—The Kinghood of Patience,	234
XVII.—Jehovah Ropheka,	252
XVIII.—Self-Winning,	269
XIX.—The Cankered Years,	285
XX.—The Goodness of God in the Land of the Living,	301

I.

THE MOUNTAINS AND GOD'S KINDNESS.

> *"For the mountains shall depart, and the hills be removed, but my kindness shall not depart from thee, neither shall the covenant of my peace be removed, saith the Lord that hath mercy on thee."*
> —ISA. liv. 10.

GOD in Scripture frequently uses nature to illustrate grace. What is still more remarkable, He uses often the sterner aspects of nature, those with which power and terror are associated, to illustrate or to emphasize His tenderness and love toward His children. The Hebrews, for instance, did not like the sea. You will find the sea in their writings employed as an emblem of terror and distress. Yet we hear the Psalmist saying, "The sea is His and He made it. O come, let us worship and bow down; we are the people of His pasture and the sheep of His hand. Let us come before His presence with thanksgiving." The forty-second Psalm is a psalm of distress and longing. It is set in the key of a stormy ocean. In it is heard the sound of the floods. "Deep calleth unto deep at the noise of Thy waterspouts. All Thy waves and Thy billows are gone over me." But out of the noise of the waves comes a voice of hope and cheerful trust. "Yet the Lord will command His loving-kindness in the daytime, and in the night His song shall be with me, and my prayer unto the God of my life. Hope thou in God. I shall yet praise Him who is the health of my countenance and my God."

The mountains are symbols of this sterner character. They suggest power and fixedness and duration, rather than love and gentleness. When associated with God, they are used to suggest His might and His eternity. They are called "the everlasting hills." To shake them implies more than human power. By His strength God "setteth fast the mountains, being girded with power." When He appears in His majesty, "the perpetual hills do bow." Yet the mountains are used, as in this text, to set forth to us the loving-kindness of God. What we should naturally suppose would repel, or at least awe us into silence and helplessness, becomes, in the hands of inspiration, full of attraction, invitation, and rest. The mountains bring peace.

And this association of ideas is neither forced nor arbitrary. The apparent contradiction, as we go deeper down, resolves itself into a beautiful harmony of thought. For weakness naturally betakes itself, not to beauty, but to power. Helplessness seeks the shadow of true majesty. True spiritual discernment detects the greatest tenderness in real strength. Hence it was most deeply natural for the pilgrim in the desert, as the night drew on and the sense of its terrors and mysterious dangers forced itself upon his mind, to say, "I will lift up mine eyes unto the hills. Whence should my help come?" God is a God of might. He made heaven and earth; but for that very reason my help cometh from Him.

He that keepeth me will not slumber. He shall preserve my going out and my coming in.

In the light of these general truths we are to read our text to-day. This chapter of the prophet Isaiah is full of comfort and hope. Its burden is consolation to the afflicted people of God; and here, therefore, the mountains and the hills are introduced, this time by way of contrast with the immutability of divine love and kindness. These vast masses which divine power has heaved up and set fast, which symbolize to human minds eternal power and stability, which seem to stand fast forever —these great bulks of nature are mutable and transitory compared with the eternal love and tenderness of Jehovah. In days of calamity, when the enemy sweeps over the plains and lays waste the homes of men, when the torrents break their banks and overflow the pleasant corn-lands, men flee to the mountains as to a friendly and inaccessible shelter. But even the mountains are not eternal. The mountains shall depart, and the hills be removed; but my kindness is beyond the reach of all convulsion or change. "My kindness shall not depart from thee, neither shall the covenant of my peace be removed." Thus saith the Lord that setteth fast the mountains; at whose touch they melt. He is the Lord that hath mercy on thee.

Possibly the prophet was not embodying a mere fancy when he uttered this comparison. Job spoke of a natural fact when he said, "Surely the mountain, falling, cometh to naught, and the rock is removed out of his place." In volcanic regions such as that in which Job lived, a mountain, undermined by subterraneous fires, often falls in and crumbles away, and the earthquake shakes and shatters the solid rocks. The simple doctrine of our text, then, is that God's kindness is like Himself, immutable. That however nature may change and decay, as it does change and decay, though the world itself pass away, as it does pass away, God's kindness to His children is above all these changes and abides forever.

Now as I have said, this is not a surface truth; and that is the reason why it is urged and emphasized in so many forms in Scripture. Naturally I think we tend to reason the other way, and to ascribe to nature a permanency which we see, or think we see, is denied to man. Do we not often find ourselves musing after this fashion, as we stand in the presence of nature's vastness: "That ocean! I shall be gone soon, and the places which know me so well will forget me, but those tides will continue to flow; those surges will break on the cliffs, those billows will bear the stately ships, long after I shall have gone. Those mountains will lift themselves toward heaven, those streams will continue to flow, those trees will stretch out their arms, and the spring shall clothe them with green and the autumn with purple and gold, when I shall have returned to dust. That sun will shine still: those stars will continue to look down from their serene heights: the earth will be running its round, and seed-time and harvest coming at their appointed seasons, when the last trace of this which now loves and hopes and strives shall have vanished." Truly it seems as if it is the natural and material that abides: as though God's care over one were short-lived. I live fourscore years or less. That mountain-peak has stood in its majesty from the day the morning stars sang together. My work is fragmentary and short-lived: but those rocky buttresses which nature piles up, those growths which strike their branching roots out and down into the bosom of the earth, those abysses filled with the briny floods—they abide. What a trifle I am beside a single Alpine peak, the lowest of them. A single rock from that mass, a mere speck compared with its total bulk, rolls down and crushes me out of life in an instant. A mass of snow comes down and I disappear forever. I, with mind and will and thought, I who can plan and hope and aspire, I am worse than helpless in the grasp of that brute bulk of water, pressed on by the power of gravity to leap over yonder precipice and break in idle foam on the rocks below.

That is the way our thought shapes itself ofttimes. It is not so unreasonable either at the first glance. It looks as though God cared more for matter than for spirit.

And I may pause to say here that that kind of reasoning (if it be reasoning) is legitimate, I fear conclusive, if the theories of modern materialism are true which go to identify spirit with matter, and soul with body. If I am of one piece with the mountains and trees, it is humiliating enough to know that I do not last as long as they do: that God has far less care for perpetuating my thinking personality than He has for perpetuating a heap of rocky layers or a huge mass of waters. If that position is the true one, then I must adjust the demands and emergencies of a nature capable of desire and hope and suffering to these rigid lines of matter as best I can. I have no hope beyond my brief connection with the economy of sea and mountain and forest. It is a little matter that I am to live in my influence, as the philosophers of this school tell me. How much does my influence count on beings who are going down to the dust like myself and of whom the dust is the end? It may make their brief day perhaps a little brighter or happier, but truly that hardly seems worth all the effort and struggle and repression which go to build up character, if annihilation is the end of the race. At any rate that does not satisfy or comfort me. Somehow I am so made that an immortality (if it be an immortality) of influence, impersonal influence, does not satisfy me. Something in me craves personal life prolonged and widened. I want eternity. Perhaps it is a presumptuous and conceited craving. Be it so. I only know it is there; and with Augustine I say, "My soul is restless until it repose in God."

Now you see that Scripture leads us away from all such musings and all such conclusions as those: and it does so, moreover, with a clear recognition, and a clear showing of all the facts in the case. For nowhere more plainly and emphatically than in Scripture is the frailty and the transitoriness of man set forth. Look at the ninetieth Psalm. There are the mountains again, those savage, purple cliffs on which Moses gazed, and turned from them to see a generation dying in the wilderness. They are thrown into contrast with the eternity of God on the one hand, but on the other hand with the mortality of man. "Thou turnest man to destruction, and sayest, 'Return, ye children of men.' Thou carriest them away as with a flood: they are as a sleep in the morning: they are like grass which groweth up and perisheth in a day. The days of our years are soon cut off and we fly away." So the apostle takes up the same theme. "What is your life? It is even as a vapor." And the prophet answers out of the past: "All flesh is grass, and all the goodliness thereof is as the flower of the field." You can easily multiply these utterances of Scripture.

But, on the other hand, in full view of this fact, nothing is so emphatic as Scripture in setting forth the eternal hope and rich promise which attaches to man, and the peculiar and high place which he holds in the eye of God. This Bible centres in him. It is made for him with its wealth of instruction and promise and consolation. There is an eye from heaven ever directed upon him; a hand stretched forth from heaven to guide and to uphold him. God takes upon Himself the conduct of His child's life. He leaves to no one inferior to Himself the regulation of his ways. "The steps of a good man are ordered of the Lord. Though he fall he shall not be utterly cast down, for the Lord upholdeth him with His hand." Exposed to sin and its seductions and consequences, God interposes in his behalf with a gigantic scheme of redemption. From the very beginning God is at work to save him and to reconcile him to Himself. For him God becomes manifest in the flesh. For him that wondrous, perfect life of the divine Son puts itself alongside of his littleness, his sin, his sorrow. Christ is the incarnation of the truth that manhood means an essential and eternal connection with God. For him are all the history and all the utterances of prophets and kings. Through his feeble instrumentality God has been pleased to work out great and abiding results. God has honored him with high commissions and vindicated him with decisive victories, and made him the herald of messages pregnant with life and hope to his kind. What privileges He has bestowed upon him: to know God, to love God, to commune with God, to be filled with His fulness, to enjoy His fellowship. For him is the promise of immortality; of seeing God as He is; of being changed into God's image; of enjoying an eternity of divine fellowship and divine ministry. The facts of human frailty and of the brevity of human life, are offset with the promise of eternal life. Death is confronted with resurrection. The world does indeed pass away, "but he that doeth the will of God abideth forever." In the light of these facts, is not the kindness of God shown to be stronger and more enduring than the hills? Does not the spirit of man, after all, appear to be, in His eyes, of more account than matter? It is only the world that passeth away. God's son and heir does not pass away. He is longer-lived than the hills. He serves a higher purpose: he is the subject of a larger divine intent: he has a higher destiny.

But in this part of the text God's eternal kindness is shown by comparison and contrast. In the second part of the text it is stated directly and absolutely, and in legal terms. It is put as a matter of agreement. God binds Himself to be eternally kind to His children, by a covenant of peace. This covenant is to stand forever. "It shall not totter" (to translate literally). My covenant of peace shall not be removed. It is a wonderful thought. Jehovah enters into a compact of eternal loving-kindness. Let us look at some sides of it.

In the first place, there is something very suggestive in that word "kindness." Kindness is originally that which is felt and shown to one's kind or kin. Kind is *kinned;* so that, according to the primitive signification of the word, kindness grows out of natural relationship. And this is really the basis of God's kindness. Men are His children: and the relation of parent and child implies kindness. And so Adam, when he came fresh from the hand of God, was compassed about with the divine kindness. Blessings poured upon him from the heavens. God came down and walked and communed with him in the paradise which He had made for him. There was an agreement or covenant implied in that relation, just as there is in the filial and parental relation everywhere: an agreement to the effect that the son, by receiving and enjoying his father's gifts, is bound to loyalty and obedience: but as long as the son lives in loyalty and love, the legal aspect of the relation falls into the background. When man, by disobedience, forfeited his privileges as a son of God, violated the sacredness of the original filial relation, God's kindness did not depart from him. He did not cease to be a son, though he was an erring and straying son. God was, from the very first, untiring in His effort to win him back to allegiance and love. The fact that he was a son of God and made in God's image was never lost out of sight in the divine counsels. Sin did not drive God out of the world. It set Him working in the world (if we may reverently cast the thought into this form) under new manifestations. It inaugurated the economy of reconciliation. And thus it brought into prominence necessarily the legal aspect of the relation between God and man; for wherever there is sin, there law asserts itself. And so from the sweet, natural, harmonious intercourse of God and man, where the kindness of fatherly love was met by filial love and obedience, we pass into an economy of invitations, promises, entreaties, covenants: we feel the strain of the chords at which man is obstinately pulling in the endeavor to break away from God, and the tension from God's side as He endeavors to hold him and to draw him back to Himself. Man has learned to distrust God's kindness. Hence God asserts it. Man has forgotten his obligations. God emphasizes them in formal laws. And yet, behind all law and ordinances, is felt the deep, strong pulsation of divine love and fatherly yearning, as if God were saying to the recreant and rebellious race, "Only see here! See what I am ready to do for you! See what power I have to enrich and bless you! See how I love you! I yearn to be kind to you. My love is like a great tide that chafes against its banks and struggles to break out of the dikes which your folly and rebellion have built. Why will you not let me be kind to you? Why will you not put yourselves where I can let loose upon you all the pent-up love and yearning of my heart?" Such is the feeling which breaks out here and there over the whole surface of the Old Testament, as when it is said, " In His love and pity He redeemed them and bare and carried them all the days of old. Forty years long was I grieved with this generation. Oh, that there were such a heart in them that they would hear me and keep my commandments. How shall I give thee up, Ephraim?"

Man's rebellion and alienation from God introduces us to an economy of adjustment. In the natural, healthful relation between father and son we hear little or nothing about terms of agreement. The terms are all included in the fact of mutual love. When the relation is disturbed, then covenants and agreements and promises come to the front. It is as if God said, "You have put yourselves off the higher ground of sonship; I will come down and meet you on the lower ground. I will agree and covenant to be kind to you." And so you will observe how this matter of stipulation with men on God's part keeps coming out in the Bible history of redemption. It is in the form of a promise to the first guilty pair that the seed of the woman shall bruise the serpent's head. It is a covenant with Abraham ratified by human symbols, as the burning lamp and smoking furnace pass between the pieces of the parted victim. It is a promise to Jacob in the vision at Bethel, and a covenant of Jacob with God, when, in his first waking moments, he sets up as a pillar the stone on which his head has rested, and pouring oil upon it, enters into solemn agreement with the Most High. Study the terms in which, again and again, God pledges Himself to bless and foster the people of Israel. Read what He says by the mouth of His prophet, Jeremiah: "Behold, the days come, saith the Lord, that I will make a new covenant with the house of Judah: not according to the covenant that I made with their fathers; but this shall be the covenant that I will make with the house of Israel: After those days, saith the Lord, I will put my law in their inward parts, and write it in their hearts; and will be their God, and they shall be my people. And they shall teach no more every man his neighbor, and every man his brother, saying, Know the Lord: for they shall all know me, from the least of them unto the greatest of them, saith the Lord: for I will forgive their iniquity, and I will remember their sin no more."

And then pass on to that memorable night in the upper chamber at Jerusalem, and see the Son of God as He lifts the cup in His hands, so soon to be pierced in ratification of His pledge, and says, "Drink ye all of this, for this is my blood of the new covenant which is shed for you and for many for the remission of sins."

Note, too, the phrase, "covenant of peace." Peace! It is the word which defines and embodies the kindness of God in Jesus Christ. The agreement which God makes with man is, in the first place, that man shall be at peace with Him: that alienation shall cease: that the man shall come back from his attitude of an enemy into his normal attitude as a son of God: that he shall be no more a stranger, but a fellow-citizen with God's own: no more a prodigal in a far country, but a son at home in his Father's house: no more working against God, but enlisted and working with Him in the interests of His eternal kingdom: having fellowship with the Father and with His Son, Jesus Christ.

Then, further, growing out of this right attitude of man toward his Father God, is God's agreement to give him peace in the sense of restfulness. "Come unto me," says Christ, "and I will give you rest." That is more than a promise, it is a covenant. There are two parties and two mutual obligations. The weary and the sin-burdened are to come to Christ—that is their part. Christ on His part stands pledged to give rest unto their souls: rest in the eternal part of their being; rest at the centre of life which touches God and eternity.

And those who have truly entered into this covenant, need no words of mine to prove to them that it is a covenant which carries with it the loving-kindness of God. Take it as related to sin. You have known what sin is. You have known its seductions and have felt its lash. You have known what it was to go seeking rest and finding none, and finally to go, bowed and burdened, covered with shame and anguish, to the feet of your crucified Lord, confessing your sin and pleading for mercy. And you can answer for it to-day that you met there nothing but kindness. Every other feeling on the part of your justly-offended Lord was swallowed up in His joy at your return. You have found what was in the heart of Christ when He pictured the prodigal's return and the father's joy, and the tumult of delight which shook the whole household. Yes, poor, sinful, contrite soul, when you came to the cross, you were met, not with heaven's thunder of indignation, but with heaven's rapturous joy over one sinner that had repented.

Since that time you have not been faultless. Your life as a disciple has been marked by numerous lapses. It has developed both infirmity and transgression. I ask you this morning if, in the face of this fact, God's kindness has been removed? Has it ever wavered? Have you not always found at His mercy-seat compassion for your weakness; a helping hand in your struggle after reformation and purity; pardon for your lapses; a healing touch upon your bruises and scars; a word of warning and of caution, but also a tender whisper—"Go into peace"?

Or trouble. You know something of life, and therefore you know what trouble is. You have been anxious and care-worn; sore beset, and worried, as with myriad stings. And yet can you say that you have not been helped through the worst; that you have not had strength descend upon you for the hardest push; that, even when your gloomiest anticipations were more than realized, you have not had power given you to do and to bear; that even in the straitest place there has not been opened for you a way out? Has the kindness of God been removed from you in your loneliness? Has it ever failed to put another and a stronger prop in the place of the broken reed on which you had leaned? And yet, perhaps, in the face of all this, you have sometimes suffered trouble to be eating out your heart when you might have cast all your care on God. Perhaps you have fretted and been anxious when you might have been at rest in the assurance of God's immutable kindness. If so, resolve that with God's help, you will gather up your faith, and with all your hearts believe that, though the mountains depart and the hills be removed, His loving-kindness shall not depart from you, neither shall the covenant of His peace be removed. Often we have sung together the old hymn, which better than any other I know, gathers up this train of thought:

> " Awake, my soul, to joyful lays,
>   And sing the great Redeemer's praise;
>   He justly claims a song from me:
>   His loving-kindness, oh, how free!
>
> " He saw me ruined in the fall,
>   Yet loved me, notwithstanding all;
>   He saved me from my lost estate:
>   His loving-kindness, oh, how great!
>
> " Though numerous hosts of mighty foes,
>   Though earth and hell my way oppose,
>   He safely leads my soul along:
>   His loving-kindness, oh, how strong!
>
> " When trouble, like a gloomy cloud,
>   Has gathered thick and thundered loud,

He near my soul has always stood:
His loving-kindness, oh, how good!"

It shall not be removed. No, the covenant of God's peace with His people is an everlasting covenant. Neither life, nor death, nor angels, nor principalities, nor powers, nor things present, nor things to come, nor height, nor depth, nor any other creature, shall be able to separate them from the love of God which is in Christ Jesus, the Mediator of the new covenant. His loving-kindness reaches into the future. The covenant is a covenant of promise. Hear how beautifully the prophet in the context puts this promise under the figure of a lovely palace which shall be the dwelling-place of God's own: "O, thou afflicted, tossed with tempest, and not comforted; behold, I will lay thy stones with fair colors, and lay thy foundations with sapphires. And I will make thy windows of agates, and thy gates of carbuncles, and all thy borders of pleasant stones."

So we look to the mountains, their foundations laid of old, those everlasting hills which lifted themselves in the beginning of time, with their vast bastions, and their steep battlements, their icy pinnacles, their lonely snowfields,—those giant forms which seem to defy the touch of time—we look to them only to look away to something more enduring, the loving-kindness of God. "They shall perish, but Thou shalt endure. Yea, all of them shall wax old as a garment. As a vesture shalt Thou roll them up and they shall be changed: but Thou art the same. Thy years shall have no end." And out of their clefts, from behind the ramparts of their power, comes a voice: "The mountains shall depart, and the hills be removed, but my kindness shall not depart from thee, neither shall the covenant of my peace be removed, saith the Lord that hath mercy on thee."

II.

THE SEED OF LIGHT.

"Light is sown for the righteous, and gladness for the upright in heart."—PSALM xcvii. 11.

LIGHT and gladness. It is natural to desire them, and God does not crucify nature. He only trains and corrects it. This text tells us that light and gladness are for the upright, and the next verse bids the righteous rejoice. An eagle desires the air, and a fish the water. Is it strange? A child of God is a child of light, begotten of Him who is light and in whom is no darkness at all. If he longs for the light, is that strange? The apostle John tells us that we lie if we say we have fellowship with Him and walk in darkness; and the wise man says that the hope of the righteous shall be gladness.

But what about the peculiar way in which this promise of light and gladness is put? Light and gladness are *sown*. A startling figure that, and a grand one too. God as a sower, scattering seeds of light. The statement is: God gives light to His children as seed. What does that mean?

If you will think for a moment, you will see that the truth is not out of harmony with much that you already know in your Bibles. You must have noticed how often our Lord uses the figure of seed, and the reason is not very far to find. The figure simply recognizes the great law of growth which everything in the universe, from a grass-blade to the spiritual kingdom of God on earth, obeys. Nothing comes into life full-grown. The tree and the grain grow up from seed. The man is a babe first. The kingdom of Heaven is like a mustard-seed. It becomes a great tree, but not at a leap. So of the fruits of the spirit in men. Knowledge, faith, love, joy, grow through successive stages, like the blade, the ear, and the full corn.

Are we then to expect that light and gladness will come full-grown into Christian experience, any more than that the sun, at his rising, will shine with noonday splendor? Are we not told that "the path of the just shineth more and more unto the perfect day"? There are, I know, childish views of Christian experience which find a sympathetic chord struck in the hypochondriac poet's verse—

"Where is the blessedness I knew, when first I saw the Lord?"

There are those who assume that Christian gladness reaches its height in the first contact with Christ; not seeming to understand that joy, like all fruits of the spirit, obeys the law of growth, and that an initial Christian experience does not put its subject on a level with a matured one in respect of joy, any more than it does in respect of knowledge. There is a gladness belonging to a ripened Christian which a new disciple can neither appreciate nor feel. The strong man revels in the light which the infant eyes cannot bear.

God, therefore, gives light and gladness to His children just as He does other things, germinally, in the seed form; not all at once, in floods, but with a large reserve into which the man is to work his way. As life moves toward God, it unfolds this seed and lets out more and more light, until eternity develops the full harvest of light.

With this figure of sowing seed are naturally associated two thoughts — hiding and diffusion: and the two inevitably run together, because, in the natural process, hiding is with a view to diffusion. The process of growth is distributive, not only in the final scattering of the seed, but in that, in the unfolding of the seed, something beautiful and promising is developed at every successive stage, in the blade and in the ear, no less than in the full corn.

If then light and gladness are to be looked for in Christian life, it is important to remember that they are growths, and that, as such, they carry with them a certain amount of concealment and delay. Let us consider some illustrations of this.

God hides away light and gladness in certain things which, for the time, give no hint of what is within, even as the rough acorn gives no visible promise of the grandeur and leafage of the oak. And here be very careful to note that when God gives us these seeds, He expects us to look for our light in them. None the less, because the acorn is hard and rough, must you look for your oak in your acorn. You will not find it by turning away to something smoother and softer. One of the very first things to which God introduces us on our entrance into His kingdom is duty. God knows that in all duty there is light which faithful doing will bring out. Often, however, He shows us very little or none of the light and promise, but only the dark furrows of duty in which the light is sown: and He says to us, "Your work lies up and down along those furrows, to keep them free from weeds, to drive away the birds, to keep the earth loose, and to watch and wait until the light shall appear." I know that I am talking to a great many men and women who have had and are having that very experience—that their life lies in contact with something which must be done, which they do not like to do, which has no hint of light or gladness in it. Only it is a duty, plain and clear. God puts this text into your hand and points to the furrows lying so darkly there, and says, "Your light is sown there. Believe it on my word. You will not find it by leaving these dark furrows for greener fields. If it spring up for you at all, it will spring up here. I have sown light for you here, and my seed always means harvest." For often we are tempted to think that our light will come in evading such duty: that God will give us light by removing the hardness. It is not so. We must get through the hard shell. The light lies under it. We must watch and tend the hopeless-looking furrow. The light lies in it.

I suppose that Abraham did not see much light when he was going up Moriah to offer Isaac. Certainly he did not see it in the heart of that dreadful duty; and yet he found it at the very altar, and in the very act of sacrifice: new and stronger light on God's faithfulness; light on the value and power and honor of faith; light in the praise and approval of God; light thrown backward from the Light of the world in the far-off future; and so Jesus himself tells us how gladness was sown for the upright in heart. "Your father Abraham rejoiced to see my day, and he saw it and was glad." God's plough went straight through Moses' peaceful life of culture and power in Egypt, and drew a deep dark furrow round by Horeb to Pisgah. There was frequent hiding of the light along the lines of that weary journey to Canaan, but it broke out now and then. Moses saw it when he stood in the cleft of the rock on Sinai, where all God's goodness passed before him, and where his human eye could not bear the full light of God's self-revealing; and it must have flooded his soul as he stood on the height from which his spirit went up to God, and looked over to the sunny corn-lands and rich verdure of the inheritance promised to his race. What a dark day that was for Israel when the law was given on Sinai. What a day of terror as the mountain smoked like a furnace, and the Lord came down in fire and spake with a voice which froze their hearts with fear. What a law was that, with its stern "thou shalt and thou shalt not." And yet what treasures of light were hidden in that law. They began to find out ere long, that walking on those lines meant peace and victory and security. There arose one in Israel, in later days, who could compare that law to the going forth of the sun in the heavens, and could say, "The statutes of the Lord are right, rejoicing the heart; the commandment of the Lord is pure, enlightening the eyes. The entrance of Thy words giveth light." And when Jesus, the Light of the world, came, and touched those old, rigid lines of law, came not to destroy but to fulfil, how they bloomed and eared into a very harvest of light which cheers and fosters our Christian homes and our Christian society to-day.

The same truth appears in the providences of God. They are full of light, but it is sown light. It is a strange fact of nature how much beauty God stores away in underground caverns where the walls are gemmed and the great stalactites hang, only awaiting the torch to fill the darkness with points of light and glories of color. We understand well enough how God hides the diamond and the topaz in the dark and overlays them with hard and coarse crusts; how He shuts up the crystal in the heart of the rough geode; and we doubt not that human skill and labor can bring them forth from their wrappings and make them blaze in the coronets of kings. Why will we limit these facts to nature merely, to God's economy on its lower side, and not see that God carries up the same facts to a higher level, and applies the same method in His spiritual economy, and conceals light and joy beneath the hard incrustations of sorrow and pain? So it is an equally notable fact that God continually leads His children into dark places to seek for light. One of the hardest lessons we ever learn is to undertake that search cheerfully and believingly;

for, as I have already said, we must not seek light somewhere else than in the providence, thinking that, if we can only get the providence out of the way, the light will shine in. We learn after awhile that it is possible to see in the dark. When we are taken out of the full sunshine into some dark catacomb, all is perfect blackness for awhile; but the eye adapts itself to the new conditions after a time. It is somewhat thus when God takes us out of the glare of worldly prosperity and joy, and shuts us up within the confines of a dark providence. We come by and by to see in the dark. The spiritual pupil adapts itself to the new state of things, and we see that the dark is peopled, and not with unkind faces. Human nature sees no light in a grave. Those first disciples of Christ saw none as they entered the door of Joseph's tomb and laid down the body of their beloved Master and friend. Peter and John and Mary had another story to tell on the third morning after. One of them at least had seen angels of light there. To-day that tomb is the central point of light for the world. We have learned that the Light of the world was sown, even as a corn of wheat, that it might bring forth much fruit. That fact goes with every train of Christian mourners to the grave's mouth, infusing the assurance that what is sown in dishonor shall be raised in glory. Not only so. The grave not unfrequently hides light for us—precious lessons which come out in the experience and the discipline of later years. All of you remember the story so graphically told by the Scottish poet, of the wizard buried in the abbey aisles with a lamp upon his breast;

and how, when the stone was removed after many years, the light from that lamp blazed up and lighted the tomb and the magic volume in the dead hand. So it is that sometimes we go back after many days to the grave where we buried as we thought all the gladness and light of our lives, to find in the hand of the dead a lamp and a lesson-book. A hard providence of God is a seed with a rough and prickly husk, but it is a seed of light, sown by Him who commanded the light to shine out of darkness, and who will shine in His people's hearts to give the light of the glory of God in the face of Jesus Christ.

The truth applies equally to the process of winning Christian knowledge and faith. We are like children at school. Study and thought and books are full of light to you now; but when you were a child, light came to you under cover of duty, by way of rules and formulas; through labor when you saw more gladness in sport; through strict discipline, when you thought that complete freedom would be perfect gladness. Would it be strange if God should deal with you in similar wise in acquiring the knowledge of His truth and will? The idea that all learning must be made pleasant, bids fair to be one of the heresies of modern education. At any rate that is not God's theory of education. He is not a harsh master, far from it; but He does not make Christian training easy. He introduces His pupils to the rest and the restfulness of faith, but none the less He makes them work out their salvation. He will not let us win the fruits of experience too easily nor be carried comfortably into the harvest-fields of light simply to enjoy what others have sown. A good many of the sparks which lighten and warm us we have to strike out. A good deal of our gladness we have to wait for along the furrows of duty and sacrifice. A good many of the problems of faith which, once solved, bring us deep peace, and yield us most effective implements in Christian work and warfare, have to be worked out till the unknown quantity is found. There are some men to whom conviction, or at least satisfaction, seems to come by some shorter process: to whom doubt never seems to be a serious obstacle: but there are others whose religious history, for a long way at least, appears to be a continuous mining and tunnelling; who get their light mostly through openings which they blast out for themselves through the heart of obstinate doubts. I have little fear for a man who sets himself honestly to face and penetrate such obstacles. He will work his way to light, though he seem a heretic for the time being. There are things which a true man would like to believe, and which it is a sorrow for him not to be convinced of, but he is a happier man after all, and gets more light on his way than the one who is afraid of his doubts, and slips past them only to be haunted by the perpetual dread that they are lurking somewhere in the rear. The man who marches squarely up to a great doubt and joins battle with it, at least knows the size and weight of his adversary. The thing which he confronts is at least no phantom magnified by his uncertainties or his fears. He strikes out light enough in the conflict to take his antagonist's measure and that is something. No man fights confidently with shadows. A modern preacher has found a beautiful illustration of the light which thus comes out of the faithful struggle with doubt, in the knowledge of the chemistry of the sun and stars, which is derived, not from the bright prismatic beams of light streaming from those bodies, but from the blank, black spaces which tell of rays arrested in their path and prevented from bearing their message to us by particular metallic vapors. The man who wins the light of solid conviction and intelligent faith out of darkness, wins purer light. He leaves the path behind him clear and with light on every step by which he has come. His faith, tunnelling down as well as out, gets down to the bed-rock. You remember the noble lines in which England's laureate describes such an one—

> "He fought his doubts and gathered strength,
>   He would not make his judgment blind,
>   He faced the spectres of the mind
> And laid them: thus he came at length
>   To find a stronger faith his own;
> And power was with him in the night
> Which makes the darkness and the light,
>   And dwells not in the light alone,
> But in the darkness and the cloud."

But let us look at the other thought—that of diffusion or distribution. Concealment or reserve in God's economy is with a view to revelation. Christ said, "There is nothing hidden but in order that it should be revealed," and though, as we have seen, God's revelations unfold gradually, that very fact results in the distribution of His revelations along the whole line of an individual life or of a nation's history. That is one aspect of the truth. A grain of wheat is wheat, not only in the full corn, but in the blade and the ear likewise, and in the growth of the seeds of light they unfold into light all along the way of the upright. Though something is hidden, though all godly living includes patient waiting, yet God does not condemn His children to walk in darkness all their days, and only then let in upon them the light of heaven in one overwhelming flood. The perfect day is at the end, it is true, but still the path of the just shineth more and more. The word is a lamp unto the feet in their daily walk. And therefore the hard duties and the hard providences, while they hide light, yet do not keep in all the light. We may be sure of one thing, that, whatever may be kept hidden, God keeps back no light which His child needs for his walk in the way of righteousness. Light is struck out in the doing of the hard duty and in the patient and trustful meeting of the dark providence. There is self-denial, for instance. No doubt it will be a good while before it will cease to be hard, or will bring its full reward: but meanwhile the practice of it is not without its gladness and light. If a great rock is between you and the orb of the moon, and you succeed in pushing the rock ever so little to one side, you let in a little light, and the farther away you push it, the more light enters. Self is the great bulk between us and God. If we push even a little of self to one side, a little of the light of heaven comes straight to our hearts and inspires us to push harder and to get more of self out of the way. And when self is so far crowded out that Christ, in the person of one of His sick or poor or orphaned ones, can step into the place, the light which is reflected from that rested and comforted soul is very bright and pure.

Take the grace of Hope. Hope has a hard fight for life in some natures; and the climb to even a low slope of hopefulness is a distressing one. Yet when one of God's desponding children does manfully grapple with his despondency and resolutely work his way upward, saying, "Why art thou cast down, O my soul? Hope thou in God. I shall yet praise Him"—light breaks in along the line of that struggle. From the first landing-place he gets a glimpse of it; and that glimpse nerves him for the climb to the point above, where the light is brighter and the view wider. The doing of duty of any kind, simply for Christ's sake and because it is duty, unfolds the seed of light. The light of conscience, for instance, burns clearer. That is a great deal. Then, since God keeps hidden His purpose in assigning this duty, the man must work on by faith and not by sight; and the light of faith becomes brighter and steadier. That too is a great deal. There is always light enough for him to see Jesus and to work his way toward Him. Then too every duty has in it some satisfaction and pleasure which one does not discover until he has grasped the duty firmly, and turned it over and over and shaken it well. Some of the things which interest you most to-day are things which you undertook most reluctantly, but they have begun to sparkle under the friction of constant and faithful handling. When you first went into a hospital, unfamiliar with suffering and death, there was no light in the duty. You dreaded it. You went simply because you ought to go. The light has been coming ever since. You have learned to love the work of ministry. Christ's own light has burned more brightly in your own heart, and clearer and fuller knowledge of the depth and meaning of His promises has been coming to you as you have tried to lay those promises on sore hearts.

Then too, light, like seed in contact with the dark furrow, multiplies itself by its contact with hard experience; for after all, it takes hard things like flint and steel to strike out light. Some of you have stood on a rocky platform among the high Alps and watched the coming of dawn. You saw the saffron light deepen behind some monster peak, and soon the first sunbeam appeared above the crest; and as it darted forth, it struck and was flashed back from a great snow-field which blushed and kindled under its touch. Another beam shot over to a cluster of ice-needles, and each one of them became a point of dazzling light. Then a long ray leaped over to that peak, far up in the calm ether, awful in the loneliness of its virgin snow, and the great cone glistened and sparkled over its whole surface, and threw back the light to another peak, and flash answered flash, and the threads of light crossed and twined until the heaving sea of hills was bathed in glory. So every Christlike effort, every Christian grace resolutely carried into practice, not only emits light, but multiplies the light at every point where it touches. Faith nerves itself for a timid venture and throws out its one feeble ray toward a hard task or a hard trial or a hard problem; and behold the thing brightens, and in its own brightening throws light on some other duty or trial, on some great snow-field of lonely sacrifice and patience. Success in the first venture of faith has robbed the larger venture of some of its darkness, and thus the pilgrim of faith walks in ever growing light. In short, the more faithfully and persistently one addresses himself to doing God's will, the more points his experience affords from which the goodness and love and faithfulness and power of God are reflected. And these points enlighten each other. One part of Christian experience illuminates another part. Each experience takes up the light furnished by the smallest, and reflects and helps to distribute it over the whole area.

Light is sown for the righteous and gladness for the upright in heart. Let us not lose faith in the fact of Christian gladness because it comes to us so often in the seed form. Let us not believe that God would have us walk in darkness because He gives us the seeds of light rather than the perfect day at once. Oh, if there be one of you whose way lies under heavy shadow, remember that the Light himself, that great Light which lighteneth every man that cometh into the world, the Father of lights who varies not, and throws no shadow by fickle changing—remember that He is with you alway even unto the end of the world. Move on in the firm faith that believing, patient, unswerving fidelity must and will unfold those buried seeds of light into their radiant harvest. God will not make everything plain to you in this life, though much which is hidden at first will come into light as you get deeper into the years; but do not forget that the perfect unfolding is not for time. Anything which is enfolded in one of God's seeds, is a grand growth. Earth is not large enough for its fruitage. It needs the ampler spaces of heaven to put forth its leafage in full luxuriance. Your path may shine more and more, but the perfect day will dawn first after you shall have crossed the ridge which shuts in this little heritage of time. Then first you shall

> "See the King's full glory break,
>   Nor from the blissful vision shrink.
> In fearless love and hope uncloyed
>   Forever on that ocean bright
> Empowered to gaze, and, undestroyed,
>   Deeper and deeper plunge in light."

Righteousness is light and gladness though its way lie through sorrow and sacrifice: and you who are pursuing that road in faith and hope may take this for your comfort that you are going forward to inevitable gladness. God has already wrought out great goodness before your eyes; but that is nothing to the goodness which He has laid up for them that fear Him. If there is assurance of harvest in the buried seed, there is even firmer assurance in the temporary hiding of God's light. If the promise of nature is sure, the promise of faith is no less sure: for "eye hath not seen, nor ear heard, neither hath entered into the heart of man the things which God hath prepared for them that love Him."

III.

THE PROMISE OF GODLINESS FOR THE PRESENT LIFE.

> "*But godliness is profitable for all things, having promise of the life which now is, and of that which is to come.*"—1 TIMOTHY iv. 8.

I HAVE many times spoken to you of the future life and of its promise. I have often urged upon you the necessity of living with the future distinctly in view, and of shaping this life with reference to the transcendent claims of eternity. I have presented to you heaven as the solution of the problems of time, the reward of faithful service, the rest from the weariness of earth. I have not a word of all this to take back. I have nothing to say which might chill your hopes of heaven, which might impair your sense of the sweetness of its rest, or which might weaken in the least the force of the stimulus and direction which it gives to your earthly work.

It is profoundly true that godliness has promise of the life which is to come. But I wish to-day to fix your thoughts upon the other member of the text—the promise of the life which now is. Because, while it is impossible to exaggerate the importance of our relations to the future life, experience shows that it is possible to contemplate the future to the neglect of the present.

The truth is that the two are parts of one life, and that any view of life which leaves out either, is one-sided and hurtful.

Not long since a friend was telling me of a sermon preached in a church in another city, a church which does not bear the name of "orthodox." The preacher spoke in bitter terms of the evil effect of church teaching about the future life upon great masses of men; how they had been encouraged to patient endurance of hard things in this life—things which were the results of men's cruelty and selfishness,—and had been kept under and quiet by the promise that the future would make everything right. From what I could gather from my friend's story, I inferred that the preacher pushed his discussion to extremes to which, probably, none of us would be willing to follow him. And yet I could not help feeling that he had at least gotten hold of one end of a very important truth: and that possibly the church, in her emphasis upon the future life, has in some measure overlooked the just claims of the present life, and the richness of the promise of godliness to the life which now is.

I take then this simple statement of the text, not overlooking the companion statement, nor attempting to deny its force: Godliness has promise of the life which now is. I think we all have a pretty distinct conception of what the apostle means by godliness: life under God's direct personal guidance; inspired by love to God; led in obedience to God, and in personal communion with God. I take it then further, that the apostle means to say that to such a life God promises good and profitable things, not only in heaven, but here upon earth. That godliness has its possibilities of joy, of usefulness, of attainment, of victory, of knowledge, of social good, of spiritual stature, in this world as well as in the heavenly world. This is substantially what I understand by Paul's words.

And it seems to me that this must be true in the nature of the case. For if godliness consists in being loyally under God's administration, then it follows, of course, that a godly man is under that administration no less on earth than in heaven. Do we not make, practically, too wide a separation in our thought between earth and heaven? I know there is a difference, a wide difference, both as to conditions and circumstances; but the central fact of both lives is the same. They are absolutely alike in that, in both, God is the supreme and controlling fact. We conceive of the kingdom of God as two worlds, separated by a wide chasm. The proper conception is rather that of one vast territory, of lowland and highland if you please. For the present we are moving on the lowlands, the highlands no doubt are misty; but the highlands are only lifts in the same surface. You do not pass into another world when you leave the plains of the West and ascend the Rocky Mountains. The railroad track is continuous from the plain to the summit. So heaven is higher than earth,—purer, brighter, happier, but earth and heaven alike are the kingdom of God; earth is merely a lower level of that kingdom. And therefore it should follow that, once within the kingdom of God, one should find the laws and the promises of that kingdom operating at the one level no less than at the other.

A sovereign whose kingdom embraces mountain-regions and valleys, does not impose one law on the mountaineers and another on the men of the plains. The administration is one, and the loyal subject at the foot of the hills shares its privileges with the mountaineer.

Conditions, I repeat, are different. Some things are possible to the dweller among the high peaks which are not possible to the dweller in the valley; but the king is the same, the law is the same; and whatever privileges of that administration are possible to the dweller in any section of it, are freely his. The great central sovereignty which makes all sections one kingdom, affects all the sections. The thought, therefore, which we are to keep prominently in view is, that on earth as in heaven we are in the kingdom of God, and in virtue of that fact are entitled to the privileges of that kingdom. Godliness has promise, must have promise for that side of the kingdom in which we are now no less than for that side to which we are going. Enoch walked with God: was he any less with God when he walked out of the gate into a part of the kingdom beyond human sight? "God took him," we are told. And as we read what Scripture tells us about the heavenly world, it is very clear that the great principles and facts which constitute the order and the enjoyment of heaven are precisely those which are commended to us as the great motors and regulators of our life here.

Love, trust, obedience, ministry, communion, worship,—they are primary facts in heaven as on earth. The law of your Christian life here is obedience to God. When you shall have reached heaven you will surely be under no other law. "His servants shall serve Him." The motive and mainspring of your Christian life here is love. There can be no other or higher motive there. "Love never faileth." The life which you live in the flesh you live by faith. You will not depend on God any less in heaven than you do here. Your joy here is in God. You surely do not expect to find any higher or purer source of joy in heaven. Your joy will be greater, to be sure, but it will still be in God.

I wonder, further, if we all realize how much the Bible has to say about this life as compared with the next. Cull out all its maxims and precepts bearing upon the principles and conduct of this life, and all the histories and incidents which go to illustrate these, and collect them into one volume, and then gather into another all that is said about the future life,—the one volume will be very thick and the other very thin. As a history, with a moral and spiritual purpose, the Bible must deal mainly with this life. A history of the angels before the creation of the world would be little better than a curiosity. It could be of no practical use to us. As a book of precepts and instructions, if it be not for this life, what is it for? Whatever the Bible may be, it is pre-eminently something to live by here. The more the significance that attaches to the future life, the stronger is the reason for giving us a manual for this life. If we are to do anything or to become anything as a preparation for the next world, we must do and become here. It is a very significant fact that a large section of the history covered by the Bible is developed almost entirely without the influence of hopes and promises attaching to the future life. There were generations of godly people who had to live without any strong light on the future, and practically without the influence of the powerful motives engendered by the Christian revelations of immortality. I say this, remembering the words of the writer to the Hebrews about those who desire a heavenly country, and who look for the city which hath the foundations; and remembering, moreover, that it is about Old Testament men that he is speaking. No doubt there were men who caught glimpses of the better thing beyond. No doubt there were special revelations to individuals; though even in these cases I cannot discover much that is definite. I know that Job had a hope and even an assurance that a deliverer would come to him, sitting and waiting in the shadow of Sheol. But that the assurance of a future life entered as a motive into the earlier religious development of the Hebrew nation at large, cannot be shown. Worldly prosperity as the sign of God's approval is the reward held out to virtue in the Old Testament. Job accepted his wealth and worldly happiness as such a token; and when these were snatched away, he was confounded; and his friends came to him and insisted that he must have sinned against God to have incurred such a visitation.

The Hebrew, in short, was thrown in simple faith and

in ignorance upon the God of his earthly life as the guarantee of his future. Meanwhile, the thing which was to be written upon his door-posts, lodged in his heart, bound about his neck and taught diligently to his children, was that God must be obeyed and worshipped here. To such loyalty God attached large promise of the life which now is. And that Old Testament economy did not make contemptible saints either. Enoch walked with God; so did Noah, who was a just man and perfect in his generation. Moses endured as seeing Him who is invisible. The moral influence of these men does not pass away with their age, but goes over into the new and better dispensation. In that dispensation they still appear, not as relics or antiques or fossils, but as types and models. Any one can satisfy himself of that by reading the eleventh of Hebrews.

Christ brought life and immortality to light; but did you ever think of the significance of that combination—life and immortality? If the Old Testament saints managed to live well and heroically without a clear revelation of immortality, does it follow that they had learned the whole meaning of life or that life has no moral and spiritual possibilities which they did not bring out of it? When Christ brought immortality to light, He threw life also into a new light by the revelation of immortality. Life was made a new thing in the light of immortality. They without us were not to be made perfect. God provided a better thing for us. So far as heaven is concerned they are there, no doubt. Mortal eyes once saw Moses and Elijah in heavenly glory; and whether the Christian saint will find himself on a higher level in heaven than the patriarchs, is a profitless question and one which need not detain us; but the thrust of the New Testament teaching on this point is that you and I are to be, with the light and help of the revelation of immortality, better men and women, of a higher spiritual type, and of a higher grade of efficiency than the patriarchs were. The truth of immortality not only reveals the future life: it lifts this life: it is intended to enlarge the mould of manhood. The head of the line which stretches back from this latest Christian century, away down through the ranks of old kings, prophets, and patriarchs, ought to be made up with characters of a far grander type than they.

So, then, Christ brings life to light in bringing immortality to light. Instead of turning away our thought from earth to heaven, He makes earth brighter and earthly life more significant with the light of heaven. The New Testament is often practically misread on this point. Some people seem to reason as if God had given up this world as a hopeless case: as if He recognized that nothing or not much could be done with man here; and therefore His plan of redemption contemplated getting men through this world with as little damage as possible under the circumstances, in order to introduce them to a new and more hopeful order of things in heaven. It seems a strange kind of doctrine to me. For, in the first place, I confront the stupendous fact that God put Himself visibly and tangibly into this world in the person of Christ. I find Christ putting His wisdom and sympathy and practical helpfulness alongside of every phase of this life of ours—buying and selling, eating and drinking, social intercourse, sorrow and pain and sickness, deformity and maiming—with a distinct and avowed purpose of setting a divine mark on each of them. To do this, evidently seemed to God a thing worth the life and death of Jesus. I read that God was in Christ reconciling the world unto Himself, making this world and this society godlike. I hear Christ saying, "I am come that they might have life, and that they might have it more abundantly." From the pains which He took with this life I cannot think that He meant the abundance to come only in heaven. I know the comparisons between earth and heaven with which the New Testament abounds, and I know that the heavenly life is better and richer than this: but I notice that when Christ says, "In this world ye shall have tribulation," He does not offset it with, "In *the next world* ye shall have peace." It is "*in me* ye shall have peace," and "I am with you always even unto the end of the world." I hear Him say, "Come unto me, ye weary and heavy-laden ones, and I will give you rest"; but when they come, He does not take them out from under burdens. He puts a burden upon them, and says "the rest is under that burden." I hear Paul saying, "I desire to depart and to be with Christ, which is far better." I do not wonder he thought so; but he says also, "for me to live is Christ." Looking forward to the crown of righteousness laid up for him, he also looks backward over his career, and says the fight was a good one, and he has fought it. There was something to be gotten out of this life and held, and he has won and kept it. I hear him talking about growing up into a perfect man, to the measure of the stature of the fulness of Christ; and he does not mean in heaven either. He is writing to those Ephesians who lived under the shadow of Diana's temple, where it was not easy to be a perfect man. I hear John saying, "The world is passing away"; but I read also, "This is the victory that overcometh the world."

In short, godliness, if it has any meaning or promise for the life to come, must, for the same reason, have a significance and a promise for the life which now is; for, as we have seen, the two are parts of one thing. Wherever God reigns, there is godliness. Wherever godliness goes, it carries its promise with it. God and godliness are facts of earth as well as of heaven, and the promise of godliness is therefore a fact of both alike. Godliness must touch and transform and lift and mould any sphere or form of life in which the godly man lives, whether it be on this side of death or on the other. We are constantly talking about eternal life as if it were a future thing. Do we forget that "he that believeth on the Son *hath* everlasting life"? It is not "*shall have.*" He hath it. Death, we say, separates one world from the other. Is that true for Christians? The Hudson River separates Dutchess and Putnam Counties from Ulster and Orange, and Westchester from Rockland, and Rensselaer from Albany; but are we any less citizens of New York in Dutchess than in Orange? The river flows through the State. It does not divide it from another State. So the kingdom of God is on both sides of death. That river will be dried up one of these days, but meanwhile it flows through God's domain. Earth is on one side, heaven on the other, but earth and heaven are only two states of one kingdom. Earth and heaven together make up the kingdom of God. That our heritage stretches farther than we can see, does not disinherit us. A kingdom of which we could see the whole would be a very contemptible kingdom, and you and I are in the kingdom of God, which is a kingdom of infinite reaches, where we can expect to see only the smallest part of our territory. I do not like to hear that passage in Isaiah about seeing the King in His beauty in a land which is very far off, interpreted to mean heaven. It does not mean heaven. Heaven is not very far off; and as for the King, we have His own word for it that He is with us alway, and something of His beauty too, if we may believe the Psalmist, who desires to dwell in the house of the Lord all the days of his life, to behold the beauty of the Lord. If we are going to make that passage of Isaiah a figure of heaven, let us read it as Isaiah wrote it. "Thine eyes shall see a land of distances—a far stretching land." Then we may read into the verse, if we please, the truth that the kingdom of heaven is larger than we think, and stretches not only far away, but close down to what we call the border line. Christ is here in the world. The powers of the world to come are at work here. It seems to me that we do not sufficiently realize that Christ came on purpose to bring heaven and earth together, in fact and in men's minds—heaven and earth

—two things which belong together, but which popular thought had separated.

How can one study Christ's parables, and not perceive that underlying their immediate application, is the great truth that heavenly laws are in operation here, and that heavenly facts have their answering facts on earth? And Christ, I repeat, is here. His touch is on society. We may be distinctly conscious, if we will not blunt our senses, of the forces of the spiritual world crowding in from every side, and pressing against the lines of our social economy, as the great ocean presses around the sides of the ship. "The things that are not seen are eternal." So they are: but does it follow that the eternal things, because they are unseen, have no bearing here and now? "The things which are seen are temporal," transitory. So they are: but does that exclude God from them? If we will but open our eyes to the most familiar facts of nature we shall read the denial of that. We see and confess the work of God in hundreds of things which are transitory and ephemeral. The blossom which to-day is starting into life only to be borne down by the wind in a few weeks—God makes it, God paints it, God brings it forth every year. The beautiful snow-crystal which melts in an hour, the insect which plays for an hour in the light of the setting sun, are God's work. Is God any the less at work in the interest of moral order and spiritual beauty in the generations of men which are passing away as the fathers did before them? Eternity! The metaphysicians say that eternity abolishes time; but we can realize eternity only as the extension of time; and they who are in Christ, and are therefore immortal, are in eternity now. He that doeth the will of God abideth forever. Our mistake is in regarding eternity as all future.

Now these are not speculations nor fancies. They are facts, every one of which can be sustained by the Bible, and facts which have an important practical bearing. And our failure to grasp these facts leads us into mistakes. It tends to keep us farther away from Christ and from heaven than there is any need of our being. The failure to see that Christ wants to be thoroughly intertwined with human life, that there is such a thing as life in Christ and Christ's life in us, has fostered, for example, the idea of a sort of external, mechanical, legal, and formal relation to Christ in the place of oneness with Christ. Unconsciously the matter has presented itself to many in this shape: That by an act of Christ their legal relation to the divine majesty is changed; and that the great central fact in Christian life is the assurance that the benefit of this change is assured to them. There is truth in this. The atoning act of Christ does adjust the legal relations of men to God; but there are those who seem to stop with this; and the practical consequence has been a class of Christians who, being satisfied that they are converted and justified, have not carried out the fact to its legitimate consequences, have lived mainly on the assurance that they are legally certified as children of God, and have not reproduced Christ's life and spirit in themselves. Such a conception does not make saints any more than acquittal makes an indicted man virtuous and a good citizen. Reconciliation to God is more than the adjustment of past differences. It is bringing the whole man into oneness with God. The essence of Christ's atoning work lies in making man at one with God, not only legally and formally, but actually; in his will, his purposes, his desires, his deeds, his spirit and temper—his whole manhood, in short. An atonement which leaves out character is worthless. Having peace with God I do not understand to mean merely making terms with God, and having one's debt settled, and then, on the strength of that adjustment, being admitted to heaven. I understand it to mean what Paul says of the union of Jew and Gentile in Christ: "for to make in Himself of twain one new man, so making peace."

The sum of Christian experience is not Christ outside of us negotiating terms with God, but Christ in us and we in Christ. And therefore the promise of godliness is a promise to make over our manhood into the mould of Christ's, here and before we die. It is not enough that we be simply declared acquitted and justified for Christ's sake. We must be Christlike. That is the Gospel ideal, expressed in such phrases as "putting on Christ," "putting on the new man," "a new creature or creation in Christ Jesus," "a life by the faith of the Son of God," "to live is Christ," and many similar ones. Inbred sin! I know it. Temptation! I know it. Natural weakness! I know it. The push and stress of circumstance! Yes, but is all the push from this side? Does not God, by the helpfulness of Christ and the mighty influences of the Spirit and the taste of the power of the world to come, bring a divine thrust to bear from the other side? Are we to assume that the push from the side of Satan's kingdom is the stronger of the two—so strong indeed that we must be pushed out of this world and into heaven in order to make Christian manhood? I know how Paul looked at that matter when he saw and felt the clutch of evil principalities and powers, and the rush of life, pulling away from Christ. "I am persuaded that neither life, nor death, nor angels, nor principalities, nor powers, nor things present, nor things to come, nor height, nor depth, nor any other creature shall be able to separate us from the love of God which is in Christ Jesus our Lord." If the Gospel is not intended to make us Christlike here, if it has not large promise of fruit in Christian character and achievement for this life, then I know not the meaning of Christ's footprints on every path where there is the mark of a human foot, and of that cross on one of the hills of earth.

So I urge that this promise of godliness be taken more distinctly and squarely and believingly into the life on earth, to make Christian lives richer and purer, and Christian action more effective in this present time.

It seems to me there is too strong a tendency to make escape rather than victory the key-note of life. To assume that the sin and sorrow of this world are so enormous and overpowering, that the best and only thing we can do is to get through all with as little harm as possible, and to get out into something better beyond. And yet I read that evil is to be overcome with good. I read, "This is the victory that overcometh the world, even your faith." I look over to where the mist has lifted a little on the other side of the river, and the outline of triumphal palms shimmers through the haze, and One stands there saying, "I will give this glory and this reward to him that overcometh."

We pray, "Thy kingdom come." What do we mean by it? How much do we mean by it? Every day we are putting up that petition; are we putting beside it in our thought a conviction of the impossibility of our prayer being answered here? When we pray it with a personal reference—Thy kingdom come *to us*—is it with a feeling that the rule of God over us must needs be partial while we stay here on earth, and that the promise of the kingdom is to be realized by us only in faint hopes and feeble faith and short spiritual outlooks and partial peace? When we pray it as a church, having in our eye the colossal misery and confusion and wickedness of this world, do we pray with a sort of hopeless feeling that the kingdom of Satan is after all the stronger? If that be so, depend upon it that feeling will tie our hands, will contract our enterprise, will cramp and belittle our church life, will make our movements halting and aimless. Godliness has promise of the life which now is. The kingdoms of this world are promised to Christ. Sin is mighty, but Christ is mightier. God did not make this world to lose it. He did not make humanity to have it wrested from Him by Satan. He did not make you and me to be dwarfs in holiness and weaklings in holy effort. May He give us a larger conception of His promise and a firmer faith in it; and help us, by grasping and appropriating the promise of this life, to begin even here to realize the promise of the life which is to come.

IV.

FROM BEYOND JORDAN.*

> "*O my God, my soul is cast down within me: therefore will I remember Thee from the land of Jordan and of the Hermonites, from the hill Mizar.*"—PSALM xlii. 6.

As one stands upon the walls of the old city of Granada and looks across the wide plain out of which the citadel rises, his view is bounded by a range of barren mountains. On one of their summits the expelled Moors turned to take their last look at the vast plain, studded with gardens and threaded by streams, and at the lordly palace on its commanding height, which had been so long the stronghold of their power in Spain and the scene of their prodigal luxury. To them their departure was banishment from Paradise; and the bitterness of their sorrow has been preserved in the tradition which has attached to that mountain-ridge from which they looked their last on Granada, the name of " The last sigh of the Moor."

A striking parallel with this is found in the setting of this forty-second Psalm. Under what circumstances it was composed we do not know. Some have ascribed it to David when he fled from Absalom, and, having crossed the Jordan fords, took refuge at Mahanaim:

---

* For the new year.

others to a priest of the temple carried away by the Chaldæans after the capture of Jerusalem. However this may be, the Psalm is the utterance of a man looking back out of present sorrow over a happy past. The scene is laid among the mountains on the east of the Jordan. From these the spectator had unfolded to him a magnificent view of the Land of Promise. Lebanon, the Sea of Galilee, the plain of Esdraelon, Carmel and the Mediterranean, the whole range of the mountains of Judah and Ephraim, Bethlehem and Jerusalem, could be seen from different stand-points. From these heights many an eye took its last look through falling tears at the familiar scenes of home and worship. David in his flight from Absalom, the captive Jews on their way to Babylon, had paused here to gaze upon the land of their love and pride.

The words of the text are indeed those of a man whose soul is bowed down, but their lesson does not encourage despondency, but on the contrary, hopefulness and peace. Let us try and get at the heart of that lesson to-day, as we mount the ridge which divides the past year from its successor. The lesson lies in one sentence: "I will remember Thee."

It is needless to comment upon the fact that memory is always busy at such anniversary seasons. The important thing is the material with which memory deals. And here let us note, in the first place, that if life is viewed by us merely as a succession of events, if memory is concerned only with the journal of each day's doings or gains or pleasures or disasters, it has unlimited possibilities of sadness: it is more likely to be sad than joyful. The world must pass away, friends must die, fortune will change, sorrow is inevitable.

But you observe that the Psalmist's retrospect, though it touches the sorrowful facts of change and loss, does not centre in them. The great fact in his review of the past is God: moreover, that fact is brought out more sharply by his sorrow, just as the overcasting of the sun often throws a prominent object into clearer outline. "My soul is bowed down within me, therefore will I remember Thee." God in the foreground of memory, is our theme to-day. Let us take our illustrations from the scenery of the text.

The prospect from the Hermons and from Mizar, the little hill, was full of points consecrated by their histories of God's special manifestation and help. The whole land, for that matter, had been God's gift and had been won by His saving help.

There, first, was Mahanaim. It was there that the angels of God met Jacob as he was going to meet Esau. The vision of the ladder at Bethel was repeated in another form. God's host joined itself to Jacob's band as an assurance of protection, and hence the patriarch gave the place the name of Mahanaim or "the two hosts."

Into the memories of a great many men, the thought of single-handedness enters, sometimes as a matter of boast, sometimes as a matter of bitterness. There are men so proud and self-reliant, that they would exclude from the memory of their success in life, if they could, all thought of help from God or man. They are self-made men, they tell you, owing their success to their own energy, and owing no thanks to anybody. One host has gained their victories—the body of their own resources. Jacob started from home to seek his fortunes with this ideal of success; but before he had gone far on his journey he received a reminder of another and higher ideal. The vision of Bethel, of the steps joining earth and heaven, of heavenly ministers going up and down between God and men, of God promising protection and the gift of the land whereon the sleeper lay, told Jacob that another host was to take part in his career, and that the principal part: that God had something to say and do about Jacob's future. It took Jacob a long time to realize that fact. He seemed to realize it when he rose from his dream at Bethel; but like so many men who yield for the moment to the power of a vivid impression, the lesson lost its hold on him for the time; and his dealing with Laban showed that he had far more confidence in the one host made up of Jacob's shrewdness, cunning, and persistence, than in the alliance of the host of God. This lesson of the two hosts is the key to the providential economy of Jacob's life. Again and again, under different forms, the truth was brought home to him that no man can safely ignore God in working out His problem of life: that all real life-victory is the victory of God's host.

So then the lesson to-day is to the self-reliant, self-congratulating man, as he complacently reviews his life. In sharp contrast with him as he remembers the vigorous and successful push of his energy against the obstacles to fame and fortune, his storming of the steep heights of honor and wealth, are the words of the Psalmist, "I will remember Thee." Ah, strong, proud, self-complacent man, who call yourself self-made, if you but knew the whole truth, you would seek to be known by any other name than that. Self is a bungling workman at best, and the self-made man must needs be a clumsy performance. The part of your life for which you take most credit to yourself is not of your own making. None the less because unrecognized, another hand has shaped that past of yours. The host of God has walked beside you, though unseen, through those days of struggle. The very conditions of your prosperity, life, health, sight, reason, have been of another's making. The wonderful forbearance which has tolerated so long your exclusion of God from your recognition and gratitude, and has permitted the current of your prosperity to flow on unchecked, is not of your earning. If, as you stand on the watershed between the old year and the new, you do not remember God, you are blind to the prime fact in your retrospect. Oh that He may anoint your eyes this morning, and cause all His goodness to pass before you, and bring you to your knees with confession and penitence and thanksgiving, saying, "I will remember Thee."

Or, sometimes this thought of single-handedness carries with it bitterness. The man looks back over a life of lonely struggle, saying to himself, I should have been so glad of a little sympathy or a little help in my hard places; but the hard, cold world passed me by without a word, and left me to fight alone as best I could.

It may be, and very likely is, all true as regards the world, for it is just like the world. But there is a sense in which it is not true, and the host which met Jacob at Mahanaim is the symbol of another and a sweeter truth. You have not been alone though you have thought yourself so. You have not been without sympathy and help though men have withheld them. No true man fights with one host only. And it is more than possible that, like Jacob, you have gotten in all these years an inkling of the truth. On a lonely road a man is wont to take up with whatever companion he can find; and if God set you to walk that lonely path of yours so that you might find and walk with Him, you know whether He did you a service or not. You know whether the days when you had no company but God were the most miserable days of your life. Sometimes in your travels you have found in the chance acquaintance of your solitary days a man so true and wise and helpful, that you have even changed your own route that you might journey farther in his company; and it would not be strange if, when you had come into days more fruitful in companionship and in kindly ministries of men to yourself, you should have said to the Divine Friend of your lonely hours, "Abide with me. If Thy presence go not with me, carry me not up hence." In your retrospect of your lonely days, and of your single-handed struggle as you are pleased to call it, the first prompting of your heart is to say, "I will remember Thee."

All the greater pity if you did not find Him out during all those days. All the greater pity if your eyes were holden so that you did not know Him. It was largely so with Jacob. God walked along by his side unrecognized, and yet met and helped him in the hour of his need. Oh, the wonderful, compassionate love of our Father in Heaven, who never takes His eye from us, though our eyes are turned everywhere else save upon Him. You and I have been so often self-engrossed, selfishly or morbidly as the case might be, thinking only of our own skill and resources in fighting our battles, and yet God struck for us in our need, though we had not called Him in, though perhaps we had wronged Him by thinking Him far off and careless whether we conquered or fell. We attach often a hard and severe meaning to the idea of God's reminders. And yet God does not always remind us of Himself by a blow. His most potent reminders are often in the form of an undeserved blessing. Your experience has been a very strange one if it does not include something of this kind; if sometimes you have not found in some generous act of divine love a sharper reproach than the most stinging rebuke. It was the presence of the hosts of God which brought from the worldly Jacob the confession, "I am not worthy of the least of all the mercies and of all the truth which Thou hast showed unto Thy servant."

Not far from Mahanaim was the brook Jabbok, the scene of Jacob's mysterious struggle with the covenant angel. I pity the man who can find in that story nothing but a myth or a legend. I do not pretend to understand all the deep meaning of that incident, but I am not concerned to take the supernatural element out of the Bible; for if I could succeed, I should be tempted to throw into the fire what was left: and so, until I can find some better authority than that which handles Old Testament story in that unceremonious fashion, I shall take the story of Jacob's wrestle as I find it, and shall continue to believe that, in this mysterious fashion, God met Jacob and revealed Himself to him there by the brook Jabbok.

God, by the revelation of the angels at Mahanaim, had given Jacob assurance of help: but so far, the assurance was general. God's help includes a good many things, and some which seem to the man, for the time being, like hindrances rather than helps. God's help is not confined to extricating a man from the special difficulty in which he finds himself. Sometimes indeed He does not extricate him, as when He refused to relieve Paul of the thorn in the flesh. God's chief aim in all His dealings with individual men is character. All the help, comfort, light which He gives, all the struggle, the darkness, the defeat which He permits, are with a view to make the man himself more godlike. And hence the deliverance of Jacob from the just anger of Esau was only one part, and the minor part, of God's purpose. It was a comparatively simple matter to pacify Esau, but it was a much greater matter to recast that calculating, tricky, worldly-minded Jacob into a Prince of God. And that was what God meant—to bring that life-long antagonism between selfishness and duty, between reliance on self and reliance on God, to a crisis. Not the winning of the birthright, not the purloined blessing, not the visions of Bethel and of Mahanaim, but the wrestle at Jabbok was the critical point in Jacob's moral history. The wrestle was foreshadowed at Bethel.

God's choice of that man for such a high destiny is a mystery. There is some reason for it in the moral possibilities of the man which God knows, but which we cannot detect until we come to Jabbok. It comes out there: a moral fibre which has been overlaid by his cunning and conceit all these years, but which stiffens into moral muscle at the touch of the covenant angel. The very man of all others, who, we should think, would break down at just such a moral crisis, whose life has given scarce a hint of the moral quality he develops in that struggle, comes out gloriously, with a tremendous force of will which faces God, and, breast to breast, and girdled with the arm of omnipotence, cries, "I will not let Thee go except Thou bless me." He had been brought to a point where stratagem and strength alike failed; where he could only cling to God; where the issue was God's blessing or nothing. He won His blessing, and the Supplanter was baptized anew as God's Prince.

Such crises are searching tests of a man's moral quality. All his manhood is involved in the answer to the question what he will do when he has nothing but God. All men are not equal to that test. God does not impose it on all men, though He puts hints and foreshadowings of it into their lives. But while such crises are the most awful in men's lives, the victory which they bring out of them is the most decisive and the most radical and far-reaching in its consequences. It sets a mark on character deeper than any other event of the whole life. Some of you have met such crises. In one way or another they have come to you—it may have been in business; it may have been on the line of your religious experience; it may have been that a great sorrow has been put into your naked hands and you have had nobody but God to teach you what to do with it: the struggle may have come on the line of your intellectual doubts: in any case it has marked a turning-point in your life. And the question with you, as you review the past, is not whether you have weathered the business storm and escaped financial shipwreck; not whether you have been able to forget the sorrow in later pleasures; not whether you have successfully parried or answered a question or resolved a religious doubt. No, the question is, what strengthened and deepened moral quality you have brought out of these crises. As you look back to them, is God the object which fills the field of vision? Have you come out of them with a conviction like Jacob's that nothing is of any worth without God's blessing? Have you come out with a song of praise though the wrestle has lamed you? Have you come out, able to say, though stricken and disappointed, "I have kept the faith: my moral manhood is unimpaired, because with all my losses I have kept God. The best of all is, God is with me"? Oh, my brother, it seems idle to talk of victory and praise while deep calleth unto deep, and all the waves and billows are going over you, and your soul is bowed down within you; but believe me, you have already won the greatest victory of your life if to-day you can stand amidst the flying spray, drenched and weak and weary, and say, " Therefore will I remember Thee."

But this scene of our Psalm gives us another lesson. It was from these heights that Moses looked upon the Land of Promise which he was not to enter. Sore, sore disappointment, as we view it. Was it for this that he had been taken from the river reeds, trained in the royal schools of Egypt, his faith and patience disciplined in the solitudes of Horeb: for this that he had borne the murmurings and rebellions of an ungrateful people, and had given his ripest years to fit them for citizenship and conquest, all the while cheered and sustained by the thought of that better time which was coming, only to be stopped short on the very borders of the promised land, to be shown its goodliness and beauty only to be forbidden to enter? It was his own fault, it may be said. So much the worse. Moses might have been pardoned for thinking that the strain on his patience had been harder than most men had had to bear, and that his forty years' loyal service might have been an offset to his single error. None the less it was his own fault, and Moses was not the man to rebel at God's decision. He knew very well that God would not forget his services. He knew that a longer, sweeter rest awaited him than any which Canaan could give. Probably he saw, with the wisdom which comes with years to such men as he, that he was not the man to lead the work of battle and conquest which awaited the host; but for all that it was a disappointment. He stands there on Pisgah representing to us unachieved success. Stands, as not a few of us stand to-day, with the knowledge of what we might have done, with the possible prize in sight, with the assurance that we never shall win it. You know what some men have brought out of such a retrospect: anger, bitterness, misanthropy. You can read for yourselves what Moses brought out of it. His retrospect is written down for you in the Book of Deuteronomy. It is not a record of his own trials and burdens. "God, God" is the theme which runs through it all, until with prophet-eyes, seeing the future of Israel, through and beyond all the struggles and lapses, all the blood and tears of ages—his lips blossom out into that wonderful utterance, "There is none like unto the God of Jeshurun, who rideth upon the heavens in thy help, and in His excellency on the sky. The eternal God is thy refuge, and underneath are the everlasting arms, and He shall thrust out the enemy from before thee, and shall say, Destroy them. Happy art thou, O Israel. Who is like unto Thee, O people saved by the Lord, the shield of thy help, and who is the sword of thy excellency."

To-day, the retrospect of most of us includes unachieved success. The poet gives voice to our thought:

> "To strive and fail! Yes, I did strive and fail.
> I set mine eyes upon a certain night
> To find a certain star, and could not hail
> With them its deep-set light.
> Fool that I was! I will rehearse my fault.
> I, wingless, thought myself on high so his

Among the winged. I set these feet that halt
To run against the swift."

We have thrown, and have not won. We have run, but others have been swifter, and it has settled down into certainty that we shall never win what we have striven for. What then? What are we thinking of this morning? Is it our disappointment? Is it the coldness and unhelpfulness of those who should have been our friends? Is it our wounded pride? Or are we remembering God? Have we gotten under our feet the infidel falsehood that God is on the side of the heaviest battalions? Have we gotten some grasp upon the truth that God is the God of the unsuccessful? Have we learned that he who has lost everything, and yet has kept hold on God, is successful? Yes, brother, you have failed in winning what you wanted, but you have not lost God. The time may come when you will look down on the maze of your life which now seems such a labyrinth, and see the order in the maze and learn that it was better you should fail. Had you fixed success in that particular thing as the reward of your striving? You have learned a lesson, cheaply bought at the price of your disappointment, if you have learned that God fixes His own rewards, and that they are often different and always better than those which we covet. It was one of the bitterest and most fearfully significant things that even Christ could say of the hypocrites and self-righteous, "They have received their reward." You have made honest effort and have failed. You have not gotten the reward you coveted, but you have God. You have failed perhaps through your own fault: that is the bitterest thing of all; but still you have God, long-suffering, compassionate, forgiving, who heals your backsliding, who loves you, not because you are successful or perfect, but simply out of the divine impulse of His own being. You can still serve Him, though not in the way you wished. You can still enjoy Him, if not through the medium of the earthly good you craved. Your failure has not been a curse if, as you look back on it to-day, you can say, "Therefore will I remember Thee."

Once more. From those heights Jordan was in sight. There, at the full tide of the harvest season, when the waters flowed with a deep, strong current, the floods had been arrested, and the host of God, following the ark, had passed over dry-shod. It is no wonder that that stream, the boundary-line of the Land of Promise, has passed into sacred song as the type of death, not only as the dividing-line between the old land and the new, but as the scene of God's most gracious deliverances. Some of you have cause to remember Jordan this morning, and memory peoples the bank with familiar forms, waving farewell ere they stepped down into the swift, cold stream, and vanished from your sight. Your soul is bowed down under this memory, and no wonder. And yet, I take it, you remember something more than the stream and the vanished faces. If this were all, the retrospect would be sad indeed; but you remember God. You remember how His rod and staff comforted those failing hearts. The precious treasure of your memory, embalmed for all time, which not even death can take away, is the fact that those lives were shaped and moulded by God, and lived out in fidelity to God, and ended in the peace of God, and have been taken up by God to be changed from glory to glory as by His presence, and are forever with the Lord. There is this blessing attaching to our faith, that the thought of God dominates the thought of death. And one of the most precious reflections connected with our sad memories of death, is that of the glory and perfection, of the new conditions of growth and of moral power into which death transfers these dear ones. I heard a brother minister tell a story of a poor, ignorant 'longshoreman whom he visited on his dying bed, and who was tormented by the thought of the grave and of the fearful change which would pass upon his poor body. The minister quoted to him, "I will write upon him My new name"; and, "His name shall be in their foreheads." A light came into his eyes. His harsh features were glorified. "I'm going then," said he, "into the next world like a new-born baby; and God, He is my Father; and He'll christen me with a new name; and He'll name me after Himself, just as if I'd never lived before; and neither saints nor devils will know anything of old John and his sins." And then, raising himself with the remnant of his fast failing strength, and lifting his hands, he cried out, "O, but that's glorious! that's glorious! I thank my God!" Brethren, death has not been a curse if it has enabled you to say, "Therefore will I remember Thee."

So then the past is behind us. The dawn of the New-Year reddens the hill-tops. As we look back, let us remember God. How can we help it as we review this year so crowded with His mercies? I had almost said, How can we remember anything else? We are wishing each other "a happy New-Year." We have its happiness in our own hands. We have only to put our hand in God's and the thing is done.

V.

CREATING AND CARRYING.

"I have made, and I will bear."—ISAIAH xlvi. 4.

IN this chapter the scene of the first paragraph is laid in Babylon. In vision the prophet sees the most venerated idols overthrown by the conqueror and carried away. "Bel," the tutelary deity of Babylon, "hath bowed down." "Nebo," the Babylonian Mercury, "hath crouched." Their idols are given up to the beasts and to the cattle. The images which were carried in procession by the priests and nobles, are resigned to common beasts of burden. If the great Bel and Nebo had been really gods, they would have interposed for the rescue of their images, but they have not been able to rescue the burden, and their soul hath gone into captivity.

The key-note of the passage is given by the figure of a burden or load, which the heathen gods are unable to bear. In contrast with their helplessness, the prophet emphasizes the power of Jehovah, carrying on still the figure of bearing a load. Historically, God has carried His people from the beginning. None have been able to pluck them out of His hand. This great burden of a nation to be shaped and developed, with all its ignorance and sin and perverseness, with its political complications, with its entanglements with contemporary heathenism—Jehovah has shown Himself able to carry it, and will carry it to the End. "Even to old age I am the same, and even to gray hairs I will bear. I have made, and I will carry, and I will bear and will rescue."

In our text the two ideas of creating and carrying are thrown together, and in such a way as to show that they are related: that in the fact of God the Creator, lies enfolded the fact of God the Redeemer. "I have made, and I will bear."

We must not let the fact of redemption, wonderful as it is, throw the fact of creation into the background; because the two are inseparably linked. Redemption, in one sense, grows out of creation. Because God made man in His own image, He is bent on restoring him to that image. Because God made us, God loves us, educates us, bears with us, carries on the race on the line of His infinite patience, ministers to us with help and sympathy, is burdened with our perverseness and blindness, yea, comes down in person into the sphere of our humanity and takes its awful load of sin and sorrow and pain and death upon Himself.

Let us look at this fact in certain familiar aspects. In anything that one makes he has a peculiar interest. With men, this interest is quite independent of the intrinsic value or importance of the thing. The fact that one has made a thing, intensifies the sense of proprietorship, and constitutes him its champion. The young artist knows that his first picture stands no chance in comparison with the works of his masters, and yet that piece of canvas is more to him than a Raphael or a Rembrandt. Critics find fault, perhaps justly, but he dwells on the points which he has treated with loving care and enthusiasm. Something in him asserts itself above the cold testimony of knowledge. A thousand hopes and fears and longings and cherished conceits have gone into the picture which none but himself know. It is his. He made it. The critic says it is not to be borne. He not only can bear it, but can hang it up in his room and live with it and love it because it is his own. The house which a man has erected with his own hands, though it be only a log-cabin; the piece of land which he has purchased by the sweat of his brow, and has made verdant and fruitful by his own toil, have an interest quite apart from their market-value or from architectural merit. And this sentiment reaches high-water-mark in the parental relation. One's own child! If parental love depended on the beauty or the mental endowment of children, the world would be peopled with orphans. The parental instinct, as you know, is quite independent of these things. Speak to a mother about the ugliness or the stupidity of her child, her only answer is to fold him closer in her arms. He is a poor cripple among the little ones who bound and dance around him; but for him are her tenderest words, the choicest dainties, the hoarded wealth of love. Love seems to thrive on defect. Those of you who are familiar with the poems of Wordsworth will remember how that idea is worked out in the little poem of "The Idiot Boy."

And the same fact holds on the moral side. Parental love is not conditioned on a child's goodness. Parental care does not relax because a child sins. Love follows the son down into the deeps of sin, keeps a hand on him, counts no sacrifice too dear to win him back, bears with insult and neglect. Over all the sense of personal wrong, wounded love, disappointed hope and pride, rises the thought, he is mine.

All this is familiar enough. Are we afraid to carry the truth farther up—up to God? Are we of those who say that God *must* be just and *may* be merciful—as if mercy were not one of His essential attributes as well as justice? Why should the "must" hold in the one case any more than in the other? If God must be just, He must be merciful. If justice is a necessity of His being, mercy is equally a necessity. A strange fashion this of parcelling out the divine nature into sections, drawing the boundary-lines with mathematical sharpness, and then setting watches upon the frontiers, lest mercy should encroach on justice or love on truth. Let us cease trying to lay out the infinite according to the rules of a topographical survey. The great thing for us is not to study God from without, but to be in God: then the lines of His attributes will adjust themselves to our eye. It is only when we live inland, or keep in our voyaging close along shore, that the waters take on for us the character of division-lines between provinces or of distinct bays or estuaries. When we push out into the ocean, we lose sight of all that in the impression of one mighty flood that fills all the bays and creeks. The bottom of the sea is divided by mountains and valleys, but the sea itself fills and covers them all. We care little whether a mountain or a valley is beneath our keel as we are borne on over the strong, deep swell. I know that it is the ocean tide that runs up between those trim stone wharves; but I do not look on the labyrinth of docks and say, "That is the sea." I leave the docks when I put out to sea. "We must make docks," you say, "so long as we are on shore. We must have places for mooring and unlading truth." Quite true. It is necessary that theology and ethics, dwelling here within the limits of the finite, should construct channels and basins for truth. Be it so. All well, so long as we do not mistake the channels and basins for the ocean. Justice, truth, mercy, and all the rest are in the divine nature; are all in due proportion and perfect adjustment; but they blend with each other and include each other in a way which defies our triangulating. That seer who was swept into the heavens from the savage rocks of Patmos, saw both mercy and judgment in his vision. He saw the Lamb leading His people to living fountains and wiping away all tears from their eyes: and he saw Him that sitteth upon the white horse, the Lord of war and righteousness, out of whose mouth goeth a sharp sword. But he came back and told the Church, "God is love, and he that dwelleth in love dwelleth in God, and God in him." To dwell in Love is, therefore, to be within the limits of justice and truth as well as of those of mercy.

But let us not lose sight of our point. All that is included in the word "bear" is practically pledged to us in the fact of creation. One reason why we take so slowly to the idea of God's bearing or carrying us, is because we divorce it from the fact that He made us; and we look at the bearing simply as a concession, forgetting that God the Redeemer is bound up with God the Creator. From our stand-point and with our crude notions of the relations between justice and mercy, it may seem that God is under no obligation to bear the sorrows and to sympathize with the infirmities and to deal tenderly with the errors which are due to man's sin. He *is* under no obligation imposed by any rightful claim of ours. But He is under an obligation stronger than that—an obligation imposed by the stress of His own infinite love for the children He has created. The stress of obligation does not draw Him from our side: it pushes from Him toward us. It is the mighty outgoing of His own fatherly heart toward that which emanates from Himself and which He yearns to see restored to the image in which He made it. From this point of view, the impulse to bear for and with man is just as deep and spontaneous and affectionate as the impulse to say in the beginning, "Let us make man in our own image."

You find that in the New Testament. Take the parable of the Prodigal Son. What is at the bottom of the whole story but this truth of sonship? It is that which defines the measure of the prodigal's sin. The very heart of the sin is rebellion against a father, and rupture of the natural tie. That also defines the father's longing, and the joy over the returning son, the free forgiveness and the festivity. The boy was as wretched and needy and generally disgusting when he appealed to his father, as when he appealed to the citizen swine-keeper; but it was not at all in the swine-keeper's line of thought to even pity him, much less to spread a table for him and give him the best robe and the choice fare. Only a Father would think of that for a son; and, for the father, it was the most natural of all things to think of it.

For, look you, we do not have any difficulty about this truth as between man and man. When a father turns his son out of doors, however blameworthy the boy may have been, we are concious of a kind of recoil from the act, such as we do not feel when a householder discharges a knavish servant, or a merchant dismisses a thievish clerk. We say, "Yes, he was an unworthy son, but then—he was his own son." And further, we do not think it strange or wonderful that a mother goes on loving the son or the daughter who has brought disgrace on the house; that she bears and forbears and hopes and cherishes long after the scant charity of the world is exhausted. We do not think it strange, I say, through our deep feeling of the strength of the natural tie between parent and child. Why should we think such a recognition strange on God's part? Isaiah did not think so when he said, "Can a woman forget her sucking child that she should not have compassion on the son of her womb? Yea, they may forget, yet will I not forget thee." And Christ did not think so when He said, "If ye, being evil, know how to give good gifts unto your children, how much more shall your heavenly Father give good things to them that ask Him! God, and I say it reverently, and because He has said the same thing of Himself—God is under the stress of the parental instinct to take our sicknesses and to bear our infirmities, and He yields to it, gives Himself up to it in His own divine measure. He is the God who says, "I have made, and I will bear."

I am saying nothing which goes to mitigate the essential badness of sin, or God's hatred of it, or to deny the fact of God's punishment of it. Even fatherhood has limitations. God cannot restore his erring child without conditions. Simply to forgive the past is not enough. God aims at the perfect establishment of the filial relation, and that cannot be without a filial heart in the son, and the son's cheerful obedience. If the prodigal had not come back repentant, he would not have had the robe and the ring. This parental feeling, and its manifestation on God's part, are, as already hinted, the things which throw the enormity of sin into the highest relief.

Bearing this in mind, let us now go on to consider some of the aspects under which this truth of God's bearing manifests itself.

It appears as a matter of tolerance. It is perfectly clear from the Bible that God's love for His children makes Him bear patiently with their infirmities and errors. When an enthusiastic sculptor has once conceived the idea of a statue, he is not daunted by hardness in the stone, nor by defects in the grain. He is bent on carrying out his cherished ideal. The greater the difficulties, the more his energies are called out. Are we to suppose that God conceives a purpose less sharply or works it out with less intensity than a man does? Not so indeed. From our stand-point, God's undertakings are formidable; bristling with difficulties; for He does not, as He might, decree the thing done by one arbitrary act of His will, but lets the human element into the process, with its times and seasons and rates of growth and clash of passions. None the less, through whatever process of work or of waiting, of doing or of bearing, God means that the thing shall be done, and it is. There is the history of Israel. The development of that nation was a stupendous task. You know the details of that history; there is not time to dwell on them; but one fact pervades the entire record—the long-suffering patience of God. That comes out, if in nothing else, in the element of time which marks the history. It is a long history. Take one single fact, that it required all the years from the Exodus to the carrying away into Babylon to get the idea of one only living and true God practically lodged in the people's heart. It was lodged at last. But God could wait and bear. How long He waited, and how much He bore. How He tolerated characters and customs at which Christian sentiment revolts; institutions which it has banished; men like Jacob and Samson; women like Rebecca and Jael, until the time was ripe for a John and a Mary, a Phœbe and a Priscilla. How He bore with national petulance and apostasy, and saw His own sun shine day after day on the idol altars upon every hill-top: smote the people, yet ever called them back and forgave and blessed them when they came.

"Bare and carried them all the days of old." Yes, and cherishes them still in His heart. Israel, though scattered and despised, has a place yet in Jehovah's love. The eye which followed her out of Egypt on the night of the Exodus, and through the sea and the desert, is on her still, and some old prophecies which lie back in darkness and dust shall flash into new meaning some day when Israel shall return unto the Lord.

God's wonderful patience shames us. We get into bitter, pettish frames of mind over the prevalence of fraud and of godless luxury, over the high-handed insolence of demagogism; and we are tempted to say, perhaps do say, "Why does not God arise in His might, and sweep away the whole mass at a stroke?" Doubtless that is what some of us would do if we could. We would call down fire from heaven. We would root out the tares at once. Well for us, well for humanity that we cannot. Meanwhile God bears. The tares spring up with the wheat. The wicked has no doubtful success. He is in great power and spreads himself like a green bay-tree. God bears. He has not only His purpose, but His method. Let us never forget that Christ resisted the temptation to step at once to an absolute but external sovereignty. His deeper ideal of a sovereignty founded in the free, intelligent acceptance of the principles of the Kingdom of God, would take time and blood and tears, yet would He wait and bear. He had made humanity in His own image, He would not restore it to anything lower.

We have seen God's bearing under the aspect of tolerance, and have seen it illustrated historically. The same truth is formulated in dogma, taking more distinctly into itself, along with mere tolerance, the facts of compassion, sympathy, and practical helpfulness. This idea of bearing is at the root of the doctrine of Christ's atonement. So it is foreshadowed by Isaiah in his prophecy of Him who took our infirmities and bare our sicknesses. It is of the very nature and essence of love, and pre-eminently of parental love, to bear. "Love," as one has said, "is essentially vicarious." It does not wait for the burdens of its object to be laid upon it. It reaches out after them to transfer them to itself.

I have said before, and I repeat it, for it is a truth which should be bedded in the foundations of your Christian thought, that we must try and reach a larger conception of the atonement of Christ than the one which is popularly held, and which makes it substantially a mere business adjustment between God and a sinful world: a settlement of accounts; a setting of men right as regards the letter and the penalty of the law. A real atonement must touch the inmost personality of the man, and must include his transformation into the image of God no less than the adjustment of his legal relations. Pardon is included in atonement, but atonement is more than pardon. That governor may pardon a criminal, but the pardon does not make the criminal over into an honest and pure man. I repeat, God will be satisfied with nothing short of the restoration of man to His image: nothing short of a filial na ture in the man: nothing short of an inward oneness of man with God answering to the relation of Christ with the Father. That is Christ's own plainly-stated ideal: "That they may be one even as we are one: I in them, and Thou in me, that they may be perfected into one." The purpose of the atonement is vastly larger than to keep men out of perdition. It is to save men, but also to make men, and to save them by making them. Such a work as this involves mediation. Job saw dimly, centuries before Christ came, saw through the driving mists of his own bitter agony, that man needed a daysman—one who could stand between him and God and lay a hand on them both: one who could stand between human weakness and sorrow and sin, and the infinite holiness of the divine: one who could unite in himself the susceptibilities to the influences from both sides: who could be one with God, yet touched with the feeling of our infirmities. And therefore, in a world of erring children of God where a process of reconciliation is at work, the cross must have a place and the highest place—the cross which is the expression of burden-bearing love. Atonement means love shouldering man and carrying him out of sin up to God: and in order to do this some one must go down into the sin where he is, and put himself within reach of the thrust of all its anguish and sorrow, and lay his heart open to its feeling while He pushes and guides the man steadily upward.

That is what God in Christ does. He bears man on His heart. I see that man of sorrows, Christ Jesus, go away under the olives of Gethsemane. It is not for human thought to fathom the awful secrets of that hour. In the light of Scripture and of Christ's avowed purpose and of His work in the world, we can catch some glimpses into the depth of that agony. Of the two, I am not sure that the agony of Gethsemane was not to Him more bitter than the agony of Calvary. He never prayed on Calvary as He did in the garden, "If it be possible let this cup pass from me." Now and then a true, thoughtful man, who studies and discerns the signs of the times, and follows the evolution of religious thought in the world, is driven into a kind of desperation as the elements of the vast problem of a renewed humanity crowd thickly upon him: as history sends up its testimonies, and the discordant voices of the time pour in at his windows, and the promises and declarations of the word of God present themselves in such apparently startling contrast with the facts. Such an one may possibly get a glimpse of the tide which rolled in upon Christ's soul there under the olive trees: the history of humanity from the beginning; the track of sin through the old empires; the carnivals of blood and lust; the gropings of blind souls for the truth; the awful secrets of the great cities; the stubbornness of human pride; the foul idolatries of human fanaticism; altars reeking with blood; alternate butchery and sensuality: then the long perspective of the years to come, through which his simple and pure truth should fight its way, and gradually draw men nearer to God; the stabs in the house of His own friends; the coldness and apathy of the Church for which His blood was to be poured out. It all came rushing together upon His soul. No man could help Him there. He must tread that fearful wine-press alone. He must face that awful mass of woe and corruption, past as well as future, and know in His inmost being that He, He alone stood between all this and God. Do you wonder that His sweat was of great drops of blood? Do you wonder that the humanity of Him cried out: "If it be possible, let this cup pass from me"? There is the comment on our text. There it is translated into flesh and blood: "I have made, and I will bear."

The truth also comes out experimentally in the Christian life of each one of us. I cannot dwell here. I can only refer you to your own experience, which, if you will read with open eyes and heart, will be a very fruitful comment on this truth. Every one of us, if he is honest with himself, knows that God has had much to bear with him, and knows, too, how patiently God has borne it: and every one of us has had experience of God's bearing in the sense of sympathetic love and helpfulness. How many of us know from most blessed experience what it is to have a great High Priest touched with the feeling of our infirmities. How many of us have known what it was to have Him bear our heavy load for us; and therefore, in the way that lies before us, can we not trust in larger measure the love of Him who made us to bear with us? We are stubborn subjects, hard material; can we not believe in God's purpose to shape us? Shall we believe that every knot and gnarl which He encounters in the process only excites His anger? Has He dealt with the knots and gnarls thus far like one who was wroth with us? Look up. We are in the hands of Him who made us. God makes nothing in vain. When He made man in His own image, He did not make him to gratify a caprice, or in mere wantonness of power. He made him with a solemn, an awful, a glorious purpose over which He took heaven into counsel: and be sure that he will accomplish that purpose, that his patience shall not fail, that He who made will bear until He shall have perfected His work.

And meanwhile let us not forget the lesson of His bearing as it speaks to us of duty. Let us not presume on it. The fact of this loving purpose and of the patience, the tolerance, the sympathy with which He carries it out, throws into strongest relief the enormity of the sin which resists the purpose and tramples upon the patience.

> "He that shuts love out, in turn shall be
> Shut out from love."

VI.

THE REFUGE FROM TALK.

"Thou shalt keep them secretly in a pavilion from the strife of tongues."—PSALM xxxi. 20.

THE author of this Psalm had evidently suffered much from the talk of society. He had been reproached by his enemies; he had heard the slander of many who took counsel together against him. The wicked had not been silent, and lying lips had spoken grievous things proudly and contemptuously. The strife of tongues had raged, and the arrows thereof had wounded him.

In this, as in so many cases, the Psalmist strikes an answering chord in the common experience of men of all times. A large share of good men's troubles come out of the talk of others. Nor is this fact confined to great men or to public men. Every man has his own little public, and that public talks; and even when it does not talk about him, the persistence and the endless variety of its talking, and many of the themes of its talk, often worry and annoy him so that he cries out for the wings of a dove, that he may fly away and be at rest in the wilderness from the strife of tongues.

The text gives us two points: the strife of tongues and the hiding-place from it.

The strife of tongues! What an expressive phrase that is. How the element of contention asserts itself in the great mass of the world's talk. I remember being once at a fair in a foreign city, and before each booth stood a crier, sometimes aided by musical instruments; each crier endeavoring to raise his voice above the others in advertising the attractions of his show. It was a good picture of the world at large, where so many people have something to say, something which they are determined the world shall hear, no matter who else goes unheard.

Then, how much debate there is. How much talk over questions, and those not always the most important: how much wrangling and idle declamation over issues parted only by a hair's breadth. What waste of rhetoric and what seething of passionate words over matters which will be forgotten in a year, perhaps in less.

Or again, while so many are fighting to tell the world something for its own good, as they declare, still more are they who are pleading with the world for their own good, and adding to the general din their blatant claims for the world's honors and emoluments.

And then there is the hiss of slanderous tongues striving against the innocent, and of gossiping tongues striving which can tell most news—bad or good, false or true—it matters not. Is the picture of the old English divine overdrawn after all? Hear a few of his stately periods. "Every gossiping is as it were a court of justice: every seat becometh a tribunal; at every table standeth a bar, whereto all men are cited, whereat every man as it happeneth is arraigned and sentenced: no sublimity, no integrity or innocence of life, no prudence or circumspection of demeanor can exempt any person from it; not one escapeth being taxed under some scandalous name or odious character, one or other. Not only the outward actions and visible practices of men are judged; but their retired sentiments are brought under trial, their inward dispositions have a verdict passed on them, their final states are determined —yea, God himself is hardly spared, His providence coming under the bold obloquy of those who, as the Psalmist speaketh of some in his own time, whose race doth yet survive, speak loftily and set their mouth against the heavens."

Now men, as we have said, get weary of this. There is no man who has not yearned to be where he could hear only the beatings of his own heart, out of reach of what men say of him or of any one else. We grow blinded and stunned by this excess of talk. The multitude of explanations and comments confuses us as to the truth. We want leisure to think, and to weigh and adjust things. We want men to stop talking so that we can talk to ourselves. If perchance a great seed-thought has floated to us on those winds of oratory and debate, we would fain give it time to strike its roots deep down into our minds and hearts. We ourselves are weary of hearing what men say of us and of what we do. We should be glad to have for a time the gift of being invisible and of being ourselves, and of doing our work without the constraint and incubus of the feeling that our simplest deed may be misinterpreted, and our frankest word twisted out of recognition. We are tired of hearing men talked over; of hearing our best friends suspected, and the men we honor and trust most set aside with contempt, until we ourselves catch the taint and begin to ask, "Is there any pure man? Is any man trustworthy? Who shall show us any good?" We want to get away where we can think our own thoughts of men: where we can indulge our hero-worship if it so please us, and give ourselves up, unchallenged, to the delusions (if delusions they be) of affection and admiration.

And, once more, we grow ashamed of ourselves, if there is any true manhood left in us, because we are so often drawn, ourselves, into this current of talk about our neighbors. We hear the gossip, and we happen to know a fact or to have heard a piece of news, and almost ere we know it, in it goes into the common stock: and, if we are not very careful, we find ourselves falling into censorious talk, flinging out sharp arrows of sarcasm or pulling a neighbor's defects a little farther out into the light; and when we come to sit down and think over what we have said, unless we are very much hardened, we feel ashamed and sorry, and indignant at ourselves, and are tempted to wish that we might never again be in society where people are talked over.

Now, it will not do for us to defy public talk, and to show ourselves so independent of what men say as to do, wantonly, what shocks social sentiment and multiplies talk. For the talk of society is by no means an unmixed evil. It hurts a good many men, and that unjustly: but it also keeps not a few men steady. The fear which it begets in a certain class of minds is wholesome. No man should defy public sentiment on any issue short of an issue of moral principle. The man who declares his contempt for the opinion of his neighbor, and who wantonly goes in the face of it, proves himself not a brave man but a very unwise man. There have been cases where one man has been right and the rest of society wrong: but such cases are not as numerous as is sometimes supposed; and while the voice of the people is by no means always the voice of God, a manly respect for public opinion, a manly desire for society's esteem are wholesome, divinely-planted, conservative elements of sound character.

Defiance of society then is not our refuge from the strife of tongues. What is it?

The world does not afford it. To get out of the reach of talk is to get out of society altogether; and to get out of society is not only no man's duty, but it is the sin of any man who attempts it. There is a sentiment which finds its way into books now and then in very attractive guise, and which appeals powerfully to overworked men, the tendency of which is to exalt the life of pure contemplation as the ideal of a perfect life. It gives rise to very sweet talk about the calm of nature and about musing on God and studying Him in His works, away from the din of cities and the ambitious strivings of men. But in reality it is the old monastic ideal of living, with the monastery left out. The principle is the same— harmless isolation from mankind. But the Bible, which says a great deal about various refuges for troubled men, says nothing about this kind of refuge. God provides better for men than by withdrawing them from the world where their work lies. Man is delivered from temptation, not by being taken out of it, but by being helped to conquer it. Paul was not relieved of the thorn in the flesh, but was given grace to bear it and to be a grand man in spite of it. Similarly man is not hidden from the strife of tongues by being withdrawn from it. God has a better refuge than that, and that is Himself. "Thou shalt hide them in the secret of Thy presence from the pride of man: Thou shalt keep them secretly in a pavilion from the strife of tongues." In putting a man in right relations with Himself, God puts him in right relation to the world's talk. Let us look at some illustrations of this, growing out of what has been already said.

There is the matter of slander and abuse. God does not always exempt good men from these. The man of science delights to show you how he can handle fire, and even go into the fire unhurt. That is a greater achievement than keeping away from the fire. In like manner God shows His power to keep the feet of His saints, by letting the tongues of men run riot, and their fire concentrate its fury upon them, while they walk in peace and come out without the smell of fire on their garments. A good man is given to thinking that, if his good name in the world is gone, if the world's talk casts up nothing but mire and dirt, it is all over with him. God shows him that he can live, and live quietly and cheerfully, on the simple fact that the integrity of his heart and the cleanness of his hands are known to God. And sometimes, when men withdraw their praise, the slandered or misunderstood man finds out for the first time how sweet God's smile is. Sometimes when men withdraw their company, and leave him shut in with God, he discovers that in His presence is fulness of joy. There was Daniel. What a talk he made at court. The spies were on the watch at the hour of prayer, and surely enough, spite of the king's decree, Daniel appeared at his open window three times in the day, and prayed and gave thanks before his God. What a buzz of talk. How the spies hastened to the king's presence, bursting with the news. Daniel prays! We saw him praying three times! His window was open; he did not even pretend to conceal his contempt for thy law, O king! And so the whisper stole into the court, Daniel has disobeyed the king! Daniel has prayed! What a rich morsel of court gossip it was. What unconcealed delight that the unpopular Hebrew had at last fatally committed himself. What wise sayings were doubtless retailed over the luxurious tables about the folly of the act. The thing took its own course. God was at no pains to save Daniel from the flood of talk, nor from the lions' den. He let slander do its worst. He suffered His servant to go down among the lions, and there Daniel found himself in the secret of God's tabernacle. God was there, and it mattered not what men or beasts were there beside. The world talks as if when everything but God fails a man, he is in desperate straits. The Bible puts it that at that point he is at his very best, most safe and most blessed.

Sometimes God saves one from the strife of tongues by putting him where he cannot talk and where others cannot talk to him. He sends a calamity so overwhelming that his friends do not know what to say to him, and the man himself cannot reason about it, cannot argue, cannot explain, is simply reduced to silence. All that he can say is, "I am dumb; I open not my mouth because Thou didst it." He must find his only explanation in that simple fact, God did it. God seems to say to him, "Be still! There is only one thing you can know about this matter. Be still and know that I am God." And the man is forced to sit down and fix his eye on that one illuminated text shining in his darkness, "I am God." And for awhile it is like the handwriting on Belshazzar's wall; but oh, how the meaning grows. What wonderful lessons men have learned by silently facing and pondering those three words: what inferences they draw, every one of which is a new hiding-place for the troubled soul, irradiated with divine light. "I am God, and therefore thy creator, and therefore have a right over thee and thine. I am God, and therefore thy redeemer and sanctifier, and therefore I am purifying thee in the fire. I am God, and God is love, and therefore this trouble veils love. I am God, and therefore there can be no mistake. I am God, and therefore I will give thee grace to meet thy trouble. I am God, and I who have torn can heal." Is not this a refuge better than all the wise talk of the world, better than all its endless discussions on the origin and meaning of sorrow?

Again, God shields good men from the world's talk by hardening them against it. We all know that exposure is often the best remedy for certain bodily ailments, and that is a kind of cure which God not unfrequently employs for moral infirmities. Often He will level every bulwark on the side on which one most craves shelter. Often He will expose one to the very thing from which he most shrinks. Again and again we have seen how the sensitive spirit which avoids publicity, which shivers at the world's comments, which hates the strife of controversy, is put under a steady fire of these. There is many a man who stands out in clear view, a mark for all the shafts of the tongue, who, you perhaps think, cares nothing for them; who speaks his word and does his work as though deaf to all the babel of popular gossip; but who, nevertheless, conceals a womanly sensitiveness under his bold front, and has had to learn how to school a timid heart not to flinch at censure. It is hard discipline, but oh, how much one learns under it. How one who has only God's purpose in his heart and God's work on his hands, gradually learns that the hardest things men can say are not so terrible after all. Archbishop Whately, of Dublin, who died in 1863, was among the sturdiest men of his time, a man of undaunted courage, and withal of that genuine originality which awakens comment and opposition. Much of his official life was passed under a fire of censure. He once said of himself: "My stumbling-block most to be guarded against, the right hand and right eye that offended and was to be cut off, was the dread of censure. Few would conjecture this from seeing how I have braved it all my life, and how I have perpetually been in hot water, when, in truth, I had a natural aversion to it. So I set myself resolutely to act as though I cared nothing for either the sweet or the bitter, and in time I got hardened. But no earthly object could ever pay me for the labor and the anguish of modelling my nature in these respects. I have succeeded so far that I have even found myself standing firm where some men of constitutional intrepidity have given way. And this will always be the case more or less, through God's help, if we will but persevere, and persevere from a right motive."

Again, God hides His servant from the strife of tongues by filling his hands with work for others. The more one is interested in the welfare of men, the less he will care for their talk; for a good deal of sensitiveness is merely selfishness, after all. When people are self-conscious and more anxious about the impression they are making than about doing God's will in serving their neighbors, they are keenly alive to what is said of them. That is a kind of sensitiveness which may be cured; and the best way of curing it is to get the life filled with Christ's spirit of ministry. Get hold of some object which stirs up the deep places in your heart: some work which lays the pressure of its "must be done" not only on your conscience but on your love, and the kind of figure you are making will pass out of your thought. What the world may be saying of you will go by like the idle wind. I am talking of what I know. I had one lesson (if you will pardon the personal reminiscence) written deep on my heart, when, with several others, I went with the Christian Commission during the war to assist in nursing the sick and wounded. I was peculiarly sensitive to the sight of physical suffering, and my friends laughed at me, and said, "You will faint at the first sight of blood": and in my inmost heart I was afraid I should, and shrank from the ridicule I should bring upon myself. And I well remember how I trembled inwardly when they put a little pail and sponge into my hand, and sent me down to a barge which they were loading with wounded men to carry them to the hospitals in Washington, and told me to moisten the stiff bandages and cool the hot heads and hands. Ah! what a sight it was! God grant this fair land may never witness such scenes again. But from the moment that I sat down beside the first man that met my eye, a poor fellow with a musket-bullet through his jaw, and tried, while I applied the cooling water, to drop a word or two about Christ and His rest for the weary—all my shrinking vanished. I thought only of those wounded men. I had little or no self-consciousness left. I saw only that colossal misery. That experience was worth a great deal to me, and that is the reason I tell it to you, for it illustrates a universal truth. Get yourself thoroughly interested in other people's bodies and souls; get the question "What can I do for them?" uppermost in your thought, and the world's gossip about you will attract as little notice as the drifting sea-weed borne to your feet on one tide only to be swept out by the next.

And I need scarcely add that this is the best way to keep ourselves from being sharers in the world's gossip. He who dwells in the secret of God's presence learns to take God's attitude toward infirmity and error—the attitude of One who is touched with the feeling of men's infirmities; of One who remembers that His children are dust, and pities them accordingly. The tongue of such an one will not be a weapon of strife. It will send forth better and sweeter things than censures and sarcasms and ungenerous criticisms.

These are some of the methods in which God hides His people from the strife of tongues; and all these methods are embraced in this one comprehensive fact—that He hides them in the hiding-place of His presence. If we sum up in a word that which meets our craving to escape from the strife of tongues, we say, our hiding-place is God. The hiding-place of Thy presence, Thy tabernacle—those are parallel expressions, the one literal, the other figurative, and they are very suggestive. Literally the first means "the hiding-place of Thy countenance." Think of it. Hidden in the light of God's face. Hidden in that splendor where His power is hidden. And if we want the New Testament key to this passage, we have it in Paul's Epistle to the Colossians: "Your life is hid with Christ in God." There never was a man so talked about and cursed and criticised and reviled as was Christ; and yet His attitude to the world's talk is very easily perceived. He does not grow irritated at the constantly repeated challenges and demands for explanation of His work and purpose. His heart is full of pity. He weeps because Jerusalem will not hear His words of life, and utters those paradoxes as they must have seemed to His disciples, "Blessed are ye when men shall say all manner of evil against you falsely for my sake." "Woe unto you when all men shall speak well of you." And the secret of all was that He dwelt in God, in absolute oneness with the Father. One whose sympathies were all with God's, whose purpose lay in the exact direction of God's, whose life was the larger life of God, could well afford to despise men's talk. It must have seemed to Him the most infinitesimal of trifles, so far as it related to Himself or to His work. And this condition it is the privilege of God's servant to share with Christ. Like Christ's life, with Christ's life, his life may be hid in God; and just to the degree in which his life is so hidden is he out of the range of the world's talk, and it ceases to harm him. There he is safe from the arrows of slander. There he is occupied with better and higher things than those which form the staple of the world's talk. There he is in the presence and under the eye of the infinite Judge, and feels how small a thing it is to be judged of men. There he is on intimate terms with the wisest of counsellors, and needs not to shape his course by the labored, prejudiced, contradictory wisdom of men. There he sees only right and not worldly policy, and learns to be right and to let policy take care of itself. "If any man walk in the day he stumbleth not, because he seeth the light of this world." He who walks in the sunlight needs no torches to guide his steps. He need care nothing if all the torches in the world be extinguished. And thus he who lives in the unclouded light of God's presence needs not the lights of men's kindling which flicker and flare in the changing gusts of popular opinion. He is like one who looks down from a chamber irradiated with pure light upon men stumbling and groping through a dimly-lighted street, and crying to him to come down and walk by their light.

And therefore, to quote the beautiful words of a living preacher—living in the best sense—"If we are really Christ's, then back into the very bosom of His Father where Christ is hid, there He will carry us. We, too, shall look out and be as calm and as independent as He is. The needs of men shall touch us just as keenly as they touch Him, but the sneers and strifes of men shall pass us by as they pass by Him and leave no mark on His unruffled life. It will be just as impossible when that time comes, for us to work ourselves into a passion about yesterday's gossip as it was for Jesus to become a partisan in the quarrel about the divided inheritance: and yet for us, just as for Him, this will not mean a cold and selfish separation from our brethren. We shall be infinitely closer to their real life when we separate ourselves from their outside strife and superficial pride, and know and love them truly by knowing and loving them in God."

This, then, is the conclusion of the whole matter. In this world we must be exposed to the strife of tongues.

It's arrows will drop over into the quietest and obscurest retreat which we make for ourselves. Its jargon will penetrate to our most retired chamber. We must hear what men say, and our very nature, the very nature of our life, makes us sensitive to that, and carries with it a temptation to shape our life by it. And yet, we are annoyed by it; we would be glad of a refuge from it. Our refuge is God. Our blessed Saviour, who knew and felt the strife of tongues as no other ever felt it, beckons us to Himself, and says, "Come hither with me into the hiding-place of God's presence. Hide your life with me in God." You who are worried by men's talk; you who are tempted to respect it as a rule of living; you who care so very, very much about what the world says, hear His voice. Give your minds to character and not to talk. Concentrate your effort and your thought upon being like Christ, and then the talk will wag on its own way and will not touch you as you walk the path which shineth more and more unto the perfect day. He shall hide you in the secret of His presence from the pride of man. He shall keep you secretly in a pavilion from the strife of tongues.

VII.

STRENGTH IN WEAKNESS.

"For when I am weak, then am I strong."—2 COR. xii. 10.

PAUL, as you perceive from the context, has been speaking of that great personal trial which he has described as "a thorn in the flesh." Speculations over the peculiar nature of this affliction have been to little purpose; and this is just what we may expect from the Bible, which is a most tantalizing book to those who are concerned about the circumstances of truth rather than about the truth itself. Thus while curious students have been trying to show that Paul's thorn in the flesh was a pleurisy, or a weakness of the eyes, a headache or an earache, temptations to unbelief or to sensuality, torments of conscience about his past life, epilepsy,—we are as much in the dark as ever upon these points: and that makes little or no difference, so long as the great spiritual lesson, God's strength in human weakness, is clear as the sun, and is charged with warning and comfort.

Of this trial we know:

That it was exceptionally severe. The apostle's metaphor would never have been selected to describe an ordinary affliction. The word "thorn" properly means the sharpened stake which was used in the barbarous punishment of impaling, being driven by force through the living body. Again, it is described as the torment of Satan; Satan's messenger sent to buffet him. When Satan is allowed to exercise his power upon men, we know what torments he applies, from the story of Job, and from our Lord's words to Peter, "Satan hath desired to sift you as wheat."

We know that this infirmity hindered Paul's work, or seemed to him to hinder it. If it were a disease of the eyes, it compelled him to dictate instead of writing. If it were epilepsy, its spasms might seize him in the midst of some impassioned appeal to the Church, and make him an object of pity and disgust to those whom he was trying to instruct. Some have thought that this was in his mind when he wrote to the Galatians, "My temptation in the flesh ye despised not, neither rejected, but received me as an angel of God." There could be no sorer trial to him than one which seemed to interfere with his work; for he was burdened with a sense of the value and of the danger of men's souls, and of the critical condition of the infant Church. The love of Christ constrained him; and the Gospel was as a fire in his bones which would not suffer him to be silent night or day.

Hence he besought the Lord to remove this trial; earnestly, thrice entreating that it should depart from him. His request was refused. He was told that the thorn must remain for the present; that he must be content to suffer, to feel the pain, to see himself humiliated, to see his work apparently suffer for the lack of his presence and counsel.

But the refusal was qualified. Certain words were added which converted it from a hopeless finality into a revelation: which changed the messenger of Satan into a messenger of God. Whereas it might have seemed that God was frowning on his labors and impeding them, it now appeared that God was forwarding them by means of this very trial, and was giving him in it the highest testimony of His love. Whereas it might have appeared that God had chosen a weak and inefficient instrument to carry on His work, and that the work was going to be weak and inefficient for that reason, it now appears that through this very instrument, and by means of this fragmentary work, God is going to reveal His own perfect strength. And the moment Paul gets hold of that view of the matter, he accepts it and rejoices in it; for he forthwith says, "Most gladly therefore will I rather glory in my infirmities, that the power of Christ may rest upon me. Therefore I take pleasure in infirmities, in reproaches, in necessities, in persecutions, in distresses for Christ's sake: for when I am weak, then am I strong."

In considering this topic, you will observe:

That God's answer to Paul's prayer lays down a general law. God does not merely promise to perfect Paul's strength in that particular weakness. Indeed He does not say, "*My* strength is made perfect in weakness," for the "my" is not in the text. He states the general truth, a truth not peculiar to the spiritual life, though appearing there in its noblest aspect, that strength is perfected in weakness.

Let us then look at this general law apart from its religious bearings.

Strength is perfected in weakness. You know that the converse is true; that weakness is perfected in strength; for both your reading and your experience show you that the greatest manifestations of weakness are constantly seen in those whom the world deems the strongest. The weaknesses of great men form an element of literature. This is partly because their real strength betrays them into weakness. A strong man is likely to be a self-reliant man; inclined to give very little heed to the counsels of others, and to insist on having his own way at all hazards: and such a man is morally certain to display some weakness in himself or in his plans. A man, again, who is consciously strong at some point, is likely to think that his strength at that point will make up for his carelessness at other points. For instance, you often see men of great intellect who are morally weak and loose, and who count on their intellectual strength to cover their moral deficiency. The man who is financially strong is now and then tempted to believe that money can carry him over the lack of courtesy or consideration for others. Scripture history is not behind secular history in the number and eminence of the testimonies to this truth. The strong men of the Bible are also its weak men. Abraham's falsehood, Noah's excess, Jacob's worldliness, Moses' unhallowed zeal, Elijah's faithless despair, David's lust and murder,

Solomon's luxuriousness and sensuality — all tell the same story which we read in the biographies of the scholars, statesmen, monarchs, and generals of later times.

On the other hand, illustrations are equally abundant of strength perfected in weakness. They are all about us in our ordinary life. Let an ignorant but conceited man go to a foreign city. Strong in his own conceit, he says, "A guide is a nuisance, and I will have none of them. I will find out the objects of interest for myself." He does not know a word of the language, he has not the faintest idea of the geography of the city, and he does not know how to use a map. And so he goes blundering along, trying to make inquiries by gestures; getting into all sorts of places where he has no business to be; exposing himself to insult and even to danger; wasting hours in his search for a palace or an art-gallery—a sorry exhibition of weakness. Another man goes into the same city, quite as ignorant, but with a little more common sense which leads him to say to himself, "I am helpless as a babe in this strange place: now let me procure the right kind of help." He finds a trustworthy and intelligent guide. He goes with no loss of time to the places he wants to visit. He receives answers to all his questions and a great deal of information besides. He is happily gaining new ideas and solid knowledge, while the strong man, so independent of help, is standing at street corners and painfully studying his guide-book. When they return home, the man who was weak enough to accept guidance, is the stronger man in knowledge.

Can you imagine any object more weak and helpless than a blind child? It is at the mercy of any cruelty which a bad heart may inspire. It is largely dependent on others for the commonest things; and yet what a strength it wins from that very weakness. How much strength it draws to itself from others. The mother's love for that child has an element of peculiar tenderness. Her heart goes out to that helpless little one as to no other member of the household. Over none does the father watch with such anxious care. Those sealed eyes, those tottering feet, those outstretched hands have a power to move those parents to labor and care and sacrifice such as the strongest and most beautiful of the household does not possess. Out of weakness the child is made strong. And then there is the familiar fact of the increased power imparted to certain faculties by the very infirmity of another faculty. Your touch is not half so sensitive and discerning as that of those groping hands. Your ear, though trained by the best masters in music or elocution, cannot detect the nice variations of sound which appeal to the ear of the blind.

Then again, the consciousness of infirmity often makes its subject so cautious, and puts him under such careful discipline, that he really accomplishes more than another who is free from infirmity. The man whose health and strength are exuberant, is likely to be careless of them. A single leap or strain, made in the overflow of his animal spirits, may maim or weaken him for life; while, on the other hand, much of the world's best work is done by men who rarely know what it is to be without an aching head or a feverish pulse, and who therefore must needs work by rule and economize minutes and bring discipline to bear on rebellious nerves and muscles. It is this power of self-mastery wrought out through weakness, which gives them power over other minds and hearts.

And now let us look at the truth on its religious side. There it comes into even stronger relief, because, in the Christian economy, weakness is assumed to be an universal condition, and dependence is therefore the universal law of the Christian life. There, it is invariably true that real strength comes only out of that weakness which, distrustful of itself, gives itself up to God. There, it is invariably true that weakness grows out of the conceit which refuses to depend, and which trusts its own wisdom or strength. There, it is invariably true that God's strength shines through human infirmity, and often selects for its best and richest expressions the poorest, weakest, most burdened of mankind.

Let us take this very case of Paul. Here is a man beset with various infirmities. He himself intimates that he lacked that imposing personal presence which carries so much weight with men. He had not the polished eloquence of Apollos. Besides, he labored under the disadvantages arising from the persistent malice and hatred of the Jews, who neglected no opportunity to blacken his reputation and to thwart his plans. There was his bodily ailment, aggravated by frequent journeys over stormy seas and roads beset with robbers and crossed by foaming torrents. There were incidents like those at Philippi, scourgings, stocks, the hideous inner-prison with its darkness and stifling heat and poisonous air; like the stoning at Lystra, like the long confinements at Cæsarea and Rome—all these, with the incessant care and anxiety for the churches. With all these, and others which might be added, Paul might well have called himself "weak," personally weak, and prosecuting his work against tremendous odds. And yet at this distance, we can see that that very weakness of Paul was his strength. Understand me. I do not mean merely that Paul accomplished a great work in spite of his weakness. I mean that his weakness helped his work, and that it was distinctly an element of the power which to-day he wields in human thought.

For Paul's weakness — conscious weakness — gave God's power its full opportunity. It is a strange gift that we have of preventing God from doing for us all that He would. Yet we have it nevertheless; and those who are strongest in self-confidence and weakest in faith have most of it. But let that pass. Paul gave up his life, weakness and all, into God's hands, for God to use whatever in it He might see fit. And you know how often God sees fit to use in such cases the very elements you and I would throw away. We do not count weakness among the factors of success. The world is at a loss what to do with weakness. It has no use to which to put it, and no machinery with which to work it up. When God takes hold of weakness it becomes another thing and works under another law. So then Paul, having abandoned the idea of doing anything by himself, having given that poor, battered self to God without prescribing or choosing what part of it should be used or how it should be used,—God took this weakness, the very thing which Paul had been asking might depart from him, and wrought out victory for Christ's cause and for Paul by means of it. You ask me, "How?"

Well, take the impression which the character and history of Paul make on your own minds. You know something of the power which Luke's record of his life and labors exerts in stimulating Christian zeal and in educating character. Do not all these things get a stronger hold on your hearts, and through them upon your convictions, through the very sympathy which the apostle's sufferings call out?

Or take the same facts in his own day. Did not his very infirmities endear him to the churches? Had not these somewhat to do with the liberal supplies from Philippi, and with the heart-breaking sorrow of the Ephesian elders at Miletus? Can any one who has known the impressiveness of an admonition from a feeble or dying friend, doubt that the spectacle of Paul's emaciated frame and the knowledge that he bore in his body the marks of persecution for Christ's sake, added wonderfully to the power of his word?

And again, after all that we read of Paul, though next to Christ he is by far the most prominent figure in the New Testament, though we heartily admire the man as we read, yet we rise from his story and from his writings with a stronger impression of Christ than of Paul. The radiance of the light eclipses the wonder of the lamp. That is as Paul would have had it; and thus, as one of his modern expositors has truthfully said, "What the apostle lost for himself by his infirmities, and what Christianity lost for the moment, has been more than compensated by the acknowledgment that he was beyond doubt proved to be not the inventor of Christianity, but its devoted and humble propagator. In his own weakness lies the strength of the cause. When he was weakest as a teacher of the present, he was strongest as an apostle of the future."

Or go farther back to the immediate disciples of our Lord. Weak, fallible men we know them to have been, and yet there stands the record of their wonderful success as ministers of the Gospel. Christ called Peter a rock; and yet at that stage of his history, Peter reminds us rather of those rocks which one meets with in clay-soil regions, which crumble at the touch, and are, least of all stones, fit for foundations. Peter, blustering, forward, boastful, with a great deal of strength of his own, which crumbled into weakness at the first touch of danger,—and yet—"On this rock will I build my Church. So strong shall it be that the gates of hell shall not prevail against it."

The church which began under the ministry of weak Peter is surely no feeble factor in to-day's society: but the Peter of Pentecost was not the Peter of Gethsemane. Between these two he had learned a great deal about the weakness of human strength and the strength which God makes perfect in human weakness. The consequence is that whereas in Gethsemane Peter asserts himself, at Pentecost he asserts Jesus. Where he asserts himself the issue is a coward and a traitor. Where he passes out of sight behind Jesus, he is the hero of the infant church, whom we love and honor.

In this text there is no encouragement to cherish weakness. Weakness is not commended as a good thing in itself. The object of Christian training is to make men strong: and the Psalmist tells us that God's children go from strength to strength. But weakness is a universal fact in human nature. Our Lord covers all humanity with the statement, "the flesh is weak"; and this text does tell us to recognize the fact and to provide against it by taking another's strength. The thing which it does commend is the permission of conscious weakness to have another's strength push up through itself and pervade and transform it; a

> "holy strength whose ground
> Is in the heavenly land."

That kind of strength does not encourage self-conceit. It does not lead a man to talk about his courage and resolution and energy. It rather hides the man behind his Lord. Paul can do all things, but only through Christ that strengtheneth him. How beautifully the context brings out this thought: "Most gladly will I rather glory in my infirmities that the power of Christ may rest upon me." Think of that for a moment. What was the ark of the covenant? Nothing but a simple box overlaid with gold, such a thing as any skilful workman could make. And yet, when it fell into the hands of Israel's enemies, the priest declared "the glory is departed from Israel." What gave it this importance and meaning? It was that which rested upon it. It was the glory which burned between the cherubim, which made its resting-place the holiest spot in the world. And so, when the power of Christ rests upon a life, all its commonplace, its littleness, its weakness, are transfigured and lifted up into power, and the weak things of the world confound the things which are mighty. Thus it comes to pass that out of the mouth of babes and sucklings God ordains strength. You have sometimes skirted a ridge of mountains, bold, rugged masses, not regular in outline, but with jagged pinnacles splintered by the lightning, cleft down to their bases here and there by some convulsion of primeval times, yet showing through these fearful rifts glimpses of woody valleys and descending waterfalls and peaceful homes. How much grander they are than the smoothly-rounded, forest-clad hills. So it is with God's strong men. "God," says some one, "often accomplishes His greatest works by ministers who, great in themselves, are all the greater because their greatness is cleft through with infirmities through which we see the divine power working within them."

However exceptional, therefore, Paul's trial may have been, this word with which Christ consoles him is for us no less than for him.

It commends to us the old truth, asserted by our Lord, confirmed by the histories of the strongest and best of all ages, daily commended to us by our own falls and mistakes—the flesh is weak.

It brings to us the same comfort that Paul received, that this weakness, so discouraging, so humiliating, so irritating, may be the very point where divine strength shall assert itself in victory. The truth of the text is wider than some of us have been wont to think. We have possibly imagined that it conveyed no more than the assurance that God would assist our weakness; would lift us when we should have fallen, and would prevent us from falling victims to strong enemies. But God means more than that. The text asserts not only that, but also the grander truth that God will make weakness itself an element of strength. That He will develop positive power out of it. We are, naturally, like one who carries round with him a rough preciousstone, ignorant of its value, and ready to throw it away or to part with it for a trifle. This thing, weakness, we do not know what to do with. It is rough. It is heavy. We should be glad to throw it away. Christ comes like a skilful lapidary and shows us its value. He refuses to take it away, because He can teach us to convert it into power which shall enrich us and the world. I remember a little church among the mountains, which sprang up through the labors of a man the best of whose life was spent in trouble—a church founded among a population little better than heathen; and in the church building there was framed and hung up a magnificent rough agate which he had picked up somewhere among the hills, with the inscription, "And such were some of you." And that stone tells the story of our text—the story of the Church on earth; a weak, erring church, formed of men of like passions with ourselves, its leaders stained and scarred with human infirmity, yet with a line of victory and spiritual power running through it like a track of fire: rough stones hewn out of the mountains, carved into polished pillars in the temple of the Lord: brands from the burning, commissioned to be priests with fair mitres and tongues touched with the convincing power of the Holy Ghost: ignorant, fallible men and women, persecuted, afflicted, tormented, despised—waxing valiant in fight, turning to flight alien armies, out of weakness made strong.

But this truth is not for the heroic side of life only. We want it most on the side which is not heroic (as men use that term); in that sphere of daily, commonplace life where our weakness is most apparent and most tested. And it belongs there. It will come to our help there.

We are weak. Let us accept the fact in all its length and breadth; but as that fact grows upon us let us fix our eyes on the other fact of God's strength. Let us retire from our own strength only to lay hold on God's. If we do, then our weakness will be a revelation. It will show us more of God. I have often seen in the woods how a storm had torn away the soil from around a tree on the edge of a bank, and in so doing had laid bare the underground history of the tree. I could see the roots, and how deeply they had struck, and how they had wrapped themselves round the rocks; and so the weakness which gives the tempests of this life their opportunity, the weakness which so often results in stripping a life of its earthly hopes and pleasures, the weakness which lays one open to remark and sneer and contempt, may yet show the roots of holy character striking deep into the life of God, and holding the life fast to Eternity.

It will bring blessed comfort when once we shall have been persuaded to take God's strength for our own:

—" to confess
That there's but one retreat:
And meekly lay each need and each distress
Down at the Sovereign feet.

" Then, then, it fills the place
Of all we hoped to do;
And sunken nature triumphs in the grace
That bears us up and through.

" A better glow than health
Flushes the cheek and brow,
The heart is stout with store of nameless wealth:
We can do all things now.

" No less sufficiency seek;
All counsel less is wrong;
The whole world's force is poor, and mean, and weak;
When I am weak, I'm strong."

VIII.

BETWEEN SOWING AND HARVEST.

> *"And He said, So is the Kingdom of God, as if a man should cast seed upon the earth; and should sleep and rise night and day, and the seed should spring up and grow, he knoweth not how. The earth beareth fruit of herself; first the blade, then the ear, then the full corn in the ear. But when the fruit is ripe, straightway he putteth forth the sickle, because the harvest is come."—*
> MARK iv. 26–29.

WHAT does Christ mean when He says, "The Kingdom of God is like" this or that? Let us be sure that He is not using a mere rhetorical figure, a superficial comparison which will not bear pressing. We may press these similitudes of our Lord. When He says a thing is like, He means a real, inner likeness. He means that a fact in the illustration, answers to a fact in the thing illustrated. In these parables, therefore, in which He expounds the nature and growth and potency of the kingdom of God, we may count upon finding the substantial counterpart of the natural fact in the spiritual fact. The kingdom or rule of God in the world and in the individual man, obeys certain laws and develops certain phenomena. The same laws and the same phenomena hold in the growth of a mustard-seed; in the work of leaven in bread; in the growth of tares among wheat; in whatever natural process, in short, may be selected to illustrate the particular aspect of the kingdom.

This fact will give us, as it is intended to give, great assurance and comfort and certainty in the practical application of these parables. Let us look at the one before us.

A farmer, an ordinary, average laborer, sows seed, of wheat let us say. He scatters it and covers it from sight in the ground. Between the sowing and the harvest a long time intervenes. For a good while nothing appears. The ground to-day looks just as it did yesterday. No stranger could tell from looking at the field that anything was sown there. What is the farmer's feeling and attitude during that time? The point of the parable is in the answer to that question. He is not nervous or worried or uneasy. So far as the seed is concerned, he is obliged to be idle. Nothing that he can do can hasten its growth. There is nothing for him to do but to let the seed lie where he threw it. So he goes on quietly with his regular routine of life. The condition of that sown field does not keep him awake at night. He sleeps, and he rises the next day, and sees the field as black and smooth as it was the day before, but he is no more troubled at that than he was overnight. He wakes and rises and goes about other business or does nothing, as the case may be.

By and by the little green shoots appear above the surface; not full heads of wheat, only slender blades. It makes no difference to him. Still he goes to rest at the appointed time, and sleeps his sleep, and rises, and possibly throws his eye over the field, but he is perfectly at his ease. He does not get out his sickles or call his men.

Meanwhile the blade is slowly developing into a stalk with the hard, crude, green wheat-ears. Still he makes no sign. Still the accustomed routine goes on. He sleeps and rises night and day, and shows no anxiety about that field.

At last the wheat is ripe. Then, of a sudden, the farmer's whole interest and attention concentrate themselves on that field. "Ho! reapers! Harvest-time is here! The wheat is ready to cut! Out into the fields! Out with your sickles! Bestir yourselves while the day is young; while the sky is clear; ere the rain come! Gather the wheat into the barns!"

Why has the farmer been so quiet and untroubled and even idle all this time? Not from indifference surely. You see how all his energy leaps into action the moment the field is ripe unto the harvest. It is from simple knowledge of a law of nature, and simple faith in the operation of that law. It is not scientific knowledge. A plain countryman, he knows nothing of the philosophy of germination. The seed springs up and grows "how, knoweth not he." But he knows that the earth beareth fruit of herself. Given the seed, he knows that the soil will do its part, and bring the seed on to harvest. Further, he knows that this process is a slow one, and is carried on by stages: that the full corn does not directly follow the blade, nor the ear the sowing: but that the process is invariable, first the blade, then the ear, then, and only then, the full corn in the ear. He trusts nature. He neither frets nor bustles during the interval between sowing and harvest. If he could hasten the growth, his indifference would vanish; but he cannot, and the impossibility does not disturb him. What seems indifference, therefore, is merely the recognition and acceptance of the fact that growth obeys a law entirely beyond his control.

Our Lord, you remember, touched the same truth as applied to human growth. "Which of you, by being anxious, can add unto his stature* one cubit?" It is folly for the boy to try and grow. He will not grow any faster by fretting for twenty years. He just moves on through happy, careless boyhood, and plays and studies, eats and sleeps, and his growth takes care of itself and perfects itself in due time. Again our Lord applies the same truth to the flowers. "Consider the lilies, how they grow. They toil not."

So then, this parable gives us three facts attaching to a process of nature. 1st. The earth bringeth forth fruit by itself, by its own natural law. Growth develops out of the contact of the earth and the seed. 2d. This process is slow and gradual. 3d. The proper attitude of man toward this process is that of patient, quiet, cheerful waiting.

Our Lord says the Kingdom of God is like this. Therefore in studying the growth of the divine life and

---

* Or "age."

the progress of the divine rule either in a single soul or in society, we may expect to find three facts corresponding to the three in nature : namely, that divine life has a power of self-development according to a law of its own : that the development is slow and gradual : that the soul's true attitude toward this development is restful, cheerful, patient waiting.

I shall not dwell at length on the first two points. We do not need to argue that the seed of the divine life has a power of self-development; and that God's life in contact with the human heart will bring forth fruit of itself. Christ indeed tells us in the parable of the sower that the seed falls into different kinds of soil, and that the character of the growth is determined by that fact. But that is not the point here. Here the favorable conditions are assumed—good seed in an honest heart. That being the case, the seed will spring up and fructify.

Moreover, the fact that this process is slow and gradual needs no proof. We see for ourselves that moral and spiritual growth is not perfected in one stage, any more than physical growth. Spiritual infancy and childhood precede spiritual manhood, just as one is a babe and a child before he becomes a man. Saints are not made at a stroke. They do not spring up like Jonah's gourd in a night. No one of the successive stages is overleaped. Conditions may accelerate growth in special cases, but the growth none the less rises through all the successive planes. Moreover, the best growths take the longest time. A Madeira vine will cover a large arbor in a single season. An oak is a matter of a century. A dog is full-grown in a couple of years. A man is not at his best in twenty.

Let us then pass to the third point: the proper attitude of a Christian toward the growth of the divine life in himself and in society.

No problem is oftener submitted to a pastor than the conscious imperfection of sincere believers. They come, saying, "I do not see that I am growing at all in the Christian life. I find so much evil in myself. I am so skeptical. My life is marked by so many lapses and stumbles. I find myself so cold and irresponsive, and therefore I fear that I have no divine life in me."

Now it is to such that Christ addresses this parable. He points them to the farmer, sleeping and rising night and day while his sown field lies black and unmarked by a single sign of growth, or while the wheat-ears are hard and green.

Let us emphasize the fact that our Lord is not encouraging indifference to spiritual progress. His illustration is as far as possible from any hint of that. The farmer is not indifferent to the growth of his wheat, but his attitude toward it is determined by the fact that, so far as the fact and rate of growth are concerned, nature has taken it into her own hands. It has passed into the sphere of the law that the earth bringeth forth fruit of itself. His apparent indifference, as has been truthfully said, "is not real apathy. It is latent energy biding its time; fervent desire controlled by the patience of hope."

And we are encouraged to take just this attitude toward our own spiritual growth. A Christian life indeed gives us something to do and to watch over at all times. It never allows us to be idle or uninterested; but, as regards this particular matter of the progress and rate of growth, we must recognize the fact that it belongs to a region and works under a law that is largely beyond our reach. The unconscious assumption which underlies much of our restlessness and anxiety about this matter, is that we have to do the work of growing; that we must make ourselves grow. And we keep our eye on the harvest-stage, and think only of that, and make ourselves miserable because we have not reached it. We carry into the time of the blade and the ear the bustle and haste of harvest-time, and to no purpose whatever. During all that intermediate period between seed-time and harvest, the farmer is not idle. He must keep away the birds from the field. He must look to his fences. There is work of various kinds to be done in other parts of the farm; but still there is a work going on in that field which he cannot do, and of the nature of which he knows little or nothing. So, whatever we may have to do day by day, as we are growing up into Christ, there is a certain work which must be done for us, independently of us, a work which will obey its own law and advance at its own rate and by its own stages.

Accepting this fact, we then come face to face with the accompanying fact that this law includes, besides the harvest-stage, the two other stages of the blade and the green ear. The core of the question is, How are we to stand affected toward these two stages?

For these have their counterpart in Christian experience. There is the blade-stage: or, as the corresponding point of a tree's growth, the blossoming-stage. How beautiful it is. How tender the blade. How fresh its living green. How delicate and exquisitely-tinted the petals of the blossom. Or carry the illustration up to human life. How unsullied and sweet are infancy and early childhood. How quick the perceptions. How natural the attitudes. How responsive to joy and pain. How bright and quaint the sayings. And similarly there is a peculiar charm about the first stages of Christian life as it emerges into the sunlight and atmosphere of Christ's love. The spiritual susceptibilities are so quick; the enthusiasm so ardent; the whole being so responsive to the breath of devotion; the will so ready; the flavor of love and holy joy so pronounced.

In nature, with all the peculiar charm of this initial stage, its transitoriness presents no difficulty or doubt to our minds. We do not dream of regarding its beauty and sweetness as a warrant for its permanency. We are not surprised nor dismayed when the tender blade gives place to the lank, unlovely stalk; when the delicate blossom is borne down the wind, and replaced by the hard, green ball; when the winsome babe passes into the rude, romping boy or girl. We do not lose hope of grain or fruit or manhood because the earlier delicacy and beauty are merged in a succeeding stage where crudeness is emphasized. But that is just what we do, or are prone to do, when spiritual growth is in question. The fact is the same. The second, middle stage of

Christian development is less lovely than the first. The life has come out into the atmosphere of conflict. The babe in Christ has begun to work out the problem of Christian manhood. The fight with temptation is on. Passion asserts itself. The life is launched upon the current of business and society. A larger and more captivating view of the world is opened. The mind has come up against the great problems of religious thought, and is learning to doubt and to question. The tender, subtle charm of the first stage has run into something harder, sharper, with more earth-stains, more marks of struggle, less rapture and brightness and warmth, less spiritual responsiveness,—just that stage of which I spoke a few moments ago, which sincere souls contemplate with dismay. I am speaking of facts—facts which most of you will recognize in your own experience: unpleasant indeed, but just as real as the hard, green ear or the crude, sour apple. And because many good people refuse to recognize this second, intermediate stage as a fact of spiritual development no less than of nature, they are frightened and restless, and disposed to believe that this stage is a violation of the law of growth in Christ. In other words, in nature we recognize in this hard, green stage a sign of growth. In religion we assume a contradiction of nature, and take the crude stage as a sign of deterioration, or of arrested growth.

But let us look farther. All through this crude stage, nature is steadily and quietly carrying out her law. The farmer knows that and is easy about it. The wind blows and the rain beats upon the stalk and its half-ripened ears. The mould stains it. The tempest tosses the bough with its load of raw, green apples or pears. But the growth is going on. A tinge of rich yellow is creeping upon the ear; a blush is stealing over the surface of the fruit; a dash of sweetness, a suggestion of flavor, are toning down the sourness. So the boy begins to show the lines of manhood in his face, and a hint of ripeness asserts itself in his speech and bearing. All these are familiar enough to us, but when we look at spiritual development we shut our eyes obstinately to any hint of riper color or flavor. We are intent only on the hardness and greenness. We will not see that growth may be going on and ripeness coming through crudeness; nay, that crudeness is included in growth, and is the prophecy of ripeness. We get no comfort out of a whole long period of our Christian growth, because we insist to ourselves that there is something abnormal and wrong in our not being ripe and ready for harvest.

And this is all wrong. God surely never meant that a stage of Christian development which covers a great part of our active life should be marked by perpetual uneasiness and despondency and worry. Those first disciples of Christ were far from being spiritually ripened, but Christ said to them, "Peace I leave with you; my peace I give unto you. Let not your heart be troubled. In the world ye shall have tribulation, but in me ye shall have peace." He gives us substantially the same lesson in this parable by pointing us to the farmer during the long interval between seed-time and harvest. It is no part of the parable that a man in Christ's kingdom should be carelessly happy all his days. Christian life develops in the face of the world, the flesh, and the devil, and must and will feel the shocks of these. The fruit and the wheat have to meet the wind and the rain. But our mistake is that we do not apprehend the real point of the struggle. Our difficulty, at the core, is, that we regard the condition which necessitates our struggle with sin as something wrong and abnormal. We quarrel with the fact of spiritual crudeness. We worry and torment ourselves because we are in the green ear and the hard bud; and thus we fight with a fact which is entirely out of our control, a fact which is as really of God's ordering as was the creation of the world; a law of slow growth through stages of crudeness, which holds as absolutely in the spiritual as in the natural world: a law which includes crudeness as it does ripeness. Paul saw it thus. He accepted spiritual immaturity, with all its consequences of wrestling and striving, as facts which he was not called upon to challenge. "Not as though I had already attained. I follow after, that I may grasp. I press toward the goal." But equally, Paul was conscious that spiritual growth and progress involved something beyond his strivings and labors; that something had to be done in him and for him; that there was a power not his own, which, in its own way and at its own rate, was ripening his Christian manhood through this immature stage; and he settled down in quiet faith upon that, saying, "If God be for us, who can be against us? I am confident that He who hath begun a good work in you will perfect it."

And the same truth holds in our estimate of others. When shall we learn that great truth of the promise and prophecy of incompleteness, which runs from the lowest point in nature through all human history? Why do we judge men only in the light of the actual, and take no account of the possibilities enfolded in their very immaturity and spiritual crudeness? Why do we refuse the teaching of nature that crudeness now means ripeness by and by? Why are we contented and hopeful over the fact of the green ear and the hard bud in nature, and fretful and impatient and hopeless over the green ear and the hard bud in God's children? Why, look at Christ's attitude toward that fact. Take the familiar case of Peter, who is a fair representative of the green-ear stage in the development of the early disciples. Our Lord knew better than any one else Peter's passionateness, his conceit, cowardice, roughness, dulness of spiritual perception. And yet all the while He saw ripeness and fruitfulness in him. He saw that Satan was going to sift him, but equally that Peter would strengthen his brethren. He saw in him the shifting sand, but also the rock of the Church. And our Lord knew that the law of the divine seed in him would assert itself and work itself out. Peter was in the hard-ear stage, but Christ did not despair of the full-corn in the ear; and He did not fret or worry or grow impatient with Peter. He was patient, loving, forbearing, not disturbed because He did not see in Gethsemane or in the high-priest's court what the multitude at Pentecost saw. The ripeness of the full corn was coming. It did come, as we know. Shall we quarrel with spiritual immaturity in our brethren? Shall we write down as not Christ's the man who develops sharp edges, obstinacy, conceit, irritability—in whom we mourn the lack of breadth, the limitation of charity? Paul teaches us a different lesson. "Brethren, if a man be overtaken in a fault, ye which are spiritual restore such an one in the spirit of meekness, considering yourselves. Bear ye one another's burdens and so fulfil the law of Christ." Our children, our Sabbath-school pupils, especially those who have professed faith in Christ—do not let us expect too much. Let us recognize the green ear as a part of God's own growth. Let us not be surprised nor disheartened at waywardness; let us not grow faint-hearted because precept and admonition seem to leave no abiding impression. The gardener must water and prune and brace up the young tree, it is true, but after all, the power of growth does not lie in the watering and bracing. We are often tempted to leave out of sight the largest factor in the process of spiritual growth—the inherent, self-developing power of the divine seed. We reason as if the whole work were of man. Let us not forget that God is at work in immaturity as well as in ripeness.

And for ourselves, let us only do our daily work and meet our daily foes with a quiet and resolved heart, and leave the growing to God, and the ripeness will come in time. Christian ripeness is a fact and not merely a hope. We do know that men grow through that immature stage, and come to take on again all that was best and sweetest in the first bloom of Christian life, together with a great deal more which could not, from the very nature of the case, be in that earlier stage. There is joy, but it is deep and tranquil rather than passionate. There is conscientiousness, but not petty scrupulousness. There is settled conviction about a few things, but quietness about things which cannot be settled. There is less thought of self and more of others. Self-scrutiny is swallowed up in the contemplation of the world's needs. There is humility about the matter of spiritual attainment. From the ripe Christian you do not hear talk of "Christian perfection." That belongs to the crude stage. The key-note is rather "I count not myself to have apprehended, but I follow after." There has dawned upon such an one so large a view of the possibilities which are in Christ and in Christian manhood through Christ, that he has come to look for completeness in heaven alone.

And withal, the life is lived in a tranquil atmosphere. You remember that beautiful passage in the Pilgrim's Progress, how, after the Slough of Despond and the Valley of the Shadow, and Apollyon, and the Giant Despair, and the Hill Difficulty had all been passed,—the pilgrims entered into the country of Beulah, whose air was very sweet and pleasant. "In this country the sun shineth night and day; wherefore this was beyond the Valley of the Shadow of Death, and also out of the reach of Giant Despair, neither could they from this place so much as see Doubting Castle. Here they were within sight of the city they were going to, also here met them some of the inhabitants thereof; for in this land the shining ones commonly walked, because it was upon the borders of heaven. Here they heard voices from out the city, loud voices saying, 'Say ye to the daughter of Zion, Behold thy Salvation cometh, behold His reward is with him.'"

IX.

THE ETERNAL GUIDE.

"For this God is our God forever and ever. He will be our Guide even unto death."—PSALM xlviii. 14.

It was an old Athenian custom to celebrate at the public expense the funeral of those citizens who had honorably fallen in war. At the close of the first year of the war between Athens and Sparta, Pericles was chosen to deliver the funeral oration. His eloquent words have been preserved for us in the pages of a Greek historian. He calls upon his fellow-citizens to fix their eyes on the present greatness of their city, and he continues: "When you are impressed by the spectacle of her glory, reflect that this Empire has been acquired by men who knew their duty, and had the courage to do it. The sacrifice which they made was repaid to them: for they received, each one for himself, a praise which grows not old, and the noblest of all sepulchres. For the whole earth is the sepulchre of famous men: not only are they commemorated by columns and inscriptions in their own country, but in foreign lands there dwells also an unwritten memorial of them, graven not on stone, but in the hearts of men. Make them your examples. Congratulate yourselves that you have been happy during the greater part of your days; remember that your life of sorrow will not last long, and be comforted by the glory of those who are gone: for the love of honor alone is ever young, and not riches but honor is the delight of men when they are old and useless."

How striking is the contrast of this utterance with the Psalm which we are to consider this morning! This too has a national character. It is supposed that it was sung to commemorate the deliverance of Jerusalem from the Assyrians. It records the defeat of the enemy, and like the speech of the Athenian, points to the unimpaired glory of the national centre. The kings marched by together. They looked upon Jerusalem, and were troubled. Fear took hold upon them, and they hasted away, broken and scattered like the great merchant-ships of Tarshish by the east wind. Zion stands unharmed. No hostile army lies at her gates. Behold her in her beauty! Let the daughters of Judah rejoice! Compass Zion, and go round about her: tell her towers, mark well her bulwarks, consider her palaces! But here the contrast appears. Israel's chief cause of congratulation is not in the bravery and well-earned honor of her captains and soldiers and counsellors; not in the enterprise and artistic skill which have founded and maintained the city. The true key-note is struck in the very first words of the Psalm: "Great is *Jehovah*, and greatly to be praised. *God* is known in her palaces for a refuge. It is He who sends forth His east wind and scatters the ships of Tarshish, that has dispersed the Assyrian host. The city is Jehovah's. God will establish it. We have thought of

Thy loving-kindness, O God, in the midst of Thy temple. As is Thy name, so is Thy praise to the ends of the earth. Let the daughters of Judah rejoice because of Thy judgments. Our future is in Thy hands. This God is our God forever and ever. He will be our Guide even unto death."

The contrast is instructive. There can be no question as to which member of it appeals to us. Our stand-point of reminiscence and of hope is the Hebrew and not the Greek one. Whether we consider our national or our individual life, we recognize God as the Author of all prosperity and the ground of all hope, and not great generals or statesmen or scholars. If we have cause for congratulation, the cause is Jehovah; if we have cheerful anticipations, they are grounded in the assurance of His care and guidance.

Naturally, at such seasons as this,* our thought runs into forecast. The character of that forecast is largely imparted by the past; and therefore it would not be strange if our anticipations and predictions of the future should be mingled with grave doubts and anxious forebodings. Many of us have lived long enough to have become skeptical of human wisdom and power in the conduct of affairs. Most of us who have reached middle life have learned by experience to distrust our own wisdom in the conduct of our own life; and our own blunders and disasters, and the magnitude and complexity of the problems which have emerged in the past, and which

---

* New Year, 1887.

cast their deep shadow into the future, tend to make us fearful and distrustful about the possibilities of the coming years. Our text to-day fits into this anxiety. The Psalm gives us our true stand-point of thought as Christians. We delight to trace God in history; let us make Him the central and controlling element of the future. "This God is our God forever and ever. He will be our Guide even unto death."

I say that the text fits into our anxiety, both for ourselves and for our nation: for guidance is our representative need. What is our true policy for the right conduct of our own future? Who is to solve for us the hard personal questions which are coming to the front? Are we to succeed or fail? If to succeed, how? Who is to guide us safely and successfully through the vexatious political and social questions which are already upon us? To these queries the Psalm makes answer: We need a Guide; we have one. This God will be our Guide even unto death.

Let us take the text in its own order.

The Psalmist makes the past throw light on the future. He reviews a crisis in national history, and shows how God has led the nation triumphantly through it. He has interposed with His strong right hand, and has dispersed and broken the enemy when he was at their very gates; and it is upon God's characteristics as exhibited in this crisis that he bases his assurances for the future. *Such* is God—so mighty, and so careful for His people. *Our* God, who has made our cause His own; *forever*, for He is always the same; as He has shown himself our guide, so will He be our guide even unto death.

And certainly, if the Psalmist had been the most learned of historians, if he could have anticipated the large and minute knowledge and the elaborate philosophies of history which mark the present, he could not have reached a wiser conclusion. For if, in our studies, we leave God out of history or of personal experience, these give us no ground of hope for successful guidance in the future. If any one is satisfied to believe that he has reached his present success, or that the world has attained its present point of progress through human wisdom alone, I wish him joy of his conclusion, and should be interested to know how he reconciles it with the facts. For history is largely a record of human blunders, whether it be the history of the world or of the Church; and the results of our own unaided wisdom in the evolution of our individual lives, are, I think, such as we should not care to have written out in full. The administration of the world has clearly proved itself to be altogether too large a thing for either the individual or the collective wisdom of mankind. If any one chooses to believe that humanity has stumbled and groped its way at haphazard up to its present attainment, I can only say his credulity is phenomenal. If, on the other hand, he recognizes in that development some element of superintendence and guidance, he cannot find it in the counsels or in the deeds of men. History without God, in short, is undecipherable; and the Psalmist, as it seems to me, reached the only satisfactory, indeed the only possible solution, when he said, "Such is God, our God forever and ever."

We go into this new year then with God as our guide, if we go into it rightly. And the next words of the text carry with them a great power of assurance. *Our* God. We carry God into the new year not merely as an abstract fact, not merely as a recognized possibility of power and wisdom, but as a personal possession. This God is our God. This permission to appropriate God is one of the most precious revelations of Scripture. Wonderful as it may seem, God gives Himself to us. We talk of God's giving Himself in Christ as if that were some new gift. God had given Himself to men long before Christ came. Long before Jesus told men to pray "Our Father," the Psalmist had said, "O God, Thou art my God." That little word "my" represents the eternal relation of God to His people; and if God is ours, then whatever in God is available for us, is ours. Not only so. We like to come into proved possessions. We like to wield the instrument which has proved potent in another's hand. We like to inherit the land which has proved its fruitfulness; and this desire is met by the word "such," which is the literal rendering for "this" God. Such is God—our God. He is our ancestral possession. He was our fathers' God. However mighty He has shown Himself in saving men, however wise in guiding, however generous in giving, however merciful in pardoning—such is God, our God: such to us as He was to them: the same yesterday, to-day, and forever. No man who can truthfully say *my* God, goes into this year poor, or helpless, or with a doubtful future. Uncertain indeed it may be as to details, but not as to quality. The modes and forms of the future we cannot know nor guess, but they will surely cover nothing but good, whatever they may be. A good many of you do not practically believe that. If you did, you would not worry and fret as you do. I tell you this to-day, and I give you God's Word for it, and yet if the Holy Spirit do not make this truth real to you, you will go home and cut down the truth to the measure of what you see. You will not accept God's large meaning. If a rich and wise man in whom you have perfect trust should come to you this morning and say, "For the rest of your life you shall absolutely command my purse, my knowledge, my experience," you would appreciate that, and would believe it, and would get substantial help and comfort from it. And yet God says to you nothing less than this. I am your God. All that you can receive as a man, I put at your disposal. That is your new-year's gift if you will believe it. God does not indeed promise to give you everything you may desire. That would be to make His gift null and void. He gives you Himself, and in accepting that gift, you take not only God's gifts, but the wisdom which selects and regulates them. Some things God will not give you because they would hurt you. Other things He will not give you because you could not use them if you had them. In giving you Himself God gives you more than all His gifts combined.

But let us go on with the Psalmist. This possession

of God is not for a limited time merely. Such is God, our God, *forever and ever*. More than this year's future is assured. The Psalmist elsewhere calls God the God of his life, and says, "I have set the Lord always before my face." You can say to-day what the king, the capitalist, the man of renown cannot say of his possessions. The king cannot say of his crown, "This is mine forever." The head that wears the crown must be laid low; the rich man's gold and bonds must pass into other hands, and the fame of the famous must fade away. But this God is our God forever and ever—with us alway, even unto the end of the world.

This thought is further developed in the second clause of the text, which brings us back to its key-note —guidance. We have been speaking of God generally as our possession: this general thought is now made specific by the word "guide": God is our God as our guide.

This idea of guidance is often attached to God in Scripture. It was symbolized in the pillar of cloud and of fire in which God manifested Himself as the leader of the host of Israel. When the angel of Jehovah appeared to Joshua, he said, "As captain of the Lord's host am I come." Moses said to the children of Israel, "The Lord will go over Jordan before thee." And in his review of the people's history, he said, "He found him in a desert land, and in a waste howling wilderness. He led him about." David says, "He leadeth me into green pastures"; Isaiah, "The Lord shall guide thee continually." And Jesus takes up the same thought in His beautiful figure of the good shepherd. "When he putteth forth his sheep, he goeth before them." Nay, the thought is not dropped from the imagery by which heaven is pictured: for the "Lamb which is in the midst of the throne shall shepherd them, and shall lead them to living fountains of waters."

Such is God, our God, our guide, an approved guide. The history of His guidance, the map of the tracks by which He has led His people, is before us. We can study it for ourselves, and can convince ourselves that God has made no mistakes; that He has never yet led any soul of man astray. The map of men's courses through life is indeed a confused one; but the confusion is made by men's wandering feet, by men's divergences from God's lines. The first instance has yet to be shown of one who has fared other than well by following God as a guide. Do you cite me the great army of the sorrowing, the persecuted, the martyrs? They have not fared ill if their own testimony is worth anything. They have had their choice. They could have forsaken God if they would, but they chose to follow Him through suffering to death. On their own testimony they fared better with God and with tribulation, than with the world and without God.

This thought of guidance is taken up again in the seventy-third Psalm, and expanded. "Nevertheless I am continually with thee. Thou hast holden me by my right hand. Thou shalt guide me *with Thy counsel.*" Guidance by counsel. Here is a voucher for the wisdom of our guide. You all remember the prophecy of Isaiah concerning Christ, in which these two thoughts of divine counsel and guidance are combined. "His name shall be called Counsellor—the Mighty God."

Now let us look at this very simply and practically. I have already said that the need which, as much as any other, is representative as we look forward, is the need of counsel—sound and wise advice. Every one of us knows that he is going forward into difficulties of some kind; that hard problems are on the way to meet him. We shall have important decisions to make, and evidence will be evenly balanced, and mistake will be easy. Moreover, every one of us must live some kind of a life, and to live rightly is not easy. It is all well enough to talk of the sharp distinction between right and wrong, but practically we shall not always find the distinction so sharp. There is essentially a sharp distinction, but, to the average moral perception, right and wrong often shade off into each other. The moral sense is a thing which requires to be educated. Now in view of these facts, which you may be sure are much more serious facts in God's eyes than in ours, what does God offer to you and me for this year and for coming years? Remember it is a fair and literal offer, and means just what it says, which is that you and I can habitually have at command the omniscient wisdom of God, if we want it; that no hard question or serious crisis will come to you this year or any year, that God will not give you His wisdom to determine in the best way; that no decision will be forced upon you in which you need make a mistake, if you will accept the solution which God shall offer you. God offers Himself as your Counsellor: He will guide you by His counsel. And that not in great matters only. God does not offer Himself to us for great emergencies only. The steps of a good man are ordered of the Lord. God offers you His wisdom for details no less than for crises, and that is important because the most of your life consists of small details, and your life in bulk will be shaped by the adjustment of these details. Is it not worth trying? Suppose that for this year you literally accept it as the law of your life, to let God take care of you. It comes to that in any event. The Father takes care of that timid, morbid, worrying child, just as He does of the sunny, cheerful, trustful one. If you ever find rest unto your soul, it will be in that way. Why not accept it then at once? Why not get some comfort out of it as you go along? Keep your hand in God's, your eye upon His face; do what He tells you; do your best, and believe with all your heart that God will do the best for you. I care not how many troubles and disappointments you shall meet—if you do not say at the close of the year that it has been the happiest, or rather the most blessed, year of your life, come to me and tell me I have misread God's promises.

But this is not all. One is constantly surprised by the correspondence between these words of the Psalms and the words of Christ. More and more it seems that the Psalms are full of Christ. And surely we cannot miss the correspondence here, "This God is our God forever and ever; He will be our guide even unto death": "Lo, I am with you alway, even unto the end of the world."

The end of the world: death. Ah! that is what troubles many of us most, after all. And yet why do we put the emphasis there on the end, as if that were the hardest thing; as if we needed guidance and counsel and help there more than anywhere? It does seem to me that if we ever come to see this thing from the right point, we shall find ourselves more concerned about living than about dying. The great thing is the journey, not the end; because, of course, if the road is the right one, the end will be right. We want the guide *at* the end, but in order to that we want Him all the way *to* the end. That is what He says we shall have. "He will be our guide even unto death." Beyond death we shall have Him if we have Him up to that point, for the great object of His guidance is to bring us to His own home. Again, the seventy-third Psalm expands the thought, "Thou shalt guide me by Thy counsel and *afterward take me to glory*." That word "take" is very suggestive. You find it in the forty-ninth Psalm, "God will redeem my soul from the power of the grave, for *He shall take me*." It is the same word which is used in the story of Enoch: "Enoch walked with God, and he was not, for God took him." Just think how significant it is, that, back in that far-off time, long before life and immortality were brought to light, the departure from life is put in this most beautiful and comforting way— being taken by God. Enoch did not die, it is true, but that does not alter the case. He had come to the end of life, and God took him, whether through the gate of death or by any other gate it mattered not, so long as he passed out of life in company with God. The point on which that story fixes our thought is, that God with whom he had walked all his life took care of him when he reached the end. It is not much for the wisdom and love which have piloted us through life, to pilot us safely out of it. Again, I say, the thing we are to be most careful about is life, not death, that God at the end may not have to take us from other hands, but simply to tighten His grasp on the hand which has been in His all along, and which mayhap trembles a little as we pass together into the valley of the shadow. We must live, we are told, "with eternity in view." Whatever is meant by that expression, we most commonly interpret it of living with some future and possibly remote thing in view, as men who walk with their eyes fixed on the city which they are approaching. That is not the right way to put it. We ought, indeed, to live with eternity in view, but chiefly as those who on their journey keep their eyes open to what is around them and at their feet. For as I have told you before, we are in eternity *now*. We who are Christians, if Christ is to be believed, are to live forever; and in living to-day have begun upon our eternal life. And the spiritual forces which bear upon us, the revelations of the things of God, the spiritual laws by which we live, the ministries to which we are called in Christ's name, communion with God, the love of God shed abroad in the heart, faith, duty— these heavenly things are not facts of a future eternity merely. They are present facts; and while we may rightly look forward to the consummate joy and fellowship and knowledge of heaven, our main business is to keep in view that side of eternity which pushes forward into to-day's life. To live with eternity in view is to live, first of all, as one who feels that that Presence which gives to eternity all its significance—God the Father, the Son, and the Holy Ghost—is with him here and now, and is the first, the greatest, the vital fact of to-day: as one who realizes that he is not merely journeying to the kingdom of God, but is already within its lines. We are on the river which leads to the sea. The passing out into the open sea is not the great thing now. The great, the pressing thing is rather to navigate the river safely. We shall best keep eternity in view by using time in the interest of the kingdom of God. When God is realized as a present fact, an eternity which is centred and summed up in God will not appear so strange a thing to us. I remember a glorious morning in the tropical sea. The ocean was one expanse of emerald and amethyst, flecked with the painted nautilus-sails, and shot through with silver flashes of flying-fish. Looking down, the purple shoals were visible through the shallow water. Around lay savage ledges of rock, and through all the ship held on her course until a lonely lighthouse on a barren island was passed, and then the color of the sea changed, as the shoals and ledges fell off into the fathomless abyss. Yet the transition was not sharp nor violent, but most beautiful. The ocean was still beneath us, though deeper. No tremor or shock marked the passage into the deep, dark blue; and so it seems to me it might be as we pass on under God's pilotage over the shoals of life, amid all its beauty and color, amid the ledges where so many have been wrecked, and onward to where the last point is passed and life falls away into immortality. We need not fear as the water deepens. The same hand is on the wheel. It is life still into which we are moving, but with a fuller swell, a larger sweep, a deeper depth of joy and rest. God will take us. If we would but learn to translate that hard word "death" into God's taking us. At the beginning of this year, as of past years, you confront the possibility that you may die this year. You shrink from the thought. There is no wrong in that; but put it to yourself in this way: I go forward into this year with God holding me by my right hand. Suppose that some time this year, as we go on together, He shall lead me out at the gate which opens on heaven. What then? He leads you; He takes you; that is the only fact worth considering. If God is your Guide here and now, be sure He will be your Guide even unto death. All the possibilities which death may bring are happily disposed of by the simple fact that He is your Guide forever and ever.

And we may carry the same truth into our larger relations as citizens. The past year has been one of unrest. There have been mutterings of thunder from more than one quarter of the heavens; tremors and upheavings of the social strata which are full of menace. We are going forward into a year of unsolved, difficult, radical problems, and our wisdom seems small and contemptible in the face of their colossal tangle. We may well be restless and fearful, if our little social theories and our crude political institutions are all that we have with which to face these things. The people of this land would have no reason to fear or to be restless, would they but accept loyally and frankly these words of the old Psalm, and take God as their guide forever and ever. That is too much to look for now. But remember that through all national convulsions, through all the confusion and wreck which men engender by refusing God as their guide, God leads safely those who put their hands in His. Many of you are familiar with Kaulbach's great fresco of the destruction of Jerusalem. You remember the awful confusion that rages round the temple porch, the laying waste of the holiest shrine, the horrors of carnage which gather round the altar where the high-priest stabs himself in despair. And you remember, too, that lovely group in one corner of the picture, a Christian family making its way out of the doomed city under the conduct of an angel, a mother with her little ones mounted upon an ass, the father by their side, and every feature and attitude of the group pervaded with a heavenly calm. The very beast, as he moves leisurely on, plucks at the green boughs in his path. God is their guide forever. The attending angel holds high in his hand the cup of covenant, and we might almost fancy them singing, " God is our refuge and strength, a very present help in trouble; therefore will not we fear, though the earth be removed, and though the moun tains be carried into the midst of the sea." Would that the whole earth, all people and nations, would accept this guidance. None the less, if they refuse, God is true to His own; He will guide them by His counsel, and afterward take them to glory.

X.

KNOWING BY DOING.

"If any man willeth to do His will, he shall know of the teaching whether it be of God, or whether I speak from myself."—JOHN vii. 17.

IT was a vain and frivolous question which those Jews raised as they listened to Christ in the temple. Curiosity and not conscience prompted it. It was not whether there was anything in the teaching worth their hearing and heeding—whether it was indeed a message from God: but how had Christ learned what He taught? How knoweth this man letters, having never learned?

Our Lord will not satisfy them on that point. That is none of their business: but He turns their thought to the question which they ought to have asked: Is this teaching of God? Now, as then, that is the first question which ought to be called out by any new teaching. Now, as then, there are those who are less concerned with the substance of a man's teaching than as to where and how he acquired it. He is in the teacher's place: by what stairway did he mount to it? What is his school of theology? Whose system does he interpret? Such questioners will find very little sympathy in the Scriptures. The test to which the Bible brings all teaching is, Is it of God? If it is, it matters nothing through what school it came, or if it came through no school at all. That is the point to which Christ aims to bring round the mind of the Jews in this answer of His. The answer thus contains two points. 1. The thing which alone concerns you in this teaching of mine is, whether it is of God. 2. In order to know this, practice it. Do the will of God: that will show you whether the teaching is divine or not. You will see then whether I learned these lessons from God, or whether I speak from myself, out of my own reason or fancy.

This old question, not the one raised by the Jews, but the one suggested by Christ, is not yet laid. Teachers there are in multitudes, too many by far, with all sorts of credentials and with no credentials. The people cannot but hear. But more than one earnest soul is asking, Whence is the teaching? This teaching about religion—much of it comes to us with the stamp of tradition, countersigned by the schools, represented by great names; but we find the great names heading parties, and the schools wrangling. How much of the teaching is of God? How much is God's and how much man's? How much are we to believe? In all this confusion of tongues over science and religion, reason and faith, new and old theology, theories of atonement and inspiration, Unitarian and Trinitarian, Calvinist and Arminian, high-church and low-church and broad-church—which voice is God's? Tell us what God says about truth and duty, and we will be content.

And not only rival books and systems make trouble for us. For a part of our teaching we are pointed to facts. We are bidden to note how God has written

Himself down in the ordering of this world. We are told that God teaches by providence no less than by the Word; and they bid us look at history and at society and see how God teaches in these. And yet—the facts are ugly facts many of them; facts with which the compact formulas of the catechisms and theologies deal about as effectively as a boy's cross-bow would deal with Dover cliffs. We ministers now and then come to places which the Confession of Faith and the Catechism do not cover. God rules the world no doubt. I believe it, but on other testimony than what the ordering of the world furnishes to my observation. The seething deeps of society throw to the surface here and there horrible practical problems; foul things not classified in the canons of Westminster and Dort; distorted lives which cannot be stretched back into symmetry on the frame of the Thirty-nine Articles. Confront a tenement-house with the words "God is love." Bring the corpse of that poor baby, smothered by a drunken mother, and let its white, pinched face look up into that pulpit from which come such eloquent and truthful words about the fatherhood of God. And then —this whole range of teaching about duty—how much of it is of God? What does God say that you and I ought to do? Among so many demands, which is the imperative demand? Many teachers tell us to do and to believe many things. How shall we know which teaching is of God, or whether any of them are of God? Faith! but what ought we to believe? The Bible! but which of its interpreters?

This is the present attitude of a good many minds; and the temptation to such is to set down summarily the whole matter as a hopeless muddle, and to conclude that the teaching of God is and must remain an unknown quantity.

And yet thus much is plain. Given the Being we are taught to believe in and worship and obey as God, an intelligible revelation of His will follows of necessity, else loyalty and duty are the veriest farce. No obligation binds me to serve a God whose will I do not know. That is the simplest of axioms. That I should know all about Him, that I should comprehend His plans and be acquainted with the reasons for His acts, is impossible. If it were possible, He would not be God. Clouds envelop the sun, we know; but if the sun be not strong enough to send light through the clouds sufficient to make a day in the cloudiest weather, even though it be a dark day, there might as well be no sun. Our great practical demand is met, if God, in any way, teaches us what we ought to do, and how we ought to feel toward Him and our fellow-men. As a fact He teaches us much more than this; but, if Christ is to be believed, all the teaching necessary to our pure, blessed, useful living is clearly given by God. Christ plainly says that men need not walk in darkness. He says that a revelation of God's will is given which is to men's moral and spiritual life what the sunlight is to the working day. If any man walk in this day he stumbleth not, because he seeth the light of this world. "The light is with you," He tells the Jews, "walk while ye have it."

Christ Himself claims to be this light. He professes to meet the demand for God's teaching. "Hear me, and you shall hear what God teaches. Follow me and you shall do the will of God. Know me, and you shall know God, for I and my Father are one, and he that hath seen me hath seen the Father. My teaching is the teaching of Him that sent me." "So far, well," says the world. "That is a fair response to our challenge. You profess to give us what we ask for—God's teaching. But how shall we test it? What evidence does it carry with it that it is of God? How shall we know?" And Christ answers, "By simple experiment. Practice the teaching and it will vindicate itself as of God. Do what God wills as you shall learn it of me, and the divinity of the teaching will manifest itself to you. If any man wills to do His will, he shall know of the teaching whether it be of God, or whether I speak from myself."

Christ thus puts practice before knowledge, or rather practice as a means to knowledge; and in this He lays down no arbitrary or unfamiliar law. The best of our knowledge, all of it indeed that is practically useful, is gained through practice. A young man goes to an engineering school, and studies algebra and geometry and trigonometry and surveying. He learns thoroughly all that is in the books. But take him directly from his books, put him down on a new line of railroad and tell him to lay out a curve, and he will need the engineer's help. You can teach a lad all about the proper motions in swimming. He will move his hands and feet just as the best swimmer does; but throw him off that pierhead into twenty feet of water, and it is ten to one that he sinks. Just so the teaching of Christ will not vindicate itself as of God by your merely studying it in the New Testament and in the light of the best sermons and commentaries. Knowledge is bound up with practice. No man ever learned to paint or to play upon an instrument by merely studying and mastering the theories of painting and music. He must handle the brush and finger the keys himself. No man ever learned the truth and will of God without doing His will. The doing is just as much a part of the learning as the studying. Doing is a mode of study.

If any man then willeth to do God's will, he shall know of the teaching whether it be of God. Practice vindicates theory. A theory which will not work is already disproved. Christ thus invites the fairest and simplest and most decisive test of His teaching. Try it and see if it works. When you are trying to make a pupil understand the ideas of a foreign author, you have to translate the author's words into the pupil's own language. The teaching of God remains an unknown tongue until it is rendered into doing. But let us look at this passage a little more closely.

The first step toward knowing the teaching of God is a determination to do it. The word of the text expresses more than a mere desire or wish. It means a resolution of the will. If any man wills to do His will. It is the same word by which Christ expresses His purpose: "I will that those whom Thou hast given me be with me where I am." "If I will that he tarry till I come, what is that to thee?" A man says, "I should like to know how to write shorthand." That is all it comes to. Another man says, "I will learn shorthand," and he goes to work at it. There is the difference. There is a great deal of vague wishing and talking, both out of the Church and within it, about wanting to know God's will: a great deal of sentimental aspiration, which is worth no more than the breath which utters it. Not a few people seem to take it for granted that the teaching of God is a hazy sort of thing, and that moral and religious action must needs be at best a groping in the twilight. And, if the truth were known, they rather comfort themselves with this haziness, and take refuge in it from the clear dictates of duty, heaving an occasional sigh, "Ah, if we only knew the will of God! If His teaching were only a little plainer." Christ nowhere concedes this haziness. As before remarked, He puts the teaching of God as a thing out in the light, definite, comprehensible. Here He says distinctly, "Man shall know of the teaching: *Any* man shall know who will take the right way to know." The first step in this right way is determination. It is not enough that a man be merely willing to know. He must will to know. Some people take the attitude of being ready and willing to know if the knowledge shall be brought to them and forced upon their conviction; but the knowledge of God's teaching is not brought to men in that way. It is something to be won, not for the man, but by him: and his professed willingness proves itself a sham if it do not translate itself into the energy of a resolved will.

This energy displays itself first in subjection. If one wills to do another's will, he puts himself under that will, absolutely, and obeys it, surrendering his own will. That is subjection. That is what Christ means when He says, "Take my yoke upon you and learn of me. Deny self and follow me." And Christ, as in so many other cases, is not laying down a new or an arbitrary law. It is a law which men everywhere recognize, that obedience is the first step in all learning:—doing what one is told, not because he understands it, but because he is told; because another wills it. When a child sits down to the piano to take his first lesson in music, he is taking the first step toward knowledge of the laws of harmony; toward getting his ear trained to grasp and analyze masses of sound; toward bringing the fingers into such perfect sympathy with the brain that they shall instinctively interpret the musical conception as it arises. But all that is in the future. He has no thought of that now. He could not understand it if he were told. He will reach it only by accepting now the teacher's word, "that key gives A, that one B, and those sounds answer to marks on such a line or space." He moves his fingers as the teacher directs. The teacher knows what all this is tending to. He does not. By and by, through the mechanical drudgery, rudimental conceptions of harmony begin to take shape. He begins to pick out and make chords for himself; to combine the rudiments into melodies and harmonies; and so on, until he grasps and interprets the works of a Beethoven or a Wagner. All learning, I say, comes to men in this way. We rise on the steps of mechanical obedience to the grasp of principles and to self-determination.

In a popular story by a well-known English writer occurs this little scene which is a good illustration of this truth. A Scotch youth is telling his companion his experience in the study of arithmetic. Says he, "I plagued the master sore with wanting to understand everything before I would go on with my sums. Says he one day, 'My man, if you will aye understand afore ye do as ye're tell't, ye will never understand anything; but if ye do the thing as I tell ye, ye'll be in the midst of it afore ye know ye're goin' into it.' I just thought I would try him. It was at long division that I boglet most. Well, I went on, and I could do the thing well enough, and aye I thought the master was wrong, for I never knew the reason of all that beginning at the wrong end, and takin' down and subtractin' and all that. You would hardly believe it, it was only this very day I was sitting in the kirk. It was a long psalm they were singing: long division came into my head again, and first one bit glimmering of light came in, and soon another, and before the psalm was done I saw through the whole process of it. But you see if I had not done as I was told, and learned all about how it was done beforehand, I should have had nothing to go reasoning about, and would have found out nothing."

I think about the whole matter is contained in that little story. You will acquire divine knowledge in the same way as you acquire human knowledge, by the road of obedience. So many fail because they do not like to obey without knowing the reason why. They want God to deal with them as equals, not as inferiors. To follow this line of implicit obedience is to become children; and that, they think, is not dignified. But there is no other way so far as I know. Christ allows no other way. "Except ye become as little children ye cannot enter into the kingdom of God." That kingdom is something which you and I can receive. Christ says so: but He says that we must receive it as a little child or not at all. Strangely enough, men do not think themselves humbled when asked to do this same thing elsewhere than in religion. If a mature man wants to learn German or French, he does what his teacher bids him; writes exercises, and learns conjugations and declensions, not knowing always the reason why. But when he approaches the greatest and most profound of all subjects, mysteries which the very angels desire to look into, he refuses the subjection he would yield to an equal and often to an inferior, and thinks himself insulted because God asks him to take the attitude of a docile pupil.

No doubt the divine teaching involves a theology and a philosophy. Beyond doubt there is a system and a plan back of all the details of obedience: but the way to these is by these details, whether their relation to the system is understood or not. If one begins at the other end, and refuses the obedience until he shall have become acquainted with the philosophy, he will gain at best a superficial philosophy, a botched theology, and will not reach the practice at all.

Teaching you by practice, God will give you lessons out of much besides books. You are resolved, let us say, to follow Christ's method: to learn God's teaching by doing His will. Well, the practical test of your resolution lies in this: are you ready to do the first thing that Christ tells you? In that case, your first teacher will probably be, not that robed priest or that grave professor of ethics. He may start up in the shape of that troublesome beggar. He may ring at your door in the person of that inquisitive, talkative, tedious man. He may come in that little child that disturbs your study hours and disarranges your books and papers. He may be that blundering clerk or that careless house-servant. Your lesson book may open at that common-place occasion which calls for a kind word and a trivial service kindly done, or for a restraint of temper or a little sacrifice of convenience. These seem trifles compared with the study of systems and the learned comparison of texts and authorities; none the less, your road to the larger and fuller knowledge of God lies through these and through meeting each of them, as it comes, in Christ's spirit and way; doing in each case what the Gospel tells you Christ did or would have done. These things will set you studying one book at least, and will furnish you with a new and strangely vivid commentary upon it.

You never will approach a truthful conception of Christ's character until you shall have honestly begun to try and do and feel as He did. You are troubled and perplexed over many hard questions about Christianity.

7*

I do not ask you to give them up as insoluble: only to give yourself implicitly to Christ in full faith that He will guide you: only to lay them aside for the present, and simply undertake, with God's help, to do the duty which lies next you. You will have quite enough to do, though your course will be simplified. You may seem to yourself to be farther than ever from the solution of your hard problems, but you will probably be getting on faster than you think. Sometimes, when you have been working your way over a long, rough road toward a town which you saw at a distance, some one has pointed you to a more direct road; but in taking that you lost sight of the town altogether for the time being, only to come upon it before you expected to. Meanwhile, in your endeavor to do God's will in whatever shape it may appeal to you, you will be getting the most satisfactory kind of evidence that Christ's teaching is of God—the evidence of experience. You have been, for instance, a care-oppressed, anxious man, burdened and troubled with the possibilities of the future. You have made an honest fight with your fears, and, accepting Christ's teaching about divine providence, have cast your care on Him, and have resolutely let to-morrow take thought for the things of itself. And you have been surprised to find how well it worked. You have been forced to say, "Such a prescription for a care-burdened mind was never framed by human science." You have learned to know God as the great care-taker; and living in the cheerful discharge of each day's duty as it came, and looking back at the old, anxious years, lying like a black cloud-bank on the far horizon, you have wondered and mourned that you did not sooner grasp that teaching of God which would have filled those years with light. You have tried to love your neighbor as yourself; to be to your fellow-man just what Christ would have you be. It has been hard sometimes, but your honest effort has brought its reward. Through your neighbor you have drawn nearer to God. Through the results of your brotherly dealing with your neighbor, you have caught a glimpse of God's ideal of a perfect society. You have come to say, "Love is the simple solution of the whole problem of civilization: God's teaching goes to the roots of the question as no human teaching does." Through your bearing your brother's burden and taking his sorrow on your heart, you have gotten a look into God's heart, and a conception of God's vast, tender meaning toward humanity underlying His teaching about love and patience and sympathy.

And so, more and more, you find yourself not only gaining new knowledge, but gaining it by a new and unsuspected way: that is to say, you are gaining knowledge of God's teaching through knowledge of God himself. You are coming to see how God's teaching is bound up with His character: how it is the laying bare of God's very heart. Now you begin to understand why Christ emphasized the bare fact of the teaching being of God. Doing God's will brings you close to God, and the better you know your teacher the better you understand His teaching. Through this doing of His will, you find God looming up larger than you have seen Him in the books and systems: you find His nature overflowing the lines of the creeds. As you mount, hour by hour, often with toil and pain, over the hard rocks of daily duty, your horizon widens, and the air becomes clearer, and new stars appear. True, you find yourself drawing nearer to the infinite. True, the conviction grows upon you that this God is not to be found out by searching. True, you have discovered that His teaching ranges beyond the farthest stretch of human thought; but you have found God himself. You have found the greatest thing in all the teaching; and that is the teacher. It was surely no loss to Job, after his fearful struggle to understand the hard lesson of God's providence, that God, instead of explaining His dealings, revealed himself. Once assured that he had touched God, he could afford to leave the why and wherefore of providence to take care of themselves. It was not the answer he had asked for, but it was a larger and a better one. It is no small gain to have gotten a grasp upon the infinite. Infinitude, to the man who surveys it through books and tries to resolve its nebulæ by systems, is despair. To the man who lays hold upon it, it is rest.

Hence, one of the elements of your new knowledge will be that there are things which you cannot know: things which God cannot or will not impart to you. If you have that truth told you by books, it will only increase your restlessness, and put you at war with God. If you learn it from your personal contact with God, it will quiet and satisfy you. You count it no small step in your child's training when he has come to be satisfied not to know on the mere strength of his trust in his father. To know God is the best solution of mysteries. To know that teaching is from God is to be satisfied that you will be taught all that you ought to know. Through this process you will have reached not only the teaching of God, but what is more important, the result of that teaching, the secret of life. For, as I have said, you will come to know God as revealed in His Son; "and this is life eternal, to know Thee, the only true God, and Him whom Thou didst send, even Jesus Christ." You shall know that life as you know your own natural life—not its ultimate mystery, but as a conscious divine force in you—Christ formed within; as an ever-burning and yearning love; as a steady impulse to duty; as a rest in toil; as a comfort in sorrow; as a controlling wisdom; as an intelligent sympathy; as a translator of the commonplace into the heavenly. Then you can go back to your systems if you choose. You will have gotten the clue of them into your hand. They will be your servants and not your masters thenceforth. They will help you to define and state much which you will have learned already in another way: but even as you study the books and tables of the astronomers, conscious all the while that the starry universe is vaster than all the books and maps, so you will be ever aware that God in Christ spans the systems and the creeds, and that His truth is more and greater than all of them combined. Then the Bible will carry a meaning for you which you never grasped in all your ransacking of the commentaries. It will be the very voice of your Father speaking to your filial heart, every inflection noted by the intuition of a loving child, and responded to with the quickness and ardor of a living sympathy. No man ever understands the Bible until he has honestly tried to live it.

The practical lesson is plain and direct. The teaching of God is the expression of His will. His will, so far as regards all that is vital in your life and mine, may be known; must be made known, if allegiance and duty are anything more than names. Do you want to know it? Is it your will to know it? Prove it, then, by beginning to do it. Strike at once into the line of simple obedience. That effort will be a revelation in itself. Walking hitherto with a vague, half-defined wish to know God's teaching, with your eyes strained as toward some far-off nebulous thing, you have been overlooking and trampling upon scores of lessons lying at your very feet. The teaching of God is a thing of to-day; a thing of this hour. "The word is nigh thee, even in thy heart and in thy mouth." Draw back your eyes. Look down at the duty of the hour. Hear what Christ has to say about your life to-day; and set your energies at work to make to-day's life Christ-like. Is there a duty in your home? Do it. Is there an indulgence to be cut off? Cut it off. Is there a right feeling to be encouraged, or a wrong one to be suppressed? Do it. Not in your own strength, oh, no. Every one of these occasions, in bringing you face to face with some difficulty or self-denial or bad antipathy in your own nature, will teach you your own weakness, which is part of God's teaching; will teach you to pray, which is another part; will teach you God's helpfulness, which is still another part. You will have made good progress by the time you shall have mastered those three. Do not be afraid of going slowly. Do not be afraid that, by your attention to these details, you are missing something greater. As well fear that you will miss that lofty summit and the prospect it commands by setting one foot before another. "He that believeth shall not make haste." It is a great study upon which you have entered, great as eternity itself, and you are not going to leap to results. The results lie along the separate steps no less than at the end, if there could be any end. And thus you shall come to the knowledge of God, not only as something grasped, but as something wrought up into your very self, and will be drawing nearer to that likeness to Him through which you shall see Him as He is.

XI.

GOD GREATER THAN OUR HEART.

> *" Hereby shall we know that we are of the truth, and shall assure our heart before Him whereinsoever our heart condemn us ; because God is greater than our heart and knoweth all things. Beloved, if our heart condemn us not, we have boldness toward God ; and whatsoever we ask we receive of Him, because we keep His commandments and do the things that are pleasing in His sight."—*
> 1 JOHN iii. 19–22.

I GIVE you here, you observe, a different rendering of this text from the one in your English Bibles, which is a mistaken one. This, I hope, will appear on our examination of the text.

The subject with which these verses deal, is an accusing conscience and its antidote. The season of approach to the Lord's table is, to many sincere Christians, a time of close self-scrutiny; the result of which is, in many cases, to awaken distressing doubts and misgivings as to their spiritual condition, and as to the propriety of their participating in this solemn and delightful rite. Such, especially, will be helped and comforted by a careful study of this text.

This chapter turns upon two thoughts—the nature of our relation to God, and its evidence. The first thought introduces the chapter in a burst of affectionate enthusiasm—"Behold what manner of love the Father hath bestowed upon us that we should be called children of God: and such we are." There is our relation to God: not *sons*, as in our version, but *children*. The difference is that sons indicates the position and privilege of one's offspring; whereas John's thought goes back of that to the community of nature. We are children of God, sprung from Him, made in His image. It is a Father's love which calls us children.

The rest of the chapter deals with the evidence of this fact. How do we know that we are children of God? John answers, "By your likeness to God. If you are of one nature, children, you will be like Him; and when your childship shall be perfected and you shall see God as He is, the perfection will consist in being like Him. But that likeness must be foreshadowed in you here and now. God is a God of righteousness and of law. Every one that hath this hope in him purifieth himself even as He is pure. He that doeth righteousness is righteous even as He is righteous. But further, God's righteous law is also a law of love. Love is the fulfilling of the law. This is the message which ye heard from the beginning, that we should love one another."

Here John brings the evidence to a focus. All evidences of our being children of God concentrate in love. "He that dwelleth in love, dwelleth in God, and God in him." To this test John attaches the highest value. To his mind it is the decisive evidence of a transition from the kingdom of evil to the kingdom of God. "We know that we have passed from death unto life, because we love the brethren. He that loveth not, abideth in death." And again, in our text—"Hereby"—that is, in the fact that we love each other in deed and in truth —"Hereby shall we know that we are of the truth."

"And," he goes on, "we shall assure our hearts before Him in whatsoever our heart condemn us." We need assurance then. This great evidence of love has misgiving to meet and to quiet. Is it strange that there should be such misgiving? Look at the standard of Christian character set up in this chapter. When one brings himself to such tests, is it strange if he hesitates? In the consciousness of infirmity, with the remembrance of error, under the pressure of daily temptation, is it strange if he is moved to say, "I cannot answer these tests. My heart accuses and condemns me"?

Now, John does not say that the heart may not accuse justly. He does not say that a child of God is sinless by virtue of his relation as a child, and that his self-accusation is quieted by being pronounced groundless. It is entirely possible that one's heart may justly accuse him of sin, and that God's judgment may confirm the accusation of the heart; but he does mean to say that the heart is not the supreme and final arbiter; and that whatever it may accuse us of, must be referred to a higher tribunal. Consequently you will observe that emphasis is to be laid on the words, "before Him." We shall assure our hearts before Him.

It is an essential characteristic of Christian life that it is lived out in the very sight of God. The true child of God sets the Lord always before his face. The prime regulator of his life is the sense of God's presence; God's manifestation in Christ is his model; God's law gives his conscience its tone of commendation or rebuke. This is a natural and necessary result of the relation assumed in the text—child of God. As children of God, in our Father's house, life is regulated by the perpetual consciousness of our Father's presence and scrutiny.

The Christian consciousness exercises a judicial office in us, approving or condemning; our heart passes judgment, but what we need especially to remember is that this office is a subordinate one, and that the decrees of the heart must, in every case, be carried up to a higher tribunal for ratification. God is greater than our heart. God knoweth all things, while our heart is ignorant and blind. Whatever light or power of discernment conscience has, it receives from God. The reason for insisting on this will be clear to you if you reflect how many self-accusing Christians there are, and that, while the self-accusation is, in many cases, just and wholesome, it is, in other cases, unjust, exaggerated, and impelled by morbid and distorted conditions. The review of life recalls a thousand lapses, a multitude of hasty words and tempers. There is the sense of shortcoming, of not having made the best of one's self; there is the fear of unconscious error and injury; the suspicion of secret fault; there is the morbid torment over fancied or possible sins: a thousand phases of this self-accusation will occur to every one of you.

And it is, moreover, an unfortunate fact that not a few Christians live habitually in this state of self-accusation. They are so absorbed in the contemplation of their own unworthiness that they see nothing else. They live in anticipation of divine judgment. Life is one continuous arraignment at the bar of conscience, spite of all their prayer and striving and study of the Word. Is this right? Is this Scriptural? Is this Christ's ideal of life in God's family? Is this what John has in mind when he says, " Behold what manner of love the Father hath bestowed upon us that we should be called children of God"? Is it the appropriate daily employment of a child of God to be a mere bookkeeper, writing down bitter things against himself?

And then, once more, it is true that too many of these self-accusing Christians do not carry up their case from the bar of the heart. They practically accept the heart's accusation as final, and do not raise the question before a higher court. And it is at this mistake that the apostle's words are aimed. He is teaching us how we may assure or quiet our heart before God, whereinsoever our heart condemn us. The whole text carries a protest and an antidote against that type of piety which is too contemplative and self-scrutinizing; which is always studying self for the evidences of a right spiritual relation and condition ; which tests growth in grace by the tension of feeling ; which limits God's presence by the sense of His presence ; which reckons the spiritual latitude and longitude by the temperature of emotion, as if a sailor should take his reckoning by the thermometer. You have heard people say that they were conscious of a presence behind them in the room, though they saw and heard nothing. That is a well-established fact; but for all that, you would not depend upon that subtle sense to inform you of the arrival of some one for whom you were impatiently waiting, and whose coming was a matter of life or death. But that is precisely the habit of such souls. They say they feel God is near, in which case they assume that He is near; or they do not feel that He is near, in which case they conclude that He is absent, and therefore condemn themselves. The apostle Paul did not put the matter in that way even when he was addressing pagans. He said: "He is not far from every one of us." And when he spoke to men who lived by faith, he said, "The righteousness which is of faith saith, The word is nigh thee, even in thy heart and in thy mouth."

In short, we cannot trust such testimonies. Feeling, religious sensibility, have their place in the Christian economy, and a high and sacred place it is: but its place is not the judgment-seat. Even the renewed heart is not infallible. Its judgments must be reviewed and countersigned before they are accepted as decisive. The pupil is not the proper judge of his own rate of intellectual progress, or of his grade of attainment. The teacher knows more about those matters; and the heart of man, which is the subject and the pupil of God's saving and educating process, which is under God's hand because it is by nature blind and deceitful, cannot be depended upon to furnish truthful and complete indications of spiritual attainment and condition. We must look outside of self for the highest tests of self. The racer in the arena kept his eyes fixed, not upon his own limbs, but upon the goal where the master of the games was sitting; and therefore the writer to the Hebrews says, "Let us run the race looking unto Jesus." Your conviction of being a child of God may create in you joyful and confident feelings, but it is not based on your feelings. You do not count yourself a child of God because you somehow have a sense that you are. You look out of yourself to the cross, to the sharply-defined *fact*, Christ died there for my sins; and you accept the fact, and rest on it, and are at peace.

And therefore in this text we are pointed away from our own hearts. It is not before ourselves that we are to assure ourselves. We cannot expect to allay self-condemnation by self-communion. We bring self and the condemning heart before Him. What we need is not to be self-assured, but to be assured by Him who is greater than our heart, and knoweth all things.

You see then that, if this passage be taken as it is commonly understood, it fosters rather than counteracts the tendency to self-scrutiny, and throws us practically back upon the lower court. "If our heart condemn us, it is because God is greater than our heart and knoweth all things." The course of reasoning in that case is,—if my heart accuses me, the accusation of God, who is greater than my heart, must be much larger and severer, because He, knowing all things, sees how much greater my sin is than my heart tells me. Do you not see that this is accepting the decision of the heart as infallible and making God confirm it?

No, indeed. Christian experience is not to be tested finally and decisively by the witness of the heart. It is before Him that we are to bring that witness.

And when we have once grasped that truth, what a wealth of assurance and comfort we find in it. How it lifts the whole life into an atmosphere of confidence and peace. So long as I go groping about my own heart for assurance and hope, I am as a man blindly feeling after God. When I come out of self, and go and stand before Him as He stands revealed to me in Jesus Christ, I see something; I get a firm grasp on something; I have gotten above the mist, and the full light of heaven concentrates itself upon Him who so loved me as to give His life for me; and I say with our apostle, "That which we have heard, which we have seen with our eyes, which our hands have handled of the word of life, declare we unto you. Our fellowship is with the Father, and with His Son Jesus Christ."

Just think what it is to escape from the maze and mist of a self-accusing spirit, and to come up into the light and comfort of a divine Father's house and presence. To exchange the dreary companionship of self for the fellowship of God in Christ. Before Him. Beloved, now are we children of God. Before Him, we are before our Father. Would not an accused child rather appear before his father than before any other judge? Would not his filial instinct tell him that there he could be sure of all patience, tenderness, and tolerance? Would he not draw comfort and confidence from his knowledge that the father knew him, knew all about his dispositions, his training, his circumstances? That is just the assurance which is given us in the fact of God's fatherhood. We carry our self-accusing hearts to our Father. We go as children of God. Such we are; and "like as a father pitieth his children, so the Lord pitieth them that fear Him. He knoweth our frame"—how you and I are made up; all our heritages of temper and disposition; all our natural infirmity; all the points where we are weakest against temptation; all our easily-besetting sins. There is not much difference between us when we stand there; at least the Psalmist recognizes none, for according to him we are all but as dust in God's sight. As children of God, all alike we are subjects of God's pity.

We shall assure our hearts before Him in whatsoever our heart condemn us. What then is the nature of the assurance? What the burden of the comfort we are to receive at His hands? Not the assurance that we are not sinners. Turn back to the first chapter of this Epistle. "If we say that we have no sin, we lead ourselves astray, and the truth is not in us." Not the assurance that we have not committed sin. Read again: "If we say that we have not sinned, we make Him a liar and His word is not in us." You and I go before God as sinful men. We bring a justly accusing heart. The testimony of conscience may be true to the letter. We are often constrained to say to conscience, even in the clear light of our Father's house: "Thou art justified when thou speakest; thou art clear when thou judgest." And yet, "we shall assure our heart before Him, in whatsoever our heart condemn us." Nor, assuming the condemnation of our heart to be just, shall our sense of the exceeding vileness of sin be mitigated in that clearer light. We shall find in our Father no compromise of His infinite holiness, no easy tolerance of sin; but as we enter that presence-chamber, this disciple whom Jesus loved meets us and puts into our hands a scroll on which is written, "'If we confess our sins, He is faithful and just to forgive us our sins, and to cleanse us from all unrighteousness." "If any man sin, we have an advocate with God, Jesus Christ the righteous; and He is the propitiation for our sins." "Hereby perceive we the love of God, because Christ laid down His life for us.' Our judge is our Saviour. We come unto "God the judge of all," but to "Jesus the mediator of a new covenant, and to the blood of sprinkling which speaketh better things than that of Abel." Beautifully says Luther, "If our conscience makes us disheartened and puts God before us as angry, God is yet greater than our heart. The conscience is a single drop, but the propitiated God is a sea of comfort."

But note that our text clearly states the great ground of assurance—the thing with which God himself assures our hearts. The great question underlying all this chapter is not the question of our individual shortcomings and faults. It is the question of our relation to God. That takes up into itself and regulates the matter of our special errors day by day. As one has truthfully said,

"As long as the relationship with God is real,—if a man is truly born of God,—sinful acts are but accidents. They do not touch the essence of the man's being." And it is upon the fact and the evidence of this relation that God throws us for assurance when we come before Him with our accusing hearts. Look at the text again. "We know that we are of the truth." How do we know it? Hereby know we that we are of the truth—that we have passed from death unto life, that we are born of God—by the consciousness of active and sincere love for the brethren resting upon and moulded by the love of Christ, and showing itself in ministry to our brethren, by deed as well as by word. All your assurance before God rests on the fact that you are a child of God; but your accusing heart often raises the question about that fact, and sets you asking, "Am I a child of God?" And when you bring that question before Him, He throws you back on the simple testimony of love. Do you love me? Do you love these other children of mine, your brethren? Do you show that you do by your life of ministry? There is nothing vague or subtle in that. It calls for no painful heart-rummaging, no tormenting self-analysis. All there is in it you get hold of every time you take your little child on your knee and ask, "Do you love me?" Your child can answer without hesitation. It knows that it loves you; though it cannot tell why or how. You know whether you love God or not. You know whether you love your brethren or not. And that is conclusive evidence. You would not and could not love either God or His children as such, if you were not of Him. "Hereby know we that we are of the truth." And so God, who is greater than our heart and knoweth all things, refers us to that simple, broad test for our assurance of being His children; and, once assured of that, all the rest—love, pardon, compassion—goes along with it. "God is greater than our heart and knoweth all things." I wonder, as I read this passage, if John, when he penned it, was thinking of that interview of Jesus with Peter by the lake-shore after His resurrection. It seems almost as if he must have been. There was poor Peter, with a heart which throbbed with self-accusation: Peter who had denied his Lord and forsaken Him; and Christ meets all this self-accusation with the simple words, "Lovest thou me?" Peter is to be an apostle, a leader: to feed the sheep and the lambs; and yet our Lord throws the whole vital matter of Peter's relation to Himself on this simple test, Lovest thou me? And Peter's reply is in the very vein of our text. God is greater than our heart and knoweth all things. "Lord, Thou knowest all things, Thou knowest that I love Thee."

You observe that John puts this fact of God's omniscience as a hopeful and comforting fact. The ordinary rendering of the verse puts it as a terrible and chilling fact, which it is very far from being. Our first instinct, perhaps, would be to shrink from bringing our self-accusing hearts before One who knows all things; but a very little thought will show us that that instinct is false and misleading. If you or I were upon trial on some grave charge involving our honor or our life, should we be willing to be tried before an ignorant judge? Should we not say, "The wiser the judge, the better for me"? It is not otherwise when we come to God's bar. Though God's holiness shames our sinfulness, though God's perfect wisdom dwarfs our folly, nevertheless the safest refuge for the most sinful is perfect holiness; and perfect knowledge joined to perfect love furnishes the strongest assurance to trembling and penitent souls. If that knowledge sees deeper into our sin than we do, it also sees deeper into our weakness. If it weighs the act in more nicely-adjusted scales, it knows what circumstances to throw into the scales. If it knows our most secret faults, it also knows our frame and our frailty. If it discerns aggravations, it equally discerns extenuations. Self-accusing hearts are nowhere so safe as in God's hands: nowhere so sure of justice, but nowhere so sure of tender mercy.

I must leave the subject here. The fact of self-accusation we know from the reproachful whispers of our own hearts; but the apostle comes to us to-day to define for us the position and the authority of the heart in heaven's chancery: to tell us that its decisions are not final, and to bid us take ourselves and our self-accusations to that higher court where supreme love and perfect wisdom occupy the judgment-seat. If the self-accusation is morbid and unfounded,—a freak of diseased religious fancy rather than a truthful verdict of a healthful conscience,—only before that bar will its fallacy be fully exposed, and the heart be assured and quieted. If it is just, only by that perfect wisdom will the error be duly weighed; only by that perfect love will it be forgiven; only by that perfect strength will the soul be invigorated to renew with fresh courage the life-long fight with sin. If we are trembling lest the things of which our hearts accuse us may be the warrant for disinheriting us of our position and privilege as children of God, we are pointed past our individual errors and lapses to the great evidence of our relation to God—love. We come to the Lord's table to-day, every one of us, with some self-accusation. We have been too worldly. We have yielded to temptation: we are conscious of an ill-developed spirituality and of an intermittent zeal. We shall meet here nothing to encourage us to continue in sin. We shall receive no assurance that sin is any less vile than our conscience tells us it is. We shall hear nothing which will warrant us in relaxing our vigilance; nothing which will go to make the struggle and the fight for holiness less intense. But these symbols beckon us away from self. They bid us to cease aggravating our struggle by self-brooding and introspection. They call us to God, the judge of all, who hath committed all judgment unto Jesus, the mediator of the new covenant. They mark the transfer of the judicial element in Christian experience from our own hearts to God. They point us from judgment to pardon. They urge the accusation of our heart as a reason and a motive for the assurance of our heart by some power outside and above itself. They lift up before our eyes Him who was manifested that He might take away sin. They tell us of divine sympathy with the tried and tempted.

They lead us up to where the complex and confused witness of our ignorant hearts is resolved into the simple test of love. You come saying, " My heart condemns me. I am so unworthy; I am an erring child; I am a stubborn, wayward pupil." But O, is there not a deeper instinct which presses through all this self-accusation upward to your lips and voices itself in Peter's words, "Thou knowest all things, Thou knowest that I love Thee"? Let us hold by that. It is the supreme evidence of our relation to God : and if we are children of God, surely in our Father's house we may be sure of all help in our struggle, all sympathy with our weakness, all pardon for our sin, all grace to help in time of need; yea, sure that, being now children of God, the time will come when the self-accusing heart will be forever stilled, the possibility of sin forever removed, when we shall be like Him, for we shall see Him as He is.

XII.

SONSHIP THE FORESHADOWING OF HEAVEN.

> *"Beloved, now are we children of God, and it is not yet made manifest what we shall be. We know that if He shall be manifested we shall be like Him; for we shall see Him even as He is. And every one that hath this hope set on Him, purifieth himself even as He is pure."*—1 JOHN iii. 2, 3.

IN every true economy of life there is a concealed side. This fact grows partly out of the nature of the case, and is partly a dictate of wisdom. There is a side of your personality, of your business, of your domestic life, which ordinary prudence and self-respect forbid you to expose to the world. There are also thoughts and plans which one man cannot reveal to another, because he cannot be understood. There are branches of science which the best teacher cannot impart to a child.

This fact of concealment, and these two reasons for it, are both apparent in God's dealing with men. Divine revelation is the exposed side of a divine economy which reaches back into darkness. "We know in part." Some things God could not tell us, because we could not understand them. Other things are equally hidden, because He does not see fit to reveal them.

But against this dark side of divine revelation human

curiosity and pride are in continual protest; speculating in the absence of knowledge, and complaining because more has not been told them, and refusing to accept what is revealed, because of what is not revealed.

God does not ignore nor forbid men's natural curiosity to know what is hidden. In many cases, indeed, He uses it in the interest of wider knowledge. The advancement of knowledge would come to a stop if all men were simply content to accept the unknown as unknowable. At the same time He does set a limit to human knowledge in certain directions: but the point which you are specially to note is that, in all such cases, God puts His revelation in such a relation to what is unknown, as to quiet the restlessness of the curious and searching spirit when it reaches the limit of knowledge. And by this I do not mean that He persuades the man to resign himself passively to ignorance; but that He teaches him to find in what He does see fit to tell him, hints and assurances which stimulate his hope and make him content to wait for further revelation. For instance, He saw fit to withhold from the Old Testament that clear revelation of a future life which came in with Christ. We cannot suppose that men in those days were not as curious about that subject as we are. But while God did not satisfy their curiosity, He set them upon a track where they could walk restfully and hopefully toward the unknown future. He did not give them simple ignorance for a companion. He walked with them Himself, and His presence and love and providential care assured them that the same presence and love and care would be with them beyond the grave. And hence we hear the Psalmist saying, "In thy presence is fulness of joy. Thou wilt not leave my soul to the pit, neither wilt Thou suffer Thy holy one to see destruction. Thou wilt show me the path of life." When we are about to ascend a high peak, it is childish to complain that we cannot see at its foot the vast prospect which the summit commands; but we are patient and hopeful and cheerful in knowing that we are on the right road to the top. In like manner God is not content with arbitrarily limiting our knowledge of the future. He puts us on the road to the larger knowledge. He clothes His revelation with hope. He assures us concerning what He does not reveal by what He does reveal. He gives us certain foreshadowings of our future in our present.

All that we have thus far said is contained and illustrated in our text. We have the concealment, "It doth not yet appear what we shall be." We have the revelation, "We are now the children of God." We have in the revelation a hint of the essential quality of the future life. We shall continue to be children of God, and our family likeness will be brought out and perfected when we shall see Him as He is. Finally, we have the practical bearing of these conditions on our lives. The hope of perfect likeness to God which our consciousness of sonship gives us, acts to make us strive for purity of heart, that we may see God. "Every one that hath this hope set upon Him, purifieth himself even as He is pure."

Let us take up these points in order. First, the concealment. Here we have a definite statement: What we are to be hereafter is not yet manifested. We need not dwell long upon a fact so familiar and so obvious. Christ reveals the fact of immortality, gives the promise of immortality, but tells us little or nothing about the outward conditions of immortality. A Christian must frankly accept this ignorance. By the terms of his Christian covenant he engages to walk by faith, and not by sight. A thousand questions, a thousand speculations, betray this ignorance. "What is Heaven? Where is Heaven? What is a spiritual body? How shall we be employed? Shall we know each other?" Literature, with its "Little Pilgrim," its "Gates Ajar," its Swedenborgian fantasies, tells the same story. Most of us construct our heaven, unconsciously, by exaggerating the elements of our earthly happiness. The Indian pictures it as a happy hunting-ground. The Mohammedan as a scene of sensuality. To the toil-worn it is a synonym of rest: to the curious, of knowledge: to the bereaved, of restoration and reunion: to the sorrowful, of joy.

Scripture concedes something to these fancies, as indeed it must if it attempt to picture heaven at all: and, besides, they are not wholly fancies. Restlessness, toil, sorrow, bereavement, ignorance, are all outgrowths of sin, and the Bible promises the abolition of these in promising a sinless heaven. Moreover, it gives us material pictures of heavenly glory in its gates of pearl, its golden streets, its trees and rivers. That is the very best our human conditions will admit of its doing for us. And yet, after all, the Bible never varies from the testimony of this text,—" It doth not yet appear what we shall be." " Now we see in a mirror, in a riddle." "We know in part." All its formulas of heavenly felicity are straitened and vague. " A far more exceeding and eternal weight of glory": " eternal life ": " a house not made with hands ": " a better country."

Still, there is revelation as well as concealment. It doth not yet appear, but we know something. Thus we reach the second element of the text. And as we study what is revealed to us, we begin to see that the concealment and ignorance which wait on this subject are not arbitrary. We have already seen that they are to a great extent necessary because of the limitations of our intelligence : that God does not reveal, because we cannot understand : but it appears, besides, that these concealments are in the interest of our knowledge on another side, and are intended to direct our researches into another and more profitable channel.

For if we rightly read the New Testament, we find it aiming not so much to put us in possession of new facts about the future life, as to put us in the right attitude alike toward what is revealed and what is hidden. Our disposition is to inquire into the circumstances of the world to come ; while the Gospel persistently counteracts this tendency by showing us that the future life is essentially a matter of character rather than of circumstances. John gives us the key to this truth in our text. Notice his words : " It doth not yet appear "—not *where* we shall be, or *in what circumstances* we shall be,—but " it doth not appear *what* we shall be ": only we know that we shall be like God. That is the great, the only point which concerns us as respects the future life. To be like God will be heaven. To be unlike God will be perdition. Character creates its own environment.

> " The mind is its own place, and in itself
> Can make a heaven of hell, a hell of heaven ! "

The Gospel lays all the stress there. It assumes that if character is Christ-like, its surroundings in heaven will be appropriate and congenial. And, accordingly, you observe that the circumstances of the eternal life, where they are touched on at all, are treated in their relation to the great facts of character. Even in the material and rhetorical descriptions of the Book of Revelation the element of personal and social holiness is emphasized. The Lamb is the light of the city. His servants shall serve Him. There entereth nothing that defileth, or that loveth and maketh a lie. The assembly is made up of the forgiven. The theme of its song is deliverance from sin.

On this side we know something of the heavenly world. We know the moral laws which govern it, for they are essentially the same laws which the Gospel applies here. We know the moral sentiments which pervade heaven. They are the very sentiments which the Gospel is seeking to foster in us here. We know that holiness which is urged upon us here is the character of God ; and that where a holy God reigns the atmosphere must be one of holiness: that if God is love, love must pervade heaven; that if God is truth, truth must pervade heaven.

Now, all this, you see, must exert a tremendous power upon the present life, viewed as a prelude and preparation for the life to come. If that future life is to have its essence in character and not in circumstance, it follows that character and not circumstance is the great thing here: that the absorbing question for you and me, in view of the inevitable future is, What am I? What can I be with God's help? That our preparation for the life to come is to be strictly on the line of character. You clearly perceive that, in the present life, you prepare for some things with reference to circumstances merely. For instance, if you are to be presented at the English Court to the Queen, your preparation is wholly a matter of circumstance. It is of no consequence whether you are a good man or a bad one: whether you are learned or ignorant. The great thing is that you know court etiquette; that you dress in a certain way; that you bow at the right time; that you do not address the sovereign directly, but only through her minister; and that you retire keeping your face to the throne.

On the other hand, if you are going to meet a company of literary and scientific men, it is of very little consequence what you wear, or whether you are to appear in a palace or in a barn. If that society is to have any meaning to you, if you are to get any pleasure out of it, your preparation must be in yourself. You must know something of the subjects discussed. You are invited on the presumption that you are a cultivated man. Your most brilliant costume, if you are an ignoramus, will only make you a laughing-stock.

You see then that the apostle strikes directly into this track of thought. In the first place he states the fact of concealment. Down between our speculations and dreams and the eternal reality falls an impenetrable veil. It doth not yet appear what we shall be. Even the eternal possibilities of holy character are not revealed to us, and the circumstances and details of the heavenly state are not thought worthy of mention. But he goes on to say, "You are on the right road to knowing. You are on the right road to becoming. Now are you children of God: that fact enfolds all that is to come. It is a matter of character here as in heaven. The true goal of your striving is likeness to God. That will be heaven; and the road to that goal is likeness to God here." Beloved, now are we children of God. That implies a family likeness. No matter what the likeness may imply when perfected in heaven. You cannot comprehend that now. The human mind cannot grasp the ultimate possibilities of holiness. The great thing here and now is that you are God's children, moving on in obedience and faith and purity of heart toward the serene heights of heaven. Two things you know amid all your ignorance: that you are on the right road to the glory that is to be revealed, and that, when it shall be revealed, your sonship will be consummated in likeness to God, whatever that may include. And if you study John's words closely, you will see that he chooses them with a nice discrimination, so as to bring out this thought with the greatest possible force. He says *children* of God, a phrase different from the common one, *sons* of God, which expresses a position of privilege, while children of God expresses community of nature, and consequent promise of development. So that very statement, " now are we children of God," tells us that even here we share the nature of God, and that in that fact lies the promise of infinite development, divine manhood, the consummate flower of character. Essentially we shall not be other there than here. The difference will be in degree, in maturity of development. We are children of God here, we shall be children of God there. When God makes us His children it is not for time merely. Hear these words of Peter: " Blessed be the God and Father of our Lord Jesus Christ, who according to His great mercy begat us again unto a living hope, by the resurrection of Jesus Christ from the dead, unto an inheritance incorruptible and undefiled and that fadeth not away, reserved in heaven for you." And you know too the parallel words of Paul: " If children, then heirs, heirs of God and joint-heirs with Jesus Christ."

But we must touch one more point before leaving this branch of the subject. Why, with all this promise, does it not appear what we shall be? Look at the promise itself and you will see the answer. The essence of the promise is, we shall be like God. Understand, not equal to God, but like God, as the finite, under the highest possible conditions, can be like the infinite. The reason for this likeness to God is given. We shall see Him as He is. This gives us the reason why it doth not yet appear what we shall be. We do not see Him as He is. We cannot so see Him here, any more than a child, in the weakness of infancy and the ignorance and perverseness of childhood, can understand and appreciate the mind and character of a noble father. The history of humanity has not been a history of clear perception of God. On the contrary, strange as it may seem, around this vital point, this most important factor of all knowledge, centre the grossest misconceptions and perversions. Ask history what has been man's thought of God, and the Oriental fairy-tales cannot furnish a more grotesque and horrible group of monstrosities. And even a nineteenth-century Christian, with Christ in the background, cannot be said to have a complete or an accurate conception of God. I think that, in many cases, it might be much fuller and more truthful; and one reason, perhaps the main reason, why it is not, I suspect, is because men refuse to accept literally the fact that God was manifest in Jesus Christ, and to go to Christ to learn what God is. They take, instead of this conception, or mix up with it, the God of the schools: the God which system-makers have pieced together and built up with attributes. Christ was given to the world as the most complete revelation of God which humanity is capable of comprehending. But even Christ appears in the limitations of our humanity. The root of the whole difficulty lies in those very limitations. We do not know what we shall be, because we cannot know what it is to be like

God. We cannot know what it is to be like God, because we cannot see Him as He is, and never shall, until He shall be manifested as pure spirit to purified spirits freed from the trammels of the flesh.

And you will further notice the truth which the text assumes, that likeness to God comes through vision of God. We know that truth already in its earthly manifestations. We assimilate to that which we habitually contemplate, and especially so when we contemplate lovingly and enthusiastically. The affectionate child takes on the characteristics of the parent whom he loves. Love has a power of transformation. A beloved object draws into its own moulds. Even material things with which one has habitually to do, set their mark upon him. The man who is working with matter on a large scale, who is projecting great structures or handling vast financial interests, takes on larger proportions than one who deals with petty things. And so the man who contemplates God, who sets Him always before his face, who looks upon Him as the supreme object of love, grows into the likeness of God; and such is the testimony of Jesus himself, as He addresses the Father in that wonderful prayer in the seventeenth of John: "This is life eternal, that they should know Thee, the only true God, and Him whom Thou didst send, even Jesus Christ."

Thus we come naturally to the third and last point of our text—the practical duty growing out of this mixed condition of ignorance and promise. For if the promise is to be fulfilled in likeness to God, if that, in short, is to constitute our heaven, and if that promise is enfolded in our present relation as children of God, then we have in that fact both a consolation and an exhortation to duty. The consolation lies in the fact that though it doth not yet appear what being like God means, yet we are on the right road to knowing in being children of God. The gardener does not know what will be the exact color and size of the ripened peach or pear, but he knows that the consummate result of ripeness is in that hard green pellet; and he guards the pellet from careless hands and wind and hail. In the fact of being children of God is contained the promise of likeness to God. The assimilation begins here. The outlines are faint, but they are real. The perfection of the ransomed and glorified spirit is foreshadowed in the first outlines of character in a child of God.

And, therefore, the whole practical duty of life concentrates itself upon maintaining and developing this condition of sonship. If you would see God as He is and be like Him, bend all your energies to being a true and loyal child of God here and now. You shall win the best of heaven by getting the best there is out of your position and relation as a child of God here. This is the logic of the Gospel. Like Him, for we shall see Him as He is. But who shall see Him as He is? Christ makes answer: "Blessed are the pure in heart; they shall see God." What then? John comes in saying, "Every one that hath this hope in Him—this hope of being like Him—purifieth himself, even as He is pure." This is our great business here, my brethren, if we have any well-grounded hope of seeing God and of winning heaven. Sonship does not stop with mere relationship. The relationship gets its real meaning in the character of each individual child. It makes little difference who a man's father was, provided the man himself does not signify. The real essence of sonship is not physical, but moral. You remember how slightingly John the Baptist treated the matter of mere physical descent when the Pharisees and Sadducees came to his baptism. "Think not to say within yourselves, 'We have Abraham to our father,' for I say unto you that God is able of these stones to raise up children unto Abraham. Bring forth fruits meet for repentance." And our Lord followed up the words to the Jews when they boasted of being Abraham's seed : "I know that ye are Abraham's seed, yet ye seek to kill me because my word hath not free course in you. If ye were Abraham's children ye would do the works of Abraham." And when they asserted that God was their father, He answered, "If God were your Father ye would love me." So that this text does not allow us merely to stand upon sonship as on a mount of vision, and felicitate ourselves on good things to come. Sonship completes itself in duty and in matured holiness of character. Hope in God means faith in God, love to God, obedience to God. We have something to do in this matter of likeness to God. Only God can purify the heart, but He enlists our service in purifying the life. In the same breath Paul tells us that God worketh in us to will and to work for His own pleasure, and bids us carry out our own salvation. Every one that hath this hope in God is purified by the Holy Spirit, yet our text says "purifieth himself." Personal devotion calls out personal effort. If we want heaven we must work for it. If we are to be true children of God we shall not become such by merely saying, like the Jews, that God is our Father. If sonship does not mean to us a fight with impurity, a study of the law of God and of the character of Christ, obedience, self-denial, fidelity, it is only a name.

But, oh, what a stimulus is there in this fact of sonship! Let us sit down, and in the light of this text ponder this ultimate meaning of sonship—likeness to God through perfect vision of God. We find the hard problem of life just at this point: to make sonship a moral reality, to be worthy sons of such a Father. How far short we come. How feeble seems our striving. What slow progress we make. How discouraged we become when we compare ourselves with Christ; but the case is not hopeless, any more than the greenness and hardness of the unripe fruit is hopeless. Sonship enfolds heaven. If we are children of God, we hold in that fact the promise of eternal life; of a state where this unlikeness to God which pains and worries us here, shall disappear in the perfect vision of God, and we shall be like Him, for we shall see Him as He is. How many of God's earnest souls have cheered themselves on their weary way with this thought. I know of no one who has given it an expression more nearly akin to inspiration than that poor Methodist shoemaker, Thomas Olivers:

"The God of Abraham praise
　Who reigns enthroned above;
Ancient of everlasting days,
　And God of love;
Jehovah, great I Am!
　By earth and heaven confessed;
I bow, and bless the sacred name
　Forever blessed.

"The God of Abraham praise,
　At whose supreme command
From earth I rise, and seek the joys
　At His right hand;
I all on earth forsake,
　Its wisdom, fame, and power;
And Him my only portion make,
　My shield and tower.

"The God of Abraham praise,
　Whose all-sufficient grace
Shall guide me all my happy days
　In all His ways;
He calls a worm His friend,
　He calls Himself my God!
And He shall save me to the end,
　Through Jesus' blood.

'He by Himself hath sworn;
　I on His oath depend;
I shall on eagles' wings upborne
　To heaven ascend;
I shall behold His face,
　I shall His power adore,
And sing the wonders of His grace
　For evermore."

And so, like all Scriptural contemplation of heaven, this text turns our thought from future glory to present duty; from victory to conflict. We may comfort ourselves with hope. We may refresh our souls with the assurance of likeness to God by and by; but the great thing now is to strive to be true and loyal sons of God here in this world; to purify ourselves as He is pure. May God help us in the struggle, and bring us all at last to behold His face in peace.

XIII.

THE GOD OF THE UNSUCCESSFUL.

"The Lord upholdeth all that fall, and raiseth up all that be bowed down."—PSALM cxlv. 14.

THE Bible, being a book for humanity, is a book for the weak, the fallible, and the disappointed. A large part of it is devoted to the erring and the unsuccessful. Take its biographies. How many do you find of perfect men? Were Abraham, Isaac, Jacob, Moses, Elijah, Job faultless, and always strong and triumphant? Does James speak any less than the truth when he says of Elijah that he was a man of like passions with ourselves? Every one of these biographies is a story of a faultful man. Then, so much of its counsel and warning is directed at servants of God and disciples of Christ. Not only guide-posts, but danger-signals, are set up all along the way of life. It was to His own disciples that Christ said, "Watch and pray that ye enter not into temptation. The spirit indeed is willing, but the flesh is weak."

By far the larger part of its promises is to the sorrowful and afflicted and disappointed. When Christ invited the weary and heavy-laden to rest, He invited a restless and burdened world. When the Bible addresses the strong it is to point them to the true source of their strength, to warn them against presuming on their own wisdom, and to commend the weak to their sympathy and helpfulness. The whole matter is summed up in the Psalmist's statement of God's attitude toward His children at large. It is that of pity based on knowledge of their infirmity. "The Lord pitieth them that fear Him, for He knoweth our frame and remembereth that we are dust."

Strange that we cannot see it as God does, and yet the world at large does not see it. Is it not the general impression that the Bible is a book for a select circle of strong and victorious saints—for men who are above human passions and temptations and errors? That God is the God of the morally successful? That if a frail, faultful, passion-racked son of earth does, by any chance, touch the hem of His royal robe and get a word of comfort or pity, the word is a morsel tossed from the table where the elect feast?

And yet, if the popular impression be the right one, the world is in evil case. I appeal to experience. What does your observation certify as to the number of those who are too successful, and too independent of the conditions of this life to need help and comfort? Do you know any house which has not its sorrow? Do you know anybody who has not his trouble? I once heard one of the most honored and eloquent ministers of this city say that he had labored, for nearly forty years, largely among the so-called prosperous classes, and knew scarcely a house where there was not a grief or a burden. Even in the world's sense of the word, how many are the successful men? How many get even a foothold?

Compare the successes with the disappointments. Do you think the number is small of the men who carry about with them at the bottom of their hearts the feeling, "I have not succeeded in proportion to my effort, nor so well as I have deserved"? Whatever power rules the world, seems to have a strange indifference to men's deserts, or what they conceive to be such. What becomes of all the failures? What becomes of the vast mass of honest work which seems to count for nothing and end in nothing so far as we can see? The waste of nature which, of fifty seeds often brings but one to bear, has its parallel in the realm of human striving.

Or, morally and religiously, how many perfect men and women do you know? How many who never swerve? We have a high ideal, and it is well that we should have, for we are the better for it even if we do not reach it. The old saying runs, that he who aims at the sun shoots farther than he who aims at the ground. We have in our minds a picture of a life flowing on with a steadily deepening and broadening current, calm and majestic up to the moment when it empties into eternity. Possibly we read of such lives in romances; but have you ever known one? Does any one of you know himself as such an one? Is it not rather your worry and your burden that you have been slipping and falling all along in the pursuit of your ideal, and that you are still so far from it? That your easily-besetting sin comes upon you again and again, and will not stay conquered? Good friend, if the Bible and the God of the Bible are for the strong and the unsoiled only, I must needs say that your case is not hopeful. If the principle of natural selection—the survival of the fittest—is to be rigidly carried out in the spiritual as in the natural world, the result must be an infinitesimal remnant. Heaven will not need to be a great city, nor will it need twelve gates.

Now you see that the Bible does not fit into any such conception as this. Nine-tenths of it is useless if this is a truthful statement of the case. On its very face it is for the many. The picture of heaven drawn by John is a picture of a great multitude which no man can number, whose song tells of sin and sorrow in the old life: who came up out of great tribulation and must needs wash the soil of earth from their garments. The Bible does not find its true place until it strikes a weak, fallible, sinful world. That moment it is at home and busy.

The ancients had an idea that God was the God of the successful. The very word which the Greeks used to denote a prosperous man, meant a man who had a deity for a patron. The idea is truthful at the root, if we couple with it a right definition of prosperity. But what they did not get hold of was the truth that a man might be under the tutelage of a good god, and yet be an unsuccessful and unfortunate man as the world goes. To the Hebrews, worldly prosperity was a synonym for divine favor. The good man should have fields and cattle, and abundance of corn and wine. To be poor and wretched and disfigured was to be smitten of God, and implied sinfulness. Jesus himself fell under that reproach. That was the sore trouble of Job. That notion was so rooted in the popular theology, that when a man like Job, who had lived in conspicuous piety and integrity, whom the eye blessed when it beheld, and who made the widow's heart sing for joy,—when such a man lost his cattle and his home and his children, and came under the power of a loathsome disease, the pious men of his acquaintance leaped at once to the conclusion that he had been living in secret sin, and had drawn upon him God's wrath therefor. And Job, being himself under the power of the same popular falsehood, was in agony over the problem raised by his affliction.

Now our text this morning gives us distinctly this truth—a truth most precious and full of comfort, because it is a truth which comes home to us all—that God is the God of those who fall and are bowed down: God is the God of the unsuccessful. "The Lord upholdeth all that fall, and raiseth up all that be bowed down."

I speak, as the Psalmist does, of men and to men who recognize and honor the law of God, and are honestly striving to keep His laws. The words do not apply to the indolent who interpret the invitation to cast their care on God as a "permit" to cast off all care about their own souls and lives. They do not apply to those who are indifferent to God and who wilfully defy His law. The Psalmist settles that in a single verse. "The Lord preserveth all them that love Him, but all the wicked will He destroy." He will not uphold them. I am speaking then to you who honor God: who are making an honest fight for the truth and the right: who are trying to keep your lives pure and to make them useful. I know that you fall as I do, and are often bowed down. I know that you are not all successes, either from a worldly or a religious point of view. I know that the way in which God leads you is often a dark and a hard way. I know that in more than one thing on which you have asked God's blessing, you have failed, at least as we conceive of failure. I know that you are not as good as you would like to be, and that conscience says to many of you that you are not as good as you ought to be; and I think it highly probable. I know that you are not without faith and honest purpose, but that you are heart-sore and self-reproached, some of you, because you have made head so slowly against your besetments and have been so often taken prisoner by them.

Now you will surely not understand me to be counselling you to make yourselves easy about such things, and to give up your hard fight with temptation, when I say that, in spite of all this, *because* of all this, God is on your side. You are saying sorrowfully to yourself, "I am not a success as a religious man or woman." I reply, God is on your side—the God who hates sin, and who fails in nothing—not to make you content with failure, but to make you a success. He is interested in you personally, as His child and servant: in you, an erring, falling, bowed-down man or woman; and that is why He upholds and raises you up.

I am very sure that you cannot study the life of Jesus, who always exhibits to us the feeling and the dealing of

God himself, without seeing that the weight of His sympathy is with the losers in life's battle. He was the friend of Mary Magdalene, but He had cast seven devils out of her. Zacchæus, poor, little, despised tax-gatherer,—He went to his house as a guest, and that one act made a man of him. That crowd of sick, squalid, filthy, blind and lame, He was their friend, and left His mark on many a restored limb and on the opened window of many a curtained eye. The man in the porch at Bethesda could get no one to put him into the healing waters; but Jesus did for him what the pool could not. The woman whom they wanted to stone, the Syrophenician whom the disciples found troublesome, she who anointed and wept over His feet—Jesus was on their side: unsuccessful people they were too. And, in His parables, you see readily which way His heart goes. It is not to the proper son, who, though he had stayed at home and not wasted his substance, had a slave's heart in him; but to the vagabond who had fed with the swine and had come penitently home in rags. It is to that lost sheep rather than to the ninety-and-nine which went not astray.

Now, first, in relation to your worldly affairs. Somehow, perhaps, you have gotten undermost in the fight. You have not obtained what you wanted. You have stumbled and fallen in the path which you thought would lead you to success and victory. Well, look at the text. The figure, as you can all see, is that of a man who has fallen down in the road. This good friend lifts him up and sets him on his feet. The text does not say that he puts him in a royal chariot and bears him smoothly on nor even that he gives him the thing he was after, as a foolish parent gives a child the sweetmeat for which he cries. He lifts him up, upholds him. It is something to be put on your feet, my friend. Something to be able to walk, if not in the direction you were going, yet in some other and possibly better direction. Something that God does not take from you the power of carrying out your own salvation. You see, God is not caring now for your glory: not concerned with your getting just what you want: He is caring for your walking. Your business in this world, now, is to walk. The glory is farther on. If you ever reach it, it will be by God's way, not by your own. So He does the best of all things for you if He puts you on your feet and helps you to walk in His way. It is the steps of a good man that are ordered. The Word throws less light upon reward than upon duty. Enough indeed to stimulate duty, but the Word is a lamp unto the feet and a light unto the path. Paul says, summing up the result of the life-battle, "Having done all *to stand*." O merciful, wise, tender love, which, even while it denies what we long for, bends over us while we lie prone and weeping over our disappointment, and sets us on our feet again and bids us follow God and not the devices and desires of our own hearts.

And, I repeat, He may thus set us on our feet that we may walk another way from that on which we were going. The fall may be a blessing in disguise, a monition to abandon that way. Many a man has found that to give up the thing he desired and take something less and lower, was not a sorrow after all. I remember how I started out one morning, under the bright Italian sky, to climb a summit which it was said commanded a wonderful prospect. For awhile the road was smooth and plain. Then I lost my way, and wandered off along the sheep-tracks, and came at last to the bottom of a grassy ravine, at the top of which, and seemingly not far off, was the hermitage toward which I was working. But I could not reach it. The descent was steep, and my feet slipped on the smooth grass, and I was alone, and my strength failed. I had to give it up. And then I sat down on that lower shoulder of the mountain, and found that I had not climbed in vain. Such a vision of beauty lay beneath and around me—hill and forest and lake and distant peak and sapphire sky. Probably the view from the summit was wider and grander, but the view from the lower slope was worth the climb and the weariness.

Or, suppose God means to admonish you by your fall to go more slowly after your desire. Because, even when men desire a good thing, they may go too fast after it. "He that believeth shall not make haste." I submit that God gives you a blessing in simply upholding you, and letting you walk on at a more moderate pace. Possibly there are things on the road which you ought to note, but which you would miss by going too fast. A man who goes leisurely through a country, sees a great deal more of its characteristics than one who rushes through in a train to accomplish something in a distant city. God will not let us pursue one remote end to the neglect of all that lies by the wayside. Success in life is not the gaining of that one end at the end. It is the right adjustment to all that lies in the track of each day. So God lets you walk, upholds you, teaches you to walk. He is doing you a greater service by upholding you, so that you can move on and win the strength and discipline and experience which come through walking circumspectly, than if He had let you go straight to the thing you coveted and sit down and enjoy that. Disappointment need not mean wreck. It will not if God is in it. God sometimes upholds and raises by means of a disappointment. There is a lift in that ugly thing. You and I have known men whose usefulness and power began with their fall in their chosen path. Failure brings our plans and desires down in an unsightly heap, and yet on that very heap one may stand and reach up to something better. A teacher of natural science and mathematics was thrown off his self-appointed course of lectures and classes, but Scotland and her poor won through that the ministry of Thomas Chalmers. Frederick Robertson wanted to be a soldier, but that brief ministry at Brighton has been more to England and America than the most brilliant military career. Saul of Tarsus had a bad fall on his way to Damascus; but the world has Paul the Christian apostle instead of Saul the persecutor. Disappointment, like fire, has a double power. It may scorch and blast a man, but it may thaw out his blood and quicken his life.

I repeat, failure is not wreck if God is in it; and sometimes it seems as if God's policy toward a man is to keep him down, and yet keep him walking and working. That develops the highest type of moral heroism. If the truth were known, there is more heroism under the world's failures than under its successes. It is a higher and greater thing for an unsuccessful and disappointed man to keep rising from his failures and to struggle on his way leaning on God's hand to the very end, than for him to succeed before the world. God has a testimony to bear to the world through His sons and daughters no less than to them; and He bears that testimony most emphatically in showing the world that His hand can keep a man a man, with an honest soul and a persistent purpose in him, amid all his falls and disappointments. Sorrow was so representative of Jesus' life that Scripture itself calls Him a man of sorrows. Ninety-nine wise men out of a hundred, standing by the cross, would have said that those thirty-three years of His life and ministry were a failure; and yet the cross is to-day the symbol of victory. Success and failure! Ah! let us not be too hasty in pronouncing upon them. Sorrow and disappointment have stony kernels and grow in hard soils, and are, therefore, of slow growth. The fruit comes and ripens late. The palm, the tree of victory, runs up a good many feet before it breaks into leaf. This life does not put the seal on success or failure. The words have a different meaning in God's lexicon from that which we give them here. Our dictionaries in that, as in a good many other points, will undergo a very radical revision in the light of eternity. I know we shall be surprised, if we ever reach heaven, at the number of people there who on earth were never thought worth minding. I doubt not we shall meet on the very threshold more than one who passed for a miserable failure in this world, and shall have to search long for some who went out of the world encompassed by the halo of success. The poor in spirit, the meek, the persecuted—the kingdom of heaven belongs to them. The world saw only their failure: God saw their fidelity. We must wait until those gates open before we fully know who have succeeded and who have failed. Meanwhile the true course for us is to take the stumbling and bowing down into our life as part of it, and to learn to look only at our walk and at the hand which upholds and guides us in it.

And as to the matter of Christian experience and the falls and stumblings which are along that line,—I know, as I have already said, that the ideal which at once beckons and reproaches us is that of a steady growth in faith and love and goodness and Christian power. It is the true ideal too. Let us never lower it: never cease striving for it. Let us never admit to ourselves that yielding to temptation is anything less than sin: that sin is other than vile. Only as a fact, we do see that Christians are human as well as other men, and that they stumble and fall like other men. The difference between a Christian and a man of the world does not lie in stumbling or not stumbling, but in the whole attitude of the man toward his stumbles and falls. It would be strange indeed if the man who sets himself to fight his way to heaven in the face of such a world as this and of the whole spiritual power of darkness, should not now and then fall into a snare or receive a blow that brings him to the ground. God nowhere promises that a believer shall walk straight on with upright carriage and serene front, compassed with the calm of holiness all the way to heaven. He tells him rather that Christian life is a wrestle. What he is specially concerned about, the point where He brings His own divine forces into the field, is the way in which the man shall bear himself in this struggle. He does promise that sin shall not have dominion over him: that though he struggles all the way to heaven, and marks his progress with a series of falls, he shall mark it also with a series of risings, and shall fall and rise and struggle through to victory. "Sin shall not have dominion over you." God will bring him at last, a saved man, out of the soil and the bruises. He will uphold him, not in sinning, but in the fight with sin. But this promise is to the honest-hearted, to the man who goes bravely and trustfully into the fight with all its certainties of blow and downfall. Even worse than a moral fall is the hopelessness which keeps a man from rising out of it: the faint-heartedness which makes him the victim of a fall instead of the victor over it: the fatal blunder which makes him say, "God is against me because I have fallen": the spiritual paralysis which keeps him lying face-downward in the mire. You are a Christian, but you are a fallible, stumbling man or woman. You confess it to yourself.

Tried by the high ideal of the Gospel, you are not a religious success, only trying hard to be. That is the saving clause. God is on the side of the unsuccessful but honestly-striving. You find in yourself a constant tendency to stumble. God meets that with the promise of the text—"The Lord upholdeth all that fall and raiseth up all those that are bowed down." He is on the side, not of the sin, but of its victim. If Satan desires to sift you as wheat, Christ prays for you. He is bent, not on raising up you and your sin together, but on raising you out of your sin and making you a man in Christ Jesus in spite of your temptation and weakness. He knows well enough that your fight is a hard one. He has measured the power of Satan better than you have. He knows it is even mightier than you know it to be, sorely though you feel it.

Take courage, then. The great thing for you is that God is on your side. Try your best to walk without falling. Lean heavily on His hand. Keep your eye on Him: keep your purpose steadfast to overcome the world. When the falls do come, think only of that hand and grasp it. When conscience tells you you are not what you should be, and reproaches you for what you are, say, "With God's help I will get farther from what I am, and nearer to what I ought to be. I can do all things through Christ which strengtheneth me; and as for life's failures and disappointments, if He see fit to disappoint me, it is still His hand in the disappointment, His hand that raiseth up them that are bowed down."

"And I, who wait His coming, shall not I
      On His sure word rely?
So, if sometimes the way be rough, and sleep
Be heavy for the grief He sends to me,
Let me be mindful that these things must be
To work His blessed will until He come,
And take my hand and lead me safely home."

XIV.

MAIMING AND LIFE.

"And if thy hand cause thee to stumble, cut it off: it is good for thee to enter into life maimed, rather than having thy two hands to go into hell, into the unquenchable fire."—MARK ix. 43.

THE New Testament revisers have rightly substituted the words "cause to stumble" for "offend"; for the popular conception of "offend" is misleading. By offending, we commonly understand doing or saying something which is annoying or distasteful to another, but not necessarily hurtful. The word in the New Testament habitually implies something dangerous. That which offends, in the Gospel sense, may be neither annoying nor distasteful. On the contrary, it may be agreeable and seductive. When Paul speaks of "meat" as an offence to a brother, he does not mean that our brother's dislike of meat is to give the law to our eating. He says, "If meat make my brother stumble,"—if my eating or drinking, or any other act, cause harm to my brother, or help to make him do wrong,—"then I will eat no meat." The common interpretation has tended to convert the weak brother into a tyrant, to set him up on his weakness as on a throne, from which his likings or scruples are to dictate to others.

It is evident, therefore, that our Lord, in these apparently hard words about cutting off and maiming, is not speaking of things which are simply troublesome; for, as a fact, we see that, in God's moral economy, a good many troublesome things are retained as permanent factors of life. Self-sacrifice, continuous vigilance, cross-bearing, hard duty, are all troublesome things, yet they enter into every genuine Christian life; while, on the other hand, it is evident that a good many agreeable and fascinating things are of the character of stumbling-blocks, and require to be taken out of the way.

The truth here stated by Christ appears to be, I repeat, a very severe and cruel one. It is simply that maiming enters into the development of life, and is a part of the process through which one attains eternal life. Let us look the truth in the face. We may find, before we shall have done with it, that it is not so cruel, after all.

Now, there is an aspect in which we all recognize and accept this truth; namely, on the side where it is related to our ordinary human life. No life is developed into perfection without cutting off something. I am speaking, you understand, without reference to moral or spiritual growth. I mean simply that no man ever attains a strong and well-rounded manhood without repressing and limiting and extinguishing certain natural tendencies; without forbidding certain appetites to indulge themselves; without setting a gateless wall round many things which crave boundless liberty. Sometimes these limitations are self-applied; sometimes they are imposed by authority. The natural tendencies of the boy are to play and eat and sleep. Left to themselves, those things will fill up the space allotted to thought and culture, so that they must be controlled and restricted. The law indeed holds, from a point below human life, that every higher thing costs; that it is won by the abridgment or suppression of something lower. The corn of wheat must die in order to bring forth fruit. The seed-life and the seed-form must go, so that the "full corn in the ear" may come. This fact of limitation goes along with the entire process of human education. The man who aims at eminence in any one department of life must close the gates which open into other departments. In order to be a successful merchant, he must abridge the pleasures of literary culture. He may have equally strong affinities for medicine and for law, but he cannot become a successful lawyer without cutting off the studies and the associations which go to make a successful doctor. And success in any sphere necessitates his cutting off a large section of self-indulgence. He must sacrifice pleasant leisure and pleasant society, and needful rest and recreation.

Moreover, it is true that men love life so much that they will have it at the expense of maiming. A man will leap from the third story of a burning house, and will take the chance of going through life with a crippled limb or a distorted face, rather than stay and be burned or suffocated. "All that a man hath will he give for his life." Mæcenas, the prime minister of the first Roman emperor, said that he preferred life with the anguish of crucifixion to death. Where is the man who will not lie down on the surgeon's table, and have his right hand cut off or his right eye plucked out rather than die? The most helpless cripple, the blind man, the mutilated and disfigured man, will say, "It is better for us to live maimed than to die." So that, on one side at least, the truth is not so unfamiliar or so cruel, after all. It represents, not an arbitrary decree, but a free choice. Men's love of life dominates their fear of maiming. Were it not so, the annals of suicide would be overcrowded. Who would willingly bear the suffering and humiliation which wait on physical mutilation,

> "When he himself might his quietus make
> With a bare bodkin?"

Now, our Lord leads us up into the region of spiritual and eternal life, and confronts us with the same alternative. Cut off anything, sacrifice anything, be maimed and crippled so far as this life is concerned, rather than forfeit eternal life.

Life in God's kingdom, like life in the kingdom of nature and sense, involves a process of education and discipline. A part of this discipline is wrought through the agency of the man himself; that is, by the force of his own renewed will. A part of it is brought to bear on him from without, through no agency of his own. And here, as elsewhere, development implies limitation, suppression, cutting off. It is hard to conceive why any one should be surprised at this feature of the Gospel economy, when it is so clearly recognized and so frankly accepted elsewhere. In our dealing with nature and with man, we never leave them wholly to themselves. We must limit both on certain sides or mischief ensues. Fire and water must not be left to follow the law of their nature. A horse is not allowed to roam the plains at will. His nature does not incline him to the rein or to the saddle; but these restraints must be applied if he is to be made useful. And, in proportion as man's nature is nobler than the beast's, his powers greater and more varied, and the range of his passions wider, the greater are his possibilities of mischief and of degeneration, and the more necessary is this law of limitation, especially in view of his possibilities as an heir of eternal life.

Accordingly, the New Testament is full of this. Paul puts it as a crucifixion. "I am crucified to the world." He puts it as death. "Ye are dead, and your life is hid with Christ in God." A whole economy of life, the fleshly, sensual, worldly economy, goes by the board when Christ takes the soul in charge. "How shall we that are dead to sin live any longer therein?" The higher life costs. It can subsist only at the expense of the lower. "No man can serve two masters." The men who have achieved Christlike character and success have done so at cost. The knife has been upon every one of those lives. What did Jesus mean when He said that His follower must hate father and mother and kindred? Surely not that Christian life is to annihilate natural affection; and yet it was quite possible that devotion to Christ might require a man to shut his heart to the appeals of natural affection. It might be, it often was, that to take Christ's part was to give up all part in the affection of father or brother. One might be compelled to turn his back on them as really as a son who hated them.

Is that an unfamiliar fact? Have you never known a woman on whom the door of her father's house was closed from the moment that she went out of it with the husband of her choice, and who gave herself to him, knowing that, in taking his part, she was cutting off and casting from her parental sympathy and all the dear associations of childhood? In our great civil war, was it not true that many a man, by taking a side, became an outcast to those whom he had loved best? Has it not been so in all the great issues of history? In Christ's own day, and much more in the early days of the Church, that happened again and again which Christ's words had foreshadowed. He who went after the despised Galilean or His apostles, must forfeit home and friends and social standing, and be called an ingrate and a traitor. He could not keep father and mother and old associates who hated his Master. They would be only stumbling-blocks to him; and he must therefore cut them off, and go after Christ maimed on that side of his life. There never was a man who had a finer opportunity of success, speaking as men speak, than Paul had. He sums up the factors of this success in his Philippian letter—his descent, his legal strictness, his zeal—and yet he cut them off. "What things were gain to me, those I counted loss for Christ."

Few can stand unmoved in the chapel of Merton College, at Oxford, before that tablet which bears the name of John Coleridge Pattieson, and his sculptured figure stretched upon a drifting canoe, with a palm-branch between the folded hands. I know few records of missionary devotion more touching and beautiful than the story of that young and finely-endowed minister, cheerfully relinquishing a home of wealth and culture, the society of doting relatives, and the prospect of congenial work in the Church in England, and going out to spend his days among the savages of the Pacific islands, and to fall a victim to their heathen rage in the prime of his manhood. Here is a significant passage from one of his letters, which shows what cutting-off meant to him: "I must forget myself, and think only of the work whereunto I am called. But it is hard to flesh and blood to think of the pain I am causing my dear father, and the pain I am causing to others outside my own circle here. There will be seasons of loneliness and sadness, and it seems to me as if it was always so in the case of all the people of whom we read in the Bible. Our Lord distinctly taught His disciples to expect it to be so, and even experienced this sorrow of heart Himself, filling up the full measure of His cup of bitterness. So I don't learn that I ought exactly to wish it to be otherwise, so much is said in the Bible about being made partaker of His sufferings: only I pray that it may please God to bear me up in the midst of it."

This text tells us that this cutting off and casting away must be our own act. "If thy hand cause thee to stumble, cut it off,"—thou thyself. We are not to presume on God's taking away from us whatever is hurtful. Our spiritual discipline does not consist in merely lying still and being pruned. That must do for a vine or a tree, but not for a living will. The surrender of that must be a self-surrender. The forced surrender of a will is no surrender. The necessary abridgment or limitation must enlist the active co-operation of the man who is limited. "Ye are God's husbandry," says Paul; but, almost in the same breath, he says, "Ye are God's fellow-workers."

There are, however, two aspects in which this self-cutting is to be viewed. On the one hand, there is, as just noted, something which the man is to do by his own will and act. On the other hand, there is a certain amount of limitation applied directly by God, without the man's agency. In this latter case, the man makes the cutting off his own act by cheerful acceptance of his limitations. Let us look at each of these two aspects in turn.

In Christian experience, one soon discovers certain sides on which it is necessary to limit himself; certain things which he must renounce. The things are not the same for all men. They are not necessarily evil things in themselves, but a sensitive and well-disciplined conscience soon detects certain matters which it is best to lay violent hands upon. Another conscience may not fix upon the same points; but to this conscience they are stumbling-blocks, hindrances to spiritual growth, inconsistent with entire devotion to Christ. It is enough that they are so in this particular case. The question is not one of abstract right or wrong: it is simply between these things and this particular man's attainment of eternal life. Of course there is no question about things which God forbids. They must be cut off, summarily, by every disciple. But observe that our Lord does not raise that question here. "If thy hand," thine own hand, not another man's, "cause thee to stumble,"—not if it be a cause of stumbling in the abstract,—then "cut it off." It is with this view that he selects for illustration a thing which is right and good and even necessary in itself. It is right to have hands and feet and eyes, and to use them, and to keep them unimpaired. Many a man may enter life with these unmaimed. But, still, it may be that a thing as precious and as needful as a hand or an eye may act as a stumbling-block. In certain cases there is an antagonism between these and eternal life. The whole question then centres there. Whatever interferes with the attainment of eternal life must go.

Thus, Paul says, "There is nothing unclean of itself," but things take their quality of cleanness or uncleanness largely from their relation to the individual conscience; and, therefore, "if any man thinketh anything to be unclean," while his thinking does not make it so in itself it does make it so for him; "to him, it is unclean." That settles the matter as between himself and God, as between himself and God's gift of eternal life. That thing he must cut off.

Eternal life is the great central object of our striving.

Each one of us moves toward that centre from a different point, and each finds different calls to renunciation and abridgment on his own line. It is as it was with the Israelites at the siege of Jericho. Every man was bidden to move straight to the city from the point where he should be standing when the trumpets sounded. One man might find a comparatively clear path on his line; another might find rocks or bushes in his way; a third might have to cross a ravine. But every man must keep to his straight line, and regulate his action according to the obstacles on that line. Very likely many would reach the city lamed or bruised. The discipline of life is different for different men. The renunciations are different. One must cut off what it is right for another to keep. The great, the only question is: What is there on my line which stands in the way of my reaching the end? Whatever it is, let me cut it off, even if the cutting off brings me to the end maimed.

> "We all are in one school:
> Each hath his daily lesson, line on line;
> But sterner chastisement and stricter rule
> God doth for some design."

Thus much for self-applied limitations, for conscious hindrances in the march to eternal life. On these we are to bring to bear the severing power of a renewed will: by our own resolve and act to cut them off. But there is another class of limitations, the need of which we do not perceive. They belong in the higher and deeper regions of character, and are linked with facts and tendencies and consequences which our self-knowledge does not cover. Such limitations we cannot apply to ourselves: they are applied to us by God; and all that our own will has to do with the matter is to concur with the limitations, and meekly to accept them whenever and wherever they may be applied. This is the harder problem of the two. In this region the discipline is the more painful. God cuts off and takes away where we can see no reason for it, but, on the contrary, where we think we see every reason against it.

And here we confront a familiar fact. Remember, I am speaking of Christians only: the truth does not apply to others. There is constantly passing before our eyes a multitude of Christian people who are going through life maimed on one side or another. There is a man with the making of a statesman, a writer, a painter, or a poet. How often we say, "What might he not have been, if he had only had the opportunities of culture and training." But he did not have them. He knows his own possibilities. He sees that he might easily have been the equal or the superior of the men around him; and he naturally asks, "Why is so much cut off from me?" Here is another, susceptible to all the influences of the finest culture. He looks upon men with splendid libraries which they cannot use; with pictures and statues which never tell them any story but the number of dollars they cost, and naturally he asks, "Why am I cut off from these, and condemned to pass my days in petty drudgery?" There is the fact that an immense volume of power, culture, holy zeal, practical talent, is hedged in by sickness and helplessness, cut off by blindness, deafness, or imperfect speech ; and it is not strange if from within those imprisoning walls should go up the whisper : " We would use our power for God : we are eager to serve, eager to speak our word for Him, eager to lay our hands to His work. Why does He cut us off ? "

We know, all of us, of men who have something worth the hearing to tell the world, but to whom the world refuses a hearing. We know of good and wholesome books which are gathering dust on library shelves, and which men will not read. Scores of people, who deserve society's attention and homage more than many who command them, do not even receive society's notice. " The world knows nothing of its greatest men." These are things hard to explain, and still harder to bear; and the only possible solution of the mystery lies in the words "eternal life." If our life is ordered simply by the laws of matter; if there is over its economy no supreme, brooding love, no absolute wisdom and power; if we are not, in short, in the hands of an infinite Father who knoweth our frame, and who is ordering our life on lines stretching far beyond this mortal environment, then I give up the mystery. It is darker than midnight. But every true disciple of Christ enters His school with absolute self-surrender; with firm trust that God will do for him just what will best help him on to eternal life; that He will cut off nothing which makes for eternal life; and, on that basis, every one of us, I think, is justified in assuming that these deprivations and suppressions which hurt us so keenly have a direct and vital bearing, though he may not detect it, upon that consummation. We are justified in concluding that we could not win eternal life with these gifts as well as without them—perhaps could not win it at all. We are justified, therefore, in saying, "We know that all things are working together for good to them that love God."

> "Nor chief, nor only those
> Who break their bonds and cast their cords away,
> Who, unsubmissive, murmur and oppose,
> He scourgeth day by day."

And so it will be better if we can but enter into life. Better, far better, to go maimed all the way than to lose eternal life. It matters little that those stately masts had to be cut down in the raging gale. No one thinks what splendid timbers were thrown overboard, on that day when the ship, battered and mastless, and with torn sails and tangled cordage, forges into the land-locked port with every soul on board safe. Better maimed than lost.

XV.

DETACHING.

"*Now He that hath wrought us for this very thing is God, who gave unto us the earnest of the Spirit.*"—2 COR. V. 5.

HATH wrought us for what? Of what has God given us the earnest? These questions we naturally ask as we read this passage by itself. We must get hold of the apostle's line of thought before we can answer them. To this end we must read the latter part of the preceding chapter. Paul is speaking there of earthly affliction, and says that it is light as compared with the glory of the world to come, and that it is, further, an element of the process by which God prepares His children for that glory. The afflictions work out an exceeding weight of glory. We who suffer, He says, are looking, not at what is seen, but at what is unseen. What is seen is transient, temporal: what is unseen is eternal; for we know that if the earthly house of our tabernacle be dissolved, we have an eternal building of God in heaven.

The figures at the beginning of this fifth chapter carry out this contrast between the temporal and the eternal. The visible, temporal things are represented by a tent or tabernacle—a frail, temporary structure, easily overthrown, its cords quickly cut, its covering easily rent: while the eternal home prepared by God, is represented by a building with solid foundations, not made with hands like the tents which Paul himself manufactured.

The thought of the affliction and trouble peculiar to this mortal and temporary state is further carried on in the next three verses, in which the figure of a building runs into and blends with the figure of clothing. In this tent of ours we are distressed: we groan: we long to be clothed upon with our house which is from heaven: to have the heavenly conditions descend upon us and envelop us like an upper garment; and to have (and here still another figure is introduced) this that is mortal swallowed up of life.

This change from the mortal to the immortal is no accident. It is the result of a divine intent. Here we strike our text. God wrought us for this very thing, and has given us the earnest, the foretaste and pledge of this change, through His Spirit.

Our text, therefore, is the expression of the truth that, in God's economy, this life is a process of disentangling and detachment from its own conditions. Mortal life, so far as related to itself, is a getting loose.

In the first place, let me recall your attention to the imagery of the context. We mortals are as dwellers in a tent. This tent is being gradually "loosened down": such is the literal meaning of the word "dissolved." The same word was used by our Lord of the stones of the temple at Jerusalem, and indicates a gradual destruction, stone after stone. So it would be in striking a tent. The tent-pins would be taken out, the cords slackened, the covering rolled up, the poles lifted from their sockets: piece by piece the tent would vanish. Paul has a similar figure in his Epistle to the Philippians, where he expresses the desire to "depart," or, literally, "to break camp."

This gradual loosening, this detachment, is a familiar fact of our life. It would be more familiar if we did not persistently shut our eyes to it; for it is not an agreeable fact. Yet there the fact is. We are breaking up; and Scripture emphasizes the fact by asserting that God's intent is to break us up. He that hath wrought us for this very thing—for the breaking up of the tent as well as for the dwelling in the building — is God. "*Thou* turnest man to destruction : *Thou* carriest them away as with a flood." One of the most puzzling things about the world is that it is made to be destroyed: that such superhuman ingenuity, such perfect finish of workmanship are expended upon things which soon crumble to dust. How exquisite is the structure of a bee or of a butterfly, and yet how short-lived they are. The Psalmist praises God because he is fearfully and wonderfully made, yet the world is one great cemetery.

These, I say, are familiar facts. Let us see what is our attitude toward them.

Plainly enough the average man ignores them. He strikes out the tabernacle from the text, and substitutes a building. He lives and plans as if both he and the world were eternal. Now, as you study the life of men around you and your own life, you notice that, in the earlier stages of life, the thought of detachment and disentanglement is practically absent from the mind. Those earlier stages are occupied with the contrary process. The life is amassing instead of throwing off. It is knitting bonds instead of severing them. The love and intimacy of the family-circle are taking the boy deeper into themselves. Then his social nature is throwing out tendrils and attaching itself to school and college friends. Then comes the determined pressure into social and business and professional life. The bonds multiply, the connections become more numerous: more and more the man is getting wrapped round and tied up. Domestic life encircles him. Children are born to him. Their interests, their future are added to his own. Business becomes engrossing: vast interests, branching out in a multitude of directions, encompass him and shut him in as in a jungle. To use the common phrase, " He has so much to live for." So the world winds round him, coil after coil. If the house of his earthly habitation is a tent, it is a substantial tent, or so it seems. It has stood a good many hard blasts. The man himself, too, has been all along growing. His bodily frame has been hardening and not weakening. His strength, his power of resistance, his knowledge, and his mental grasp have been growing. Thought has been taking a larger range and sinking its shafts deeper; and difficulty has acted only as a stimulus to energy. In short, I repeat, the thought of dissolution and detachment at this period, fall into the background. All is growth, increase, enlargement of range; multiplying points of contact with the world; a larger variety in the man's own environment.

But, as time goes on, you notice a change. The man has reached his altitude. Perhaps he shines there with a steady splendor for yet a good many years; but his position or reputation are practically fixed. His standing in the community is defined. Men know how far they can draw on him and what purposes he can serve, and into what places he will fit. He is no longer a man of promise. His age, if it do not find fulfilment, drops him. The cords on the rear of the tent begin to slacken. There have been bonds which still held him strongly to the past. A father or a mother dies. Brothers and sisters form new alliances and new homes for themselves, and their interests and his diverge. The old circle of kindred begins to break up. It goes on quietly, like the undermining of a bank, where now and then a loosened mass dropping into the stream shows that the current is at work; but some day he wakes up to the fact that his connections are mostly with his own generation, while the cords which held him to the love and wisdom and fellowship of his fathers—fibres along which something of the freshness of boyhood and youth still found its way into his maturer life—now hang slack or severed. And, as time moves on, a new and more startling fact begins to emerge—that the connections with his own generation are gradually breaking. More and more pronounced is the sense of the push of a mass of younger, fresher life, crowding him back or on one side. The world is not for him as he thought it was. It is for youth. The children, to whom he has been an authority, are developing independent ideas of their own, and are carrying them out without much regard to his approval or disapproval. A familiar face vanishes at intervals from the counting-room or the council-table. Little time to pause for this; only a day for decorous funeral ceremonial. The gap is filled. There is no vacant place to look at. Only some day he realizes that almost all his old comrades are gone. The very respect of men is suspicious. It is the formal respect they pay to the antiquated.

The break is heading toward the centres of life. He has lost some ambition. He has given up certain things he was always meaning to do. He is not so ready for the undertakings which make a drain on nerve and strength. He gives up more easily than of yore. The spring has gone out of him. Younger men may come to the front unchallenged. The front is a hot, dangerous place, under fire, and rest and quiet are growing sweeter.

And so the final stage sets in; physical wreck, mental feebleness, complete withdrawal from the busy world. Let it go on its way. He cares no longer. The tent with its loosened cords flaps and strains, then collapses. There are eulogies and obituaries and an epitaph. The earthly house of this tabernacle is dissolved: and yet He that wrought us *for this very thing* is God. God meant this: meant that our earthly house should be a tent and not a building: meant that it should be transitory and not eternal.

This is a very sad picture, if this is all. Nay, it is an insult to common sense to ask us to believe that this wondrous frame of nature and of man are made merely to be destroyed. Reverently speaking—speaking from the stand-point of thought at which God's own Word and Spirit place us—we may say that such a result would argue a wanton and arbitrary exercise of power. But this is not all. God did not make us for death, but for life. If He has appointed a tent for our sojourn, He has reared a building for our dwelling. Moses, in that old psalm, voices the truth. There is nothing eternal but God. There is no warrant of man's eternity but God. There is no eternal home for man but in God. The old law-giver looked forth from the tent where a generation was dying out in the wilderness; looked away from the purple mountains, the most impressive symbol of stability which the earth furnishes; looked away into what would have been vacancy to many another eye, and saw the eternal home there. "Lord, Thou hast been our dwelling-place in all generations. Before the mountains were brought forth or ever Thou hadst formed the earth and the world, from everlasting to everlasting Thou art God."

And so we turn to the other side of our text. God has made us for the tent, but He has also made us for the building.

The important point is that we should see these two things as parts of one economy—the tent and the building as related to each other. How death and decay came into the world is not now the question. We are dealing merely with the facts. Now, I may say here that even if sin had never entered the world, I doubt whether this human life and this human body would have been any more than a temporary stage of existence through which men would have passed into a purely spiritual life. Because I find that this is according to the analogy of God's working elsewhere, if not everywhere. God's plans unfold. They do not flash into consummation. They involve progressive stages; and immense expenditure of time and of labor is concentrated upon single stages, which, after all, seem to be little more than stand-points for succeeding stages. God's economy distinctly takes in the transitory and the temporal as well as the eternal. The line of His purpose runs out to eternity, but it runs through time. And so I repeat, that, without questioning the statement that death came by sin, I think I can understand how, even if sin had not entered, human life might have been temporary, a transition stage to something higher; and how, therefore, the apostle might truthfully say, even of God's original intent—even of the tent no less than of the building—"He that hath wrought us for this very thing is God."

Thought has tended too much to the violent separation of the mortal life from the eternal life: has tended to set them in contrast and opposition instead of in harmony: has tended to regard them as representing different economies, instead of as being included in one and the same economy. For instance, we draw the line sharply between life and death; and yet many a scientist will tell you that death is the beginning of life : and Christ and Paul tell you that in unmistakable terms. And what we want clearly to apprehend with reference to this mortal, transitory tent-life of ours, is that it has a definite relation to the permanent spiritual life of the future; that it serves a purpose of preparation and development toward that life: that it furnishes a basis, a soil in which the seeds of the spiritual life are sown ; and that, therefore, instead of being despised and neglected because it is temporary and destined to dissolution, it is to be cherished and cultivated as the real and effective ministrant of the eternal life. "He that wrought us for this very thing is God." If God made us merely to die, and if death is the end, why, then, life has very little significance. If He made us to live forever, and if our life here fits into that life beyond, and prepares us for it, then life is not only significant, but gets its chief significance from that other thing for which God hath wrought us—the building of God eternal in the heavens. We have in nature a great many illustrations and analogies of the fact that what is transitory and ephemeral directly ministers to higher and more enduring forms of life. Take, for instance, the illustration of the soil. Existence underground, in the dark, is a low form of life, and yet the seed must be cast into the ground and remain there for a time, before the beauty and fruitfulness and nourishment of the fruit or grain can become facts. And that preliminary stage in the dark mould is not merely a period of idle, passive waiting. That stage ministers directly to the higher form of life. So in animal life.

What a delicate and beautiful structure is the egg of the fowl. How perfect its outlines. How fine the texture and tinting of the shell. Yet how frail. It is made, as we all see, to be broken, and an egg-shell is a synonym for something worthless. And yet there have been lodged in that frail and temporary thing forces which minister to life. That little casket holds and protects and fosters the life of the infant bird, and in it are begun and nourished those processes of life which are taken up and carried on by a new set of ministries from the moment that the fowl emerges from the shell. So the worm rolls himself up in the cocoon, but within the cocoon the purple and golden glories of the butterfly are silently elaborating themselves.

Even so it is God's intent that the immortal, the spiritual life should be taking shape under the forms of the mortal life: that in the tent man should be shaping for the eternal building: that in this frail, fleshly environment we should be growing familiar with the powers of the world to come; should be coming more and more under their influence; should be growing more and more into sympathy with the principles and the ideas of the eternal world; growing in aspiration for their larger range, and even welcoming the dissolution of the tent as the signal and medium of entrance into the eternal building.

This feature of our mortal life is intended to show itself early. The average human life, as we have seen, tends to become more and more enveloped in the wrappings of this world, and to consider nothing else; and many practically reason that attention to the interests of the next world may be deferred until the process of detachment from the things of time has fairly and consciously set in. In other words, that a man need give heed to the things of eternity only when his breaking up warns him that he is about to pass into eternity. On the contrary, the life should be shaped for eternity from the beginning. The ministry of the soil begins with the very first stage of the seed-life. The world to come does not appeal merely to manhood and old age. It is the child that is most inquisitive about the sky; who cries for the moon; to whom the stars are a wonder. Why not the same fact in spiritual life? Why should not heavenly aspirations characterize childhood? Why should not the child-life be touched and quickened by contact with heaven? At any rate, from the time that the idea is fairly grasped that this life is a stage to a larger and permanent life—not merely a stage of waiting, but a stage of shaping for that life—from that time the larger life of eternity inaugurates its own process in child or man, and gives their life its own direction. Under the wrappings which earthly business and earthly relationship swathe round him; under the tangled lines which connect him with so many and such varied interests; under the shape into which the contact of the world presses the visible outlines of his life, a life may be taking shape whose quality and tendencies are heavenly. Within and under the life of society, the life of business, the domestic life, an eternal, spiritual manhood may be outlining itself.

When men have undertaken to shut themselves out as much as possible from the contact of this life, when they have walled themselves up in cloisters, or have sought for saintship in dismal caverns or on the top of pillars, they have mistaken the intent of this life. They have not seen that He that hath wrought us for this very thing is God. They have seen in mortal life only a contradiction, an antagonism to eternal life, and not a minister to it. It has been as though the embryo bird should refuse the nourishment for his initial life which the egg supplies, and should refuse to call it living until he had escaped from the shell into the air and sunshine.

Detachment, breaking up, come of themselves, come quickly enough in God's own order. Meanwhile, it is not for us to accelerate the process, but to keep ourselves on the line of God's great purpose to make the tent tributary to the building; to make the mortal life minister to the immortal. That this thing is made to break up, does not prove that it has no permanent purpose to serve. That you and I are short-lived and frail, that we are dust, as God tells us we are, does not prove that we cannot turn our brevity and frailty to account in the interest of our eternal life. Building is the type of the permanent, but all building involves the temporary.

Many of you remember how, for years, as the traveller on the Rhine came in sight of Cologne, the first object which greeted his eye was the unsightly mass of scaffolding around the Cathedral spires. It is all gone now, and the twin spires soar heavenward from their base, and cut the horizon with their clean, sharp lines of stone. Yet the scaffolds were necessary to the building. No scaffolding, no spires. Whether this life is to be more than scaffolding depends on the man who lives; depends on whether or not he mistakes scaffolding for building. Connections he must make. He must have earthly no less than heavenly environment. Windings innumerable, social, domestic, commercial, go into the texture of his earthly tent. The question is whether these are all: whether these things are ends unto themselves: whether the cocoon in which the mortal life enswathes itself is to be regarded as its final investiture, or as a sphere for the development of the life of heaven: whether mortality is simply to be dissolved, or whether mortality is to be swallowed up of life. It is for this, for this swallowing up of life, that God hath wrought us; and the real character will be set upon your life and mine by our recognizing or failing to recognize that fact.

If the cocoon is all that the worm comes to, poor worm! Worthless cocoon! If business, politics, social life, fame, are all the man comes to, poor man! It is a sad, sad thing if all is summed up in the dissolving of the house of this tabernacle. For it will dissolve. It is dissolving. You see and know it yourselves. Already with many of you the cords are slackening, the wrappings loosening, the shell breaking.

What then? The tent will fall. Shall you be left uncovered? Beware, beware of these same wrappings. They are folding you in closely. You are growing in reputation and in wealth, and the world is a very pleasant place to you. Your tent-strings are taut; your pins well driven, your tent-cloth of fine and rich texture; your tent is looming up and making a good appearance among the other tents: all well perhaps, if these things are not all: if, under your busy life, there is the constant presence of God, a carefully-fostered, keen consciousness of the touch of God; an unbroken connection between heaven and your tent; a daily interchange between Christ and you: if, in short, to put it as Paul does, your citizenship is in heaven, and the mark of heaven is on your words and your life and your spirit. Your tent does not shut you out from heaven's light; need not if you will see to it that the curtains are drawn back to let in the light.

God hath wrought you for this. Again I say, God hath made the tent that it might serve the building. He has made you a man in time that you may be a glorified spirit in eternity.

Hence detachment may mean for you victory and immortality. God hath wrought you for the eternal building in the heavens, no less than for the frail, perishing tent on earth. You will have gained much when you shall have learned to read in dissolution the prophecy of eternal stability; the foreshadowing of life in the approaches of death. That you may learn this, God hath given to you the earnest of His Spirit. To the eyes which that Spirit unseals, every break, every collapse, every sign of wear, is a touch, throwing into sharper outline God's own handwriting, "We have a building of God, a house not made with hands, eternal in the heavens." He that hath wrought you for *this* is God. Something within tells you you are more than mortal. Something assures you that you are not made for these wrappings which fade and rend. Something tells you that the tatters of mortality are not the final outcome of God's intent concerning man. The materialist will warn you that your wish is father to your thought: that a natural desire is not to be construed into a fact: that longing must yield to logic, and instincts be content to wither at the touch of science. None the less, instincts have wrought with wonderful power in the history of humanity. The religious *feeling*, however unscientific, has made a formidable stand against a godless materialism which reduces life to matter and force. But, more than this, the Gospel interprets and defines this instinct as a revelation of God, wrought into the very fibre of our humanity, the earnest of the Spirit. You who believe in Jesus and the resurrection may safely trust that testimony; you may rest in that prophecy with joy. You cannot arrest the decay, but you may turn it to account; you may translate it into hope: you may see in it emancipation, fulness of life, an inheritance incorruptible, undefiled, and unfading.

XVI.

THE KINGHOOD OF PATIENCE.

> *"I John, your brother and partaker with you in the tribulation and kingdom and patience which are in Jesus, was in the isle that is called Patmos, for the word of God and the testimony of Jesus."*
> —REV. i. 9.

THAT is a very remarkable phrase—"the kingdom and patience." It might almost seem to be an arbitrary and fanciful phrase. And more than this, the two ideas would appear, to some minds at least, to be contradictory. Patience does not appeal to such minds as a kingly virtue, but rather as a commonplace quality befitting people of humbler rank. As for a king, why should he wait when he has the power to accomplish at once? Why should he tolerate the slowness of others when he can command sure and swift agents? Impatience is somehow conceived as a king's privilege.

The Bible puts this whole matter directly the other way. Kinghood, instead of being dissevered from patience, is bound up with it: the kingly virtues are all intertwined with patience and dependent upon it. The kingdom, the divine kingdom, is inherited through faith and patience, and the kingly man is the patient man.

This truth, when we come to examine it, is not confined to the region of Scripture or of religion. It is, in part at least, an every-day, business truth. It is a familiar enough fact that the great successes of the world have been won by hard and patient work, and not by inspired flashes; and we are beginning to have greater respect for the power of holding on than for the power of brilliant striking out.

And, as in so many cases, Christ shows us how, in these familiar views, we have gotten hold of one end of a truth which runs up through the whole spiritual economy; a truth which takes the form of a principle: patience is kinghood.

But if that principle is to commend itself practically to mankind, it must be incarnated. Men will not believe it on the strength of mere assertion. There is a disposition, and it is a healthful one, to challenge all moral requisitions which rest on mere precept. Men say, " It is easy enough for an idealist to retire from the world, and write down rules and frame moral theories. Wait till the idealist gets down to where we are: wait till his rules and theories are set at work in this region of half-sight, of clashing wills, of natural wants, where we toil and suffer and fight: wait till these fine moral ideals are applied to the unexpected crooks and turns in human nature, and are set against the onset and shock of hard facts. Then see what they are worth. Then see what they can do." So, when this claim of royalty is made for patience, the world says, " It is nothing to us that even God says it is kingly. Let us see it on the throne. Let us see this plodding, quiet virtue, this thing so far removed from high spirit, conquer its place and grasp the sceptre. Show us a kingly man who is also a model of patience, and who wins his crown of manhood through patience."

In response to that demand Christ puts forward Himself and the lives which He inspires; such a life, for instance, as that of John, who, though the victim of an impatient, fitful, brutal sovereignty, though a sufferer and an exile, can yet salute his brethren as kings, and style himself " your brother in the kingdom and patience which are in Jesus."

We take the statement, therefore, just as it stands. In Jesus there are these two elements, dominion and patience. Let us try and have clearly before us the contrast between Christ and the mass of men whom He came to save; and this will afford us at least a practical gauge of the severity of the strain upon His patience.

Though our Saviour adapted Himself to human conditions, it goes without saying that He was, regarded merely as a man, superior to other men. That is conceded on all hands. His word was instinctively recognized as carrying a mysterious authority. "Never man spake like this man." He impressed the judge who condemned Him and the officer who executed Him. He had a strange and subtle attraction for men, from the day when He questioned the doctors in the temple, until the hour when the centurion said, "Surely this was a righteous man." Moreover, Christ was consciously superior. "Ye call me," said He, "the teacher and the Lord, and ye say well, for so I am." And when Peter declared in answer to His question, "Thou art the

Christ, the Son of the living God," so far from disclaiming the honor, He pronounced a special blessing on Peter for his confession.

But Christ's superiority was put at the service of men, to raise and to save them. It was not goodness and greatness coming before ignorance and simplicity to display themselves and to call forth stupid wonder. Christ's greatness came down to the level of the lost, that He might seek and save that which was lost.

Now, I ask you to consider the peculiar trial of patience applied to a cultured mind and a pure character in contact with dense ignorance, wicked cruelty, intense bigotry, enormous conceit, and personal degradation in every conceivable form.

Look at the matter, for instance, on its lowest side. Did you ever do a full day's work in a hospital, surrounded from morning until evening with the sick and wounded and dying, scarcely for a moment out of the sound of moans or of sights which wrung your heart? If you have, you know how weary in body you were when the night came. And yet your worst experience of that kind was probably but a faint shadow of many days in Christ's life, especially those in which He was pressed all day long by that fearful oriental crowd, thrusting their various ailments upon His attention, bringing their diseased friends to His feet, while, through the hot, dust-laden air, penetrated the moan of pain or the shriek of the demoniac. Christ's work must have entailed a severe physical strain. The tension of His finely-strung, sensitive, emotional nature must have told powerfully upon the strongest body : yet we never read of His growing irritated, or of His seeking to evade the contact with sickness. He gives Himself freely to the wretched. He ministers up to the limit of His strength, and then withdraws to the mountains and to His lonely, peaceful communion with heaven, to recruit His powers for new draughts upon His patient love.

It is not so very hard to keep patience with an ignorant person who feels his ignorance, and wants to learn. The trial comes when ignorance mistakes itself for wisdom : when it is bent, not on learning, but on asserting itself. This was what Christ had to meet daily. He came to teach men who thought they had nothing to learn about the principles and the practice of religion. In the face of taunts and abuse, surrounded by learned men who could not appreciate His broader vision and His higher ideals of religion, how patiently and persistently He repeats His lessons by word and act. To eat with publicans and sinners was to fly in the face of tradition and custom; yet so often was the act repeated that it became one of the standing charges against Him: and yet it was never done defiantly, but always in pursuance of some purpose of love. In like manner He was not withheld from doing acts of mercy on the Sabbath day by the charge of being a Sabbath-breaker. One would suppose that the narrowest spirit would have rejoiced over such a gracious deed as the healing of the withered hand ; but the Pharisees went out and took counsel how they might destroy Him. Yet how gently He reasons with them. "If you have one sheep, and it falls into a pit on the Sabbath day, do you not lift it out? Is not a man of more value than a sheep? Wherefore, it is lawful to do good on the Sabbath day." That degraded Samaritan woman, entrenched in her ignorant prejudices, and urging her stale traditions against Jesus' purer teachings — whose patience would not have been tried by her? And yet our Lord will have no quarrel with her. All sense of personal annoyance is swallowed up in His eagerness to save her; and that story, as it seems to me, ought to be read over and over again, and studied in every detail, and committed to memory by every one who seeks to draw human souls to the truth.

Wise and good men who devote their lives to the ignorant, have nevertheless some compensations. They step out of their own congenial circle, where their character and thoughts are appreciated, and down into the lower circle; but they can step back again at intervals, and refresh themselves with the contact and sympathy of congenial minds. But this compensation was denied Christ. There was, indeed, a small band that loved Him, listened to Him, and believed in Him, but even these could sympathize with Him only to a very small extent. Nothing is more evident than that they failed to appreciate His main aims and principles, and that their growth was very slow in those elements of character which He most desired to develop. How slow they were, for instance, in learning the secret of true greatness. With the spectacle daily before their eyes of a master whom they reverenced and whose infinite superiority they felt, putting Himself at the service of the lowest, they yet quarreled among themselves as to who should be greatest in their little company. Peter, who could utter that glorious confession, "Thou art the Christ, the Son of the living God," could tempt that Christ to swerve from His act of self-sacrifice and to believe that He was too good to suffer. How many times He had occasion to rebuke their slowness of faith: when the storm came down on the lake, and they rushed to Him, crying, "Lord, save us, we perish": when they stood helpless before the possessed child at the foot of Hermon: when the two opened to Him their doubts and fears on the way to Emmaus: when Thomas met the tidings of His resurrection with such obstinate, senseless incredulity. How many times He had to say, "O ye of little faith! O foolish and slow of heart to believe!" This is one of the hardest of all things for a true man of high and pure aims—to go through the world without sympathy: and not a few men have shown themselves unable to endure it. Sometimes they have lowered their ideal: sometimes they have compromised: sometimes they have grown bitter and defiant and misanthropic. Nothing is more beautiful than the patience of Christ as related to His uncompromising fidelity to His standard of duty and of truth: His holding by His principles while He holds on at the same time to those slow, backward pupils in the school of faith and of self-sacrifice.

Many a man, by his severe devotion to his moral ideals, cuts himself loose from other men. They admire

THE KINGHOOD OF PATIENCE. 241

his courage and consistency, but refuse to follow him; and a reason for this is often found in his impatience with their slowness. He scolds them because they are not as radical as he is. He sneers at their principles because they will not carry them out to the same length that he does. He will not let them go part of the way with him because they will not go all the way; and thus he not only loses them altogether, but converts them into enemies. It was the patience of Christ which enabled Him to bate not one jot of His high claims and at the same time to lose none of those whom the Father had given Him. He could mourn over slow faith and uneducated conscience and low ideals of duty, yet He could go on teaching, and continue to wait long and patiently while they toiled slowly and painfully up toward His higher level. Cannot modern radicalism learn some lessons from this? "Radical," properly understood, is an honorable title. A genuine truth-seeker is always radical, and Christ was the most radical teacher and reformer the world ever saw; but Christ's success, won by patience, is an expressive comment on a great many failures of radical teachers who want to bring in the millennium at once; and whose motto is, millennium or nothing.

Look, for instance, at Christ's patience in dealing with those who, though convinced of the rightfulness of His claims and secretly on His side, yet hesitated to confess Him openly. He used no doubtful words about the duty of open confession and the consequences of withholding it. He would deny before the Father the man who should finally refuse to confess Him before men:

and yet He could wait for that confession: He could give feeble courage time for training. He could patiently and persistently and gently apply influences to those souls to quicken their conscience and to shame them of their cowardice. A reformer who represents a new and unpopular cause, stern, brave, outspoken himself, naturally desires the same qualities in his followers. He wants them to come out boldly on his side, and he is tempted to be very impatient with any partial committal. Yet Christ had to deal with such. Let us remember that the Holy Ghost with its baptism of power and courage was not yet given. Christ himself could take the highest way, knowing that it ended at the cross, and could pursue it to Calvary; but He knew very well that not all the men under His teaching could do that yet. He had a Thomas, who, doubter as he was, proposed to go to Bethany and die with Him; and a John, who followed Him to His judgment; but He had a Nicodemus, who was afraid to commune with Him in the daytime, and a Peter who could openly deny Him, and a Joseph of Arimathea who was afraid to declare his belief in Him while He lived. Jesus could wait—wait even till after His death—for these timid ones. His patience was vindicated. Nicodemus spoke for Him, timidly it is true, in the Sanhedrim, and brought spices for His burial. Joseph refused to vote against Him in the council, and boldly begged His body of Pilate and buried it in his own tomb; and Peter's is among the loudest and clearest of the voices which ring through the history of the infant church. Jesus himself had seen over that sad, humiliating period of cowardice and treachery, to a time when Peter should be the rock of the early church. So he was, and he went to the death of the cross for Christ's sake.

And there was another case: that of the one who used His name and His power, and yet did not identify himself formally with Him: the man who was casting out devils in His name, and whom the disciples forbade because he did not follow with them. Ah! how often we have heard that same prohibition in later days! that utterance of religious partisanship which refuses to recognize the rightfulness or the virtue of a good, Christlike deed, and the nobility of a Christlike character outside of religious party-limits. When shall we learn that whatever anywhere is Christlike, is Christian? How much it would have been to Christ to have all such men openly arrayed with Him; yet what a noble tolerance breathes in His reply to the disciples: what a keen recognition of Christlike quality: "Forbid him not. After all the man shows himself on my side. He is not the friend of the demon that he casts out. He is indeed not my friend in the full sense that I could wish, but he is not my enemy. He that is not against us is on our part. No man can do a miracle in my name and lightly speak evil of me."

Once more let me briefly refer you to Christ's patience as shown in His method of securing friends and helpers. Most reformers, in their zeal to secure partisans, are willing to receive them under the influence of momentary enthusiasm. They are willing to have a man commit himself while his reason is unconvinced and only his fancy captivated. You cannot but observe how Christ guarded against this mistake, though His caution doubtless cost Him many followers. He had patience to wait for followers who should embrace His cause deliberately, from conviction ; and in this light the plainness of His statements concerning the terms and consequences of His service are worth noting. Nothing is concealed. Tribulation, self-denial, possible sundering of earthly ties—all are plainly set forth as the consequences of following Him: and then there is a commentary upon this in His words of warning addressed to enthusiastic votaries. "You wish to follow me. Count the cost as men do in their ordinary affairs. A king does not go forth to battle without knowing his adversary's force, and calculating whether he can resist or overthrow it. A man does not build a house without ascertaining how much it is going to cost him." The scribe comes to Him and says, "I will follow Thee wherever Thou goest." "Well, good scribe, come after me if you will : take me as master if you will : only remember that your master fares in worldly things not so well as the foxes and the birds." The two young aspirants, led by their fond mother, come and ask for high places in His kingdom. I wonder if they penetrated the awful meaning of the question with which Jesus met them : "Can ye drink of my cup and be baptized with my baptism?"

And now I should like to dwell upon the patience of Christ as shown in His waiting : but the time forbids.

Just a hint or two on this point. Christ's mission, in its very nature, involved long, patient waiting. It was the mission of a sower, sowing seed of slow growth. The harvest of Christ's ideas was not going to be reaped in three years nor in a hundred. He knew perfectly that He should return from earth leaving behind Him almost nothing in the way of visible results. And you will remember how He was tempted at this point at the very beginning of His ministry. Do you suppose that Satan, when he spread before the Son of man that gorgeous vision of the kingdoms of this world, expected to appeal to any shallow fondness for power and display and luxury? No. He knew Christ too well to offer Him any such cheap toy. The failure of His first temptation showed how much the Lord cared for mere sensual gratification. He could play upon a more sensitive chord than that. He could offer to the Saviour the temptation of going at one stride to His goal by asserting His kingly authority, by setting up an earthly dominion, by bringing in a condition of worldly happiness through righteous and merciful government instead of through the slower process of spiritual regeneration. He could open to Jesus a gate to a road which led round the cross. And to a nature like Christ's, so loving and so tender, to One whose dearest employment was to help and to comfort the wretched, there must have been something alluring in the thought of tiding over those long ages of blood and tears and misery which lay between Bethlehem and the new Jerusalem; the thought of going at once to the throne of the world, and by His power exerted against injustice and in the interest of good order and of the common weal, redressing so many wrongs, "stanching all those fountains of tears, and imparting all that knowledge of His Father's love." And yet Christ knew that the results of such a course would be superficial. He knew that the only sure basis for a happy society on earth was holiness. He knew that the road to the new city of God where entereth nothing which defileth, lay, not only for Him, but for the world, by the way of the cross. And so He deliberately turned from the vision of worldly power. His answer to those who charged Him with aspiring to kinghood was invariably, "My kingdom is not of this world." He was content to await the slow growth of the Gospel seed, the slow pervasion of the Gospel leaven; to wait for the consummation of a sovereignty based on the spiritual transformation wrought by the Gospel. His course in this stands out as the sublimest illustration of patience in all time, and stamps Him as the true King of the ages.

Thus, then, we see this element of patience wrought into the very fibre of Christ's kinghood. With all His other qualities He could be the king He is, and shall be confessed, only through His patience. Even from these few illustrations, which might be multiplied indefinitely, we begin to understand John's phrase, "the kingdom and patience of Jesus Christ."

And Christ, therefore, by His own example, no less than by His word, commends to us this kingly virtue of patience. The apostle James has caught the meaning of His life and its relation to our lives when he says, "Let patience have its perfect work, that ye may be perfect and entire, lacking in nothing." Surely he does not mean that a man who is merely patient is perfect: but he does mean that a man who is not patient cannot be perfect. He does mean that this quality of patience is indispensable to the growth and maturing of every other Christian quality. Love! Can there be any true love without patience? Does not love bear all things? Is it love when we merely love those who never try us, who always please us, who are always congenial? "If ye love them which love you, what thank have ye? Do not even the publicans the same?" Look at the love of God in Christ Jesus. God so loved the world that He gave His only-begotten Son. Was the world lovely or lovable? Was the society into which Jesus boldly threw Himself, and upon which He poured out His heart and His gracious ministries, a thing calculated to inspire love, in our sense of the term? Even from what we have seen in this brief review, is it conceivable that Christ's love should have had any power or any result without patience? Nay, let us come nearer home. Let us look at ourselves as we stand related to God in Christ to-day. Take the element of patience out of God's love, and what becomes of us? Are we indeed so lovable, so free from fault, does our fidelity and our conformity to the Divine standard of character so commend itself to our heavenly Father that He has simly to approve it? Or is it not rather the case that we stumble and blunder all the way to heaven; that we appeal by our wavering and our carelessness and our vanity, more to the forbearance than to the approbation of God? And so of all the other virtues. What is faith if it be not persistent? Do we think of faith merely as a single act of belief? Is it not rather a hard, persistent holding on against the efforts of earth and hell to shake us loose? Are we not bidden to be followers of those who through faith and patience inherit the promises? Take that series of graces arrayed in the first chapter of second Peter —faith, virtue, knowledge, temperance, godliness, love of the brethren, love—and strike out patience, and does not the whole chain fall to pieces? Can any of these thrive and grow without patience?

So, then, if you and I are expecting to win moral and spiritual dominion, this element must come to the front in our lives. Suppose we want to be good, truthful, pure in heart, single in purpose, Christlike in temper. Are these things wrought in us on the instant? What is the story our own experience tells us? Some of us have been trying for a good many years. Have we gotten past the necessity of going to God's throne with confession and penitence? Are there no fresh scars upon us from recent stumbles? Have "passion's unruly nurslings" been "rocked to sleep"? Is the fire all gone out of our tongues? And has there been born to us a sense of rest as of those who feel that the strain is over and the hardness of the fight past? No, brethren, you and I know it is not so. We know that each morning we wake to a twofold fight, with the world outside and with the self within. God help us, if patience fail. God help us, if there be not something within which keeps firm hold of the exceeding great and precious promises; which will not suffer faith to fail, that He that hath begun a good work will perfect it; which is not disheartened at slow progress, and which, spite of the tears and the dust, keeps our faces turned toward the place where we know the crown and the glory are, though we cannot see them.

So, too, like Christ, we have a work to do among men. We shall not do it without patience. We are constantly tempted to a false and selfish view of our relation to society: to think that society exists for our pleasure and comfort only, and to lose out of sight the other truth, that, as Christians, we exist for the good of society. And therefore our tendency is to eliminate from society all that is uncongenial, everything which can possibly be a tax on patience, and to put it on one side as a thing with which we have nothing to do. But that is not Christ's way. If we are to be true followers of His we must frankly accept the contact with the uncongenial and the unlovable as part of our lives, and the trial of patience which comes with it. If we want the kingdom of Jesus Christ, we cannot have it without the patience of Jesus Christ. We must try and get a firmer hold of the great principle of Christ's life: " not to be ministered unto, but to minister"; and when we shall have gotten it clearly into our minds that our main purpose in life is not to be blessed by the world, but to bless the world, then we shall find ourselves on the road where every day and every hour will beget a prayer for the patience of Jesus Christ. Bearing, waiting, enduring,—these do not seem to be means to kinghood; but if we aim at spiritual kinghood, dominion over our hearts, dominion over self, dominion over character—the kingdom of Jesus Christ—that and that only is the way to it.

And we must try to put ourselves, moreover, at Christ's stand-point, in our outlook upon religious progress. I think the patience of Jesus grows upon us as we, here nearly at the end of nineteen centuries, see what His prophetic vision saw—how much yet remains to be done ere Christ's spiritual dominion shall have become a world-wide fact. The prayer, "Thy kingdom come," is taking on a new meaning and a new intensity to some in these later days; and, what is more, is being put up ofttimes under a gigantic shadow of doubt. The kingdom seems so slow in coming. The blows are redoubled at the old foundations. The cold materialism of the age is so pronounced. We want faith at this point, but we want patience and much of it. We need not doubt Christ's word. His kingdom will come, is coming, coming straight and steadily: but we must try and get back to where He stood on that mountain of vision, and with Him accept the fact that the kingdom of God is a plant of slow growth. Watered though it has been by the prayers and tears of the faithful through all these centuries, it does not quicken its rate. And I think that perhaps one reason why we are tempted to grow impatient is that we do not realize fully the magnitude of the result which the Gospel contemplates.

At any rate, Christ could afford to wait and to be patient, and so can we. He did not despair, neither need we. He predicted success; on His word, as the testimony of His infinite foresight, we may be sure of it. It is not for us to grow sick and disheartened and angry at the times. Not for us to cry, "Who shall show us any good?" Not for us to say in despair, "The foundations are being removed." You and I are to be patient, not with the patience of idleness, not in the spirit of helpless acquiescence with things as they are, but with the patience of hope; the patience of firm holding by God's truth and promises in His word; the patience of persistent warfare against sin; the patience of constant, faithful preaching and living of the word of God; the patience of Jesus Christ. The kingdom of Jesus Christ will follow in due time. Things never looked less like the triumph of Christ than when Nero was raving and burning at Rome, and the Roman Empire was rotting at the roots, and John was driven by the storm to desolate Patmos. But it was in Patmos that John saw the vision of a perfected society which was to be a fact some day; and it was from that vision of the city of God coming down out of heaven, that he came to tell the Church of all time of the kingdom and patience of Jesus Christ.

XVII.

JEHOVAH ROPHEKA.

"*For I am the Lord that healeth thee.*"—EXODUS xv. 26.

WHEN one has escaped from great danger or distress, every other feeling is for the moment swallowed up in the joy of deliverance. This very joy contributes to make any subsequent trouble the harder to bear.

If the Israelites, in their delight at their newly-won freedom, supposed that their troubles were at an end, they were soon undeceived. The old conditions in which they had been reared did not quit their hold easily. Pharaoh was not slow in awaking to a sense of the disaster to his kingdom involved in the simultaneous migration of a slave race of two millions, and was resolved to retrieve his mistake; and so the Israelites had hardly gotten clear of Egypt when they found him, like a thirsty bloodhound, on their track. That danger was very summarily disposed of, and Pharaoh put beyond the possibility of further harm to them or to any one else. Then there were great rejoicings, songs and timbrels and dances. It was like a second exodus. Two such signal escapes do not often occur close together in the history of a people. And now they set their faces toward their future. The working out of the new national problem began, as it always must, on the line of commonplace work and daily drudgery. The march commenced over the sand with its dry depressions and stunted herbage and bare limestone hills. Soon came the danger so common to Eastern travel. The water supply failed: but they had scarcely time to grow frightened and discontented ere the wells appeared. Again trouble seemed to be at an end. The eager crowd surrounded the cisterns. The water was hastily drawn. Thousands of parched lips touched the coveted draught; and then a general cry of disgust and anguish rang through the host. Any one who knows what the water of desert wells in the East is, knows that the best is bad enough; and can imagine how loathsome this must have been, when men and women of no delicate taste were obliged to throw it away.

And strangest of all is the fact, so often repeated in this history, that the people did not appear to think at all of God, to whom it was but natural that their thoughts should turn at once. One would think that after two such divine interpositions within the last few days, they might have seen a way out of this last difficulty: but no, they stood there by the wells and cried out against Moses, and asked, "Where shall we find water?"

God has wonderful patience with men. He does not expect too much from His new pupils in the school of faith. It was evident in this case that the principle of faith had to be developed from the very roots; and therefore God at once interposed with a twofold object; to relieve the present distress, and to give an elementary lesson in faith and obedience. He pointed out a tree which He bade Moses cast into the water, and the water became sweet.

We need not allegorize this story in order to draw a lesson from it. It deals with facts, which, under different forms, are constantly reappearing in all our lives. It is a fact, for instance, that the rapid alternations of safety and danger, triumph and terror, joy and mourning, which marked this stage of Israel's history, mark the course of human life in every age. No human experience is uniformly joyful or sorrowful. A great triumph is succeeded by a great obstacle and sometimes by a great defeat. To-night there is the joy of escape from bondage: to-morrow the tyrant's chariots are in hot pursuit. To-day the Red Sea is passed and Miriam's timbrel and song resound over the waters: to-morrow come the pangs of thirst: the next day Elim with palms and sweet wells: soon the desert and the rock. To-day you are prosperous, satisfied, every want met: to-morrow you are asking how to win your bread. To-day you stride forth with the easy swing of health: to-morrow the door of the sick-chamber shuts you in, and you languish with weakness and are consumed with fever. To-day surrounded with friends and kindred: to-morrow the circle is broken, and you are weeping beside your dead. So it has been from the foundation of the world; so it will be, until the new order shall have entered, and there shall be no more death, neither sorrow nor crying.

But there is another equally constant fact to offset

this. As we look at this alternation of Elims and Marahs in our life, and recognize it as a law of our human experience, we find it supplemented by something else which is equally a law; and that is the economy of God by which this alternation is happily adjusted. In other words, I mean this: that if it is a law of our life that joy and sorrow succeed each other, it is equally a law of our life that God interposes and keeps the joy from corrupting and the sorrow from crushing us. If He tempers our joy by a sorrow or a danger, He has always a branch to cast into the bitter water which our lips refuse, and to sweeten it. If sorrow is a part of God's economy, healing is equally a part. If the apostle can state it as a law of God's administration that He chastens those whom He loves, and scourges every son whom He receives,—God states another law in the name by which He here commends Himself to Israel: I am Jehovah Ropheka, the Lord that healeth thee. And thus we find these two ideas side by side in the familiar words of the prophet Hosea, "Let us return unto the Lord, for He hath torn and He will heal us; He hath smitten, and He will bind us up."

We have gained very much when we have gotten hold of this truth, that human sorrow and human joy are two parts of one complex law, the mutual working of which is adjusted by heavenly wisdom. We have sure standing-ground here, from which we can look calmly forth upon the joyful and the sorrowful possibilities of life alike. If we had only the divine prophecy, "In this world ye shall have tribulation," it would seem to us, and justly, that life was one-sided and unbalanced, and must be thrown out of its orbit into utter confusion and wreck by the overwhelming, unremitted pressure from one direction. Not so when we read also, "in me ye shall have peace." Peace is perfect poise. Life takes on proportion and symmetry when we see the tribulation and the peace, the bitterness and the sweetness alike controlled by Jehovah.

Our ordinary, natural reasoning, and the philosophies of life which men construct out of their own brains and with the material furnished by their larger or smaller experience, do not give us anything corresponding to this. To perhaps the majority of minds, sorrow, while it is recognized as a constant factor of human life, appeals as something lawless. They look upon happiness as their natural right, and consequently upon every interruption of happiness as an intrusion, a disorderly thing. The idea of an economy of life which deliberately includes and provides for sorrow, is as strange as it is unwelcome. And therefore the idea of an economy or law of healing sorrow is equally strange. The alleviations of sorrow do not, to such minds, obey a law any more than the sorrow itself. You hear abundance of popular proverbs and sayings to the effect that clouds have often silver linings; that calamity usually stops short of the very worst; that time dulls grief; that nature reacts from its depression, and much more of the same sort, all which may be more or less true, but which do not cover the same ground as this blessed name, "Jehovah that healeth thee": which throw man for his compensation for sorrow merely upon nature and circumstances. Both are lawless and accidental, the alleviations no less than the sorrow itself.

But there is a radical difference between a grief which is accidental, and a grief which falls in with happier things into an order arranged to make the man purer and more blessed. There is a radical difference between accidental mitigations, and the firm, wise, tender touch of an omnipotent Healer upon a sorrow: and there is a radical difference between that conception of sorrow which makes it an intrusion and an interruption, and a conception which sees both sorrow and healing as parts of one divine plan, adjusted by that same divine hand all along the line of man's life. It is one thing for a man to start out upon a journey through an unknown country, taking it for granted that he will be able to pick up something somewhere to meet the needs and to repair the accidents of the way; and it is another thing for him to undertake the same journey under the auspices of one who knows the route, and anticipates the difficulties, and who has provisions and means of transportation to meet him at proper points, and appliances for every conceivable disaster. This was the case with Israel. Had they started from Egypt trusting to the desert to supply their needs as they arose, they would have perished, and that very early. Things were as bad as they could be at Marah. They must have water, and there was no water. And in this as in all other emergencies, when they received help or healing it was not accidental; it did not come through their skilful turning of circumstances to advantage. No combination of circumstances which they could make would have furnished manna; there was no water in such a circumstance as that rock at Kadesh: no way out from that writhing mesh of fiery serpents which enfolded them as they journeyed toward Edom. The help and the healing were parts of the same economy with the barren desert and the bitter wells.

God's child, then, has this firm standing-ground; this divine assurance that Jehovah that healeth is identified with the whole course of his life: that while that course leads beside many a bitter well and dry rock, and through many a desert place, he may be sure he shall meet the Lord, the Healer at each.

With the alleviations of sorrow which come in what we call the natural order of things, I have therefore nothing to do here. That nature has certain recuperative powers is a familiar fact: that God often uses these or other natural means in His own processes of healing, as a physician uses for medicine the herbs and flowers which he gathers by the roadside, is an equally familiar fact. But we are not concerned with the question of means. Our text leads us back of the means. That to which alone sorrow can grapple securely is not means, but God. God, on this occasion, though He uses a branch to sweeten the water, also uses it to direct the attention of the people to Himself. When He gives Himself a name by which they are to know and remember Him all through this desert journey, it is not, "the God of the branch," nor "the God of the rod," nor "the God of the strong east wind," but simply, "I am Jehovah that healeth thee." No matter what means I use. If He had called Himself the God of the rod, the people would have despaired of healing in any case where there was not a branch or a rod present. He would have them know that healing was in Him, by any means or by no means as He might choose.

And thus it is well for us to bring every bitter experience of life at once to God—directly. The fountain of healing is there, and there is no need of our taking the smallest trouble in seeking any lower source of comfort. If you live close beside a great lake of fresh, cold water, and want a cupful to drink, you do not hesitate to take it from the lake because it is so large. The lake which can fill your largest reservoir can certainly fill your cup, and Jehovah, who can heal your worst affliction, can certainly heal your lightest one. Since the great Physician thus puts Himself at your disposal, you may as well submit every case to Him, and not wait until you are driven to Him by some great emergency where no one else can help you. God is not like certain great medical authorities who leave all minor maladies to subordinates and hold themselves in reserve merely for consultation on cases of life and death. He wrought the great miracle at Marah, not only to relieve the people's thirst on that occasion, but to encourage them to seek His help in smaller matters. He is the Lord that healeth thee; and so He takes thee with all thy maladies great and small under His care, and would have thee cast all thy care upon Him, for He careth for thee. And if we do not get in the way of seeking God's healing in little troubles, we shall not so easily find it in great ones. The man who has trodden a mountain-path every day for years in the course of his ordinary toil, is the one who knows how to thread it in the darkness of midnight when his life depends upon his sure footing.

And that midnight darkness, that condition in which a man is alone with God and his own bitterness of soul, where no human help or sympathy or utterance is of any avail, where no diversion is possible, that, I say, is a not uncommon experience of God's children, in the presence of which one learns, often for the first time, what possibilities of healing are hidden in God. Do you remember those words in the ninety-fourth Psalm, "In the multitude of my thoughts within me, Thy comforts delight my soul"? Do you suppose that this means that the Psalmist reasoned out his way to comfort with a multitude of thoughts? Not so. There is a graphic little picture in those words. They mean literally, "in the multitude of my *tangled* or *intertwined* thoughts," a confused mass of thoughts like the interlacing twigs and boughs of a tree swept by a tempest. His thoughts are too confused to think out anything. That suggests a common feature of sorrow. When a great calamity has overtaken one, the first experience, and a dreadful one it is, is that of utter confusion, of inability to think connectedly at all. The man is simply driven like a leaf before the storm. Now he is hopeless, now desperate. He is as one in a jungle and cannot cut his way out. It is there, amid the multitude of tangled, conflicting thoughts, that he finds healing if he can get hold on God. It is a comfort if he can only realize that God is in the dark with him. He does not trouble himself much about the mode of the comfort. He merely clings to God and finds the more comfort the closer he gets to Him. In the midst of a severe and complicated disease one does not try to comprehend the medical problems involved in his case. His thought narrows down to his doctor. It is his business to know the problems and their solution; and it is better for the patient when he can dismiss all thought about those. He is always the worse for trying to keep track of his own case.

That is one element of the sweetness which God throws into our Marahs — that element of simple rest in Him. God sometimes reduces a man to terrible straits so that he may learn that lesson. The branch which He throws in is this: "Rest in the Lord and wait patiently for Him." When one is in such confusion and bewilderment, a great deal of the distress is thrown off in the throwing off of all responsibility for the way out. Helplessness under the touch of the great Healer is converted into restfulness. Many years ago, while in Rome, I went down into the Catacombs. I had not gone five feet from the entrance when I saw that if I should try to find my way back, I should be hopelessly lost. Passages opened out on every side, and crossed and interlaced, and my life was literally in the hands of the cowled monk who led the way with his lighted taper. But that was a relief. Having no responsibility for finding the way, and having faith in my guide, I could give myself up to the impression of the place. There is a beautiful passage in the one hundred and forty-second Psalm which brings out this truth. The Psalm is ascribed to David when he was fleeing from Saul's persecution and wandering in a labyrinth of caves and secret paths. "When my spirit is overwhelmed within me, Thou knowest my path." Few things are more painful or humiliating than the sense of having lost the way. The sweetening branch then is just this blessed consciousness that divine omniscience knows the path: that the knowledge is with one who knows just how to use it, who knows the path through, the path out, knows what the trend of the trouble is and what its meaning is. Thou knowest my path. No matter whether I know it or not. My ignorance is bliss, provided it can rest on Thy wisdom. I am no longer confused or distracted when I know that Thou art in the way before me, and can hear Thee say, "I am the Lord that healeth thee."

But then, while God reveals Himself as the ultimate source of all comfort and healing, He does not always withdraw from us secondary sources of help. The great Healer knoweth the frame of His patients. All constitutions will not stand the same treatment, and God's love in healing is balanced by His wisdom in applying remedies. One of the most familiar of these secondary agencies is human sympathy. Some men God can detach entirely from human help and set them to work out the hard problem of sorrow with Him alone. He could do so with Job. He not only swept away one material comfort after another, but He withdrew him from human sympathy. The very wife of his bosom was appalled at his lot and refused to face it and work it out with him: and his three friends only aggravated his torment. God knew the man with whom He was dealing, and could let him beat round wildly for a time, held only by a single thought, God did it, knowing that by that his faith would mount by and by to victory and to clearer vision. But God could not have dealt with every man in that way. Christ did not deal so with Thomas the doubter: and I think that, in the great majority of cases, our Healer makes use of the sympathy of our fellow-men as a branch with which to sweeten our Marahs. And, say what we will of the impotence of human words to reach the depth of great sorrow, human sympathy and human help are sweet, and help to make the burden lighter. We may not reject them. They are the choice medicine of the Lord that healeth. Not many days ago I received a letter from a dear friend who had recently suffered a terrible bereavement, and his words are an expressive comment on this truth, especially as he is one of those strong, thoroughly-tempered natures who would face such a fact boldly and fight his way through it. "I thank you with all my heart for the hand which you reach out to me in the dark. I never knew till now the real worth of the love of men. It takes on toward God —this human leading of hearts which one believes in and loves." Yes, we may honestly thank God for the branches of human love which bend down over the bitter springs. God does not blame us for craving this. He does indeed aim to teach us that He alone is sufficient for us, but He leads us up to that knowledge gently and by the touch of brothers' hands.

But let us not forget the other great truth of this story, a truth quite as important as the first, and perhaps quite as hard to learn; and that is, that God's healing is a lesson no less than a comfort. After God had showed Moses how to make the waters of Marah sweet, we read that "he made for them a statute and an ordinance, and there he proved them, and said, 'If thou wilt diligently hearken to the voice of the Lord thy God, and wilt do that which is right in His sight, and wilt give ear to His commandments, and wilt keep all His statutes, I will put none of these diseases upon thee which I have put upon the Egyptians: for I am the Lord that healeth thee.'" There was a danger in the freedom of the Israelites. The reaction of feeling upon the deliverance from bondage would naturally tend to throw the idea of masterdom into the shade. From hard servitude the stride to lawlessness was very easy. And hence you see that God insists on obedience in contrast with the loosened bonds of Egypt. He did not long delay warning them against the thought that they had no master, now that Pharaoh's yoke was removed. The new economy was to be, as really as the old, an economy of service, fidelity, obedience, only to a better and kinder master. How this feature of the story chimes in with the words of the Saviour as He calls men to rest from the heavy burden and weariness of sin, but still to take on themselves His yoke and His burden.

God couples even His tenderness with His law. Into

His most affectionate, sympathetic, gentle dealing with men, He introduces the claims and the obligations of duty. The law is, as the Psalmist puts it, like the sun in the heavens. "There is nothing hid from the heat thereof." And therefore this wonderful lesson of God's healing is coupled with a lesson of obedience and a warning against neglect of duty. The aim of a physician's treatment is not merely to relieve his patient from pain. It is, further, to get him on his feet for active duty. God did not sweeten the waters of Marah in order that the people might stay there. Marah was only a stage on the way to Canaan; and the draught at the sweetened spring was but to give strength for a long march. And God never heals His people simply to make them easy. If He takes off a load, it is that they may walk the better in the way of His commandments. We limit too much the meaning of that good old word "comfort" which God uses so often. In our minds it is too much identified with ease and rest and satisfaction with the present. Whereas the original word has a nervous, vigorous force, a meaning of bracing and strengthening. The Holy Spirit in His office of Comforter, does not come to lull us to repose. It is the Comforter who reproves the world of sin, of righteousness, and of judgment. The idea conveyed by "comfort" is tonic as well as restful. God comforts us with His healing that we may take up His work, and address ourselves vigorously to faith and prayer and obedience. That is healing indeed which not only frees the patient from pain, but makes him a living, active power. Indeed God's healing, as many of you know very well, does not always take away pain. God healed Paul of the thorn in the flesh, but He did not remove the thorn. His healing lay in the gift of His grace to bear the thorn; and many a one rises up from beside the well which God has sweetened for him, strengthened and refreshed indeed, girding up his loins and grasping his staff, and striking out with a firm step into the desert, yet knowing full well that he will carry that old heartache to the very end of the journey—that longing for "the touch of a vanished hand and the sound of a voice that is still." God's healing enables him to work well and faithfully and even cheerfully in spite of the aching heart. Most of us have known something of sickness, not a few of us of dangerous sickness. We are often reminded of the lesson and the warning of the sickness, and we have little difficulty in reading that lesson: but I wonder if we as readily apprehend the lesson of recovery. Are we not sometimes blinded by the joy of recovery to its teaching? Ah, my friends, the lesson of Marah is as good a one for us to-day as it was to the murmuring Israelites. Whatever God may say to us by sickness, when He comes to us as the Lord of healing He says, "I will raise thee up that thou mayst do that which is right in my sight; that thou mayst give ear to my commandments and keep my statutes." You remember how forcibly this is put in the one hundred and sixteenth Psalm. The writer tells how the sorrows of death compassed him: how he was brought low and God helped him; and then he breaks out, "Return unto thy rest, O my soul, for the Lord hath dealt bountifully with thee. For Thou hast delivered my soul from death, mine eyes from tears and my feet from falling. I will walk before the Lord in the land of the living." I have been saved from the land of the shadow of death: it is that I may walk in the path of obedience in the land of the living.

This, then, is the teaching of the bitter spring. We live under an economy of which sorrow is a part, but of which God's healing is also a part. We are under the care of Jehovah that healeth; a wise healer, a tender healer, a thorough healer. The alternation of joy and sorrow in our life is not accidental, it obeys a law; it is all regulated, the joy and the sorrow alike, by infinite wisdom and infinite love. Healing has a lesson as well as sorrow; it is not an end unto itself, not an encouragement to indolence and slackness, but a monition pointing us to make use of recovered tone and strength on the path of duty and ministry. God, in calling Himself our healer, appeals to no sickly sentiment in us. Healing means more toil and more burdens and more conflict, and these will continue to the end. But let us remember that God never forgets to give rest along the road, and refreshment at the right places to His faithful ones. Even on earth there will be intervals of sweet rest, though the desert lie on beyond. After Marah came Elim with palms and abundant wells. shade and flowing waters, and they were suffered to encamp there by the wells and to stay awhile. By and by the desert will be passed, the palms of the heavenly Elim will rise into view, and the faithful shall walk with the Lamb who is in the midst of the throne, who shall lead them to living fountains of waters, and God—the Lord that healeth—shall wipe away all tears from their eyes.

XVIII.

SELF-WINNING.

"In your patience ye shall win your souls."—LUKE xxi. 19.

"IN your patience possess ye your souls" is the familiar reading of this verse. The words have passed into a proverb—" Possess your souls in patience." But have you ever stopped to think what meaning that phrase conveys? A very vague one, I think you will find. What definite thought do you get from that—"possess your soul in patience?" On the other hand, the true rendering of the text gives a very clear and sharp and almost startling statement: Ye shall win your souls in your patience. Leading your life in patience, you shall save yourself: you shall get your life into your own power: you shall save it out of the throng of wrecking forces which encompass it.

Only, it comes to us, perhaps, with a flavor of novelty that a man must win his own soul. Is it not a contradiction in terms? If one's soul is his own, why must it be won? We hear a good deal, and rightly, about the Christian duty of winning souls—our neighbors' souls. Scripture tells us that "he that winneth souls is wise." Doubtless you and I have a duty to the souls of our neighbors, but that is not what Christ is talking about here. It is our duty to our own souls; and if winning souls is a mark of wisdom, surely it is the highest wisdom for a man to win his own soul if that must needs be done; not only for his own safety and happiness, but as the indispensable condition of winning other souls.

Does this seem strange to you? Look at it for a moment. Popular saws often tell us truths, though quite as often, possibly, they tell falsehoods. We have a common saying that such a man is afraid to say his soul is his own. There is a case where we distinctly recognize the fact that a man has not won his own soul. He dares not assert it. He has no such possession of his deepest self as to make it tell in the conflict with other men. His inner life is not gathered up and massed in convictions which he can wield as weapons and make men feel their edge. He is possessed by other men's convictions, carried their way, a mere shuttlecock obeying the blow of the racquet from either side. His soul is not his own.

Now here, as in so many other cases, our Lord is simply using a familiar and commonplace truth. The peculiarity of His teaching is that He always sets these commonplace truths in a new and startling light; so that the truths themselves seem strange to us because their applications are novel.

Why, is it not true, and do you not know very well that a man's self—all that makes him a man—has to be won out of a mass of circumstances which would annihilate him if they could? Do you not know very well that such winning is not once and for all, not of the nature of a sharp, quickly-gained, decisive victory, but rather through patient, long toil and struggle and discipline? Take the life on its physical side. There is a healthy, well-developed babe. All the possibilities of manhood are in him. Thirty years hence he will be a model of manly strength. Hard matter will yield at his firm grasp or well-directed blow. His healthy frame with its quickly-bounding pulses, will throw off the sickly influences of the atmosphere. His exuberant energy will carry him through days and nights of severe toil and exposure. But now these are only possibilities. Now, healthy and vigorous though he is, he is only a healthy and vigorous babe, whom a child of five years might easily stifle. The strength of manhood has to be won, through the slow, gradual knitting of bone and muscle, the protection of stronger arms, the hard teaching which comes through falls and bruises. He wins his way to the power of locomotion, first to creeping, then to walking, then to running.

So it is with other faculties, beginning from the very roots of the physical life, and all the way up to the faculties which border on the spiritual region. This baby has to learn to see. He has eyes, sound, clear, lovely orbs into which a mother's eye looks as into deep wells of love, but when he emerges into consciousness and begins to take note of things around him, hold up a ball before him, and see how aimless is his grasp at it. His eye has not yet learned to calculate distances. You know how the blind, when restored to sight, have to learn to see: sight and seeing are not the same things. Sight is a gift of nature. Seeing has to be won. That blind man whom Jesus healed did not at once receive power to see. At the first touch he said, "I see men, for I behold them as trees, walking," in vague outline, confused, like the blending of trees in a grove. When Jesus laid His hand upon him a second time, he saw all things clearly. We see the same truth as related to special training of the senses. We have all heard the story of "eyes and no eyes." One man will see the material for a volume where another sees nothing but stocks and stones. You go up into the northern woods, and as the night settles down, the whole forest is vocal. To you it is a hopeless chaos of sounds; but the trained ear of the woodman will pick out this and that sound and tell you what animal or insect or bird makes it. The natural, untrained ear does not catch the beautiful modulations and harmonies of a symphony. The hand which brings melody out of the piano or organ or viol must be long and patiently trained. It is needless to multiply illustrations. You see that, on the side of the senses and of the physical being generally, power and effectiveness have to be won. They are not born with the man. There is no royal road to them either. It is through patience and toil that a man wins practiced perception and deft manipulation.

Now the law does not hold any the less when we get down to the core of the man, this which makes a distinct self. Power and gifts are latent in that self or soul, but they are only possibilities. I think we have all been impressed with the unused mental and moral forces in certain men. We have all seen men with the instincts and powers of artists or poets, who yet had no mastery over their power. They could not use it. The untrained hand could not embody the vigorous conception of the brain: the untrained ear and pen could not cast the poetic thought into verse. They had not won their own native powers. And, going still deeper, there is that moral something which we call self-mastery. In how many do you see it? How many men do you see who make their thoughts work on given lines; who have their hand on the gates which shut out vain and wicked thoughts; in whom the whole moral and spiritual nature is obedient to law, and is marshalled and massed and directed by a supreme will? We say a man is self-possessed. What do we mean by that, but that there resides in the man a power which holds all his faculties at command, and brings them to bear in spite of all distractions? There can be no better phrase to express it. He possesses himself. He can do what he will with that side of the self which he chooses to use. Nothing takes away his courage. He has that in possession. Excitement and tumult do not take away the clearness of his mental vision. He keeps his eye on his theme. He has possession of his tongue. No confusion takes from him the power of lucid speech: and, above all, that deep-lying personality of the man is not thrown off its feet. It asserts itself. Men as they look and listen, yea, as they rave, say, " The man is himself. He is not what our threats or our tumult or our opposition make him. We cannot take his manhood away from him. He has himself in hand. He is self-possessed."

And all this comes through a long and severe discipline, which is all vain without patience. Patience is the element in which discipline lives and thrives. It is only through patience that natural endowment is converted into possession and mastery.

Natural endowment is only possibility. It is something which a man has, and yet does not have until he wins it. So in the spiritual realm. Spiritual self-mastery, full command of the deepest self, possession of all the soul's resources of faith and hope and sanctified will—all are born of discipline and struggle working in the atmosphere of patience. They have to be won. Man, along the whole scale of his being, from its lowest physical point up to the very acme of his spiritual life, is in contact with forces which oppose and thwart the possession and masterdom of self. Leave him passively to nature, and she will make short work with him. Niagaras and Atlantics will suck him down and sweep him away. Her fire will consume and her frost petrify him. If man has by constitution a principle of self-determination, a way of his own, so has Nature; and Nature, no less than man, likes to have its own way. It will possess if it be not possessed. It will master if it be not mastered.

> "Like us, the lightning fires
>   Love to have scope and play.
> The stream, like us, desires
>   An unimpeded way.
> Like us the Libyan wind delights to roam at large.
> Nature, with equal mind,
>   Sees all her sons at play;
> Sees man control the wind,
>   The wind sweep man away."

Man's self must develop powers of resistance and control. It must be so completely in hand that he can say to wind and water, "You shall not possess me and carry me whither you will. Rather shall you do my bidding, and grind my corn, and turn my lathe, and carry me whither I will." "Nature, red in tooth and claw," roars and pants and rages after him. He must win his life from her jaws.

And no less does the truth hold higher up. As we follow human nature upward, it is only the antagonists that change. The contact and the conflict are perpetuated. The Bible is full of this. It may indeed be said that the underlying truth of the whole Bible, working itself out through the successive stages of history and the infinite varieties of human experience, is, how shall a man win his own soul? A whole economy of secret, spiritual forces is arrayed against this consummation. Hence it is that Paul says, "We that are in this tabernacle do groan." Hence we are told of a wrestle which is not with flesh and blood, but with spiritual hosts; marshalled and organized evil in the spiritual realm; princes of darkness. So too our Lord told Peter of an unseen, terrible power, fired with malignant desire to sift him as wheat. And under the stress of this fact, the whole current of New Testament teaching settles down into one sharply-defined channel; that spiritual mastery, self-possession, self-wielding, are the outcome only of patient effort and discipline protracted up to the very end. Accordingly we hear an apostle, far on in his Christian career, saying, "I keep my body under." I treat it as the boxer does his adversary, bruising it into subjection, lest after having held out to others the hope of spiritual victory, I should become a castaway. Religious sentimentalists tell us of a condition where spiritual conflict ceases. Do not believe that hollow delusion. The man who fancies he has reached such a stage as that, displays his ignorance instead of the depth of his piety. He is walking on enchanted ground, in an atmosphere of falsehood, and is the very one to be most easily betrayed into sin. I do not mean that Christian experience is all fight and agony. By no means. It has its rest, and its sweetness: but you remember our Lord's blessed invitation to the weary and heavy laden, "Come to me. I will give you rest": but also, "Take my yoke and learn of me, and ye shall find rest, rest unto your souls." Rest is a gift, but it is also something to be won. God, when He commences the education and salvation of a soul, begins by centring it: by giving it a firm resting-place; but He puts the soul there as on a basis from which to work out something, and there is another and a deeper rest than that of forgiven sin, which a man finds in that working out; in that struggle for dominion over self and the world; in that resistance of the flesh and of the devil.

Look at these words of our Lord which precede the text. See what a fearful campaign is mapped out for these disciples of His. War and natural convulsion in the earth; the machinery of civil government arrayed against the faith; domestic affection changed to gall; kindred turned into persecutors; hatred from every quarter. But you see the point on which Christ fixes the disciples' attention. It is not how all this persecution and sorrow are going to affect fortune and life and domestic relations. That needs no comment. It is not how the disciple is going to be able to break the force of these blows. He will not be able to break it. It may put an end to his life. But it is what the disciple is going to win and bring out of it all. Something is to be suffered. He does not conceal that: but something, and that the greatest thing, is to be won.

And that is the point for us to consider no less than for those disciples; because our life, and every Christian life, if not assailed by the troubles which are predicted here, has to make head against obstacles of some sort. The life never loses the character of a conflict though the enemies change ; and the enemies do not all change either. The world, the flesh, the devil, take on new forms with the new ages, but they beset the nineteenth-century Christians as they did the Saviour in the wilderness. Let us have it clearly before us what we are aiming at. If we are true to our Lord's ideal, we are not aiming chiefly to keep clear of trouble, to cushion ourselves against the shock of disaster: not to lose as few friends as possible; not to spare ourselves loss of caste; not to go through with the sacrifice of the fewest dollars; not to avoid as many discomforts and humiliations as possible. If, I say, we are true to our Lord's ideal, our first aim in life is to make Christian manhood. Amid all the shocks and disappointments and cruelties of time, Christ never allows us to lose sight of that. The fact that a man lives in the midst of trouble and confusion does not excuse him from the effort to win his own soul, to become a man in Christ Jesus. The way to this lies straight through the trouble and confusion, as our Lord's words very clearly show. Judicial ban, domestic hatred, social disturbance, convulsions of nature,—through all, in all, ye shall win your souls. The conflict does not mean first getting the better of the men who trouble you; adjusting the circumstances which impede your business and your prosperity; getting your party into power in politics. It means, first of all, a rightly-pointed self. It means a clean heart and a right spirit. It means an honest fight with besetting sins and a victory over passion. You are more important than your circumstances. It is more important that your soul should be saved than that you should save your fortune. It is more important that you should be a man strong in faith and pure in character than that your bed should be soft and your table luxurious.

The great feature of this text is that Christ points us away from circumstances to souls. You stand some day by the ocean swept with a tempest. It is a grand spectacle. A score of things in the clouds and in the waves appeal to you. You mark the height of the billows, their tremendous volume and swiftness and power, their mad struggle round the sunken reefs; but after all it is not the grandeur or the terror of the scene which most enchains you. Your interest is concentrated on that ship yonder. You forget the spectacle of the maddened ocean as you watch her fight with it. The question which fills your mind is not how long the storm is going to continue, or whether it is likely to become more severe. It is whether the ship will ride out the gale. And so all circumstances take their character from their relation to man's soul. The question is whether the man will ride out the storm of circumstance; the whole significance of circumstance turns on whether it will conquer the man or be conquered by him; whether it will swallow up the soul, or whether the man will bring his soul alive and entire out of the tempest. This is the way in which Christ, as He is pictured in the text, looks out upon that horrible tempest of blood and fire; and this is the attitude of the whole Bible toward the struggle and convulsion of this world. Through it all God has His eye on man's moral destiny. To us, often, the principal things are the war and the confusion, the dislocation and the overturning. To Him the principal thing is the destiny of that soul in the midst of the storm. Will the man win his soul or not? Circumstances will adjust themselves if men are right. The great struggle in God's eyes is not between parties or sects or opinions. It is between the soul and the world. Victory is the man's overcoming the world; not one side of the world getting the better of the other; not the victory of the man's native force of will and physical power over the things which assail his fortune or his reputation, but the perfecting of his spiritual manhood in the teeth of all the loss and damage and pain which this world can bring to him. You and I will win this battle if we shall win our souls. If we shall go through all, gaining in self-mastery, in faith, in love to Christ, in conformity to the character of Christ, the end will not be escape, but victory. In your patience, ye shall win your souls.

And that enters into the true conception of patience. Patience is active as well as passive. It includes the persistent energy which wins no less than the submissiveness which bears. The popular conception of patience is too narrow. One is always tempted to smile at the popular phrase, "As patient as Job," applied to a man who submits to trouble without murmuring. For, in this aspect, Job's patience is not a model. Job was impatient. He chafed under his trouble, not so much indeed at his bodily suffering as at his inability to understand what God meant by it; and he murmured, and impugned God's justice, and well-nigh blasphemed in his frenzied wrestle with this problem. And yet the core of this struggle reveals the very truth we are illustrating. The man's thought was absorbed, not by the relations of this calamity to his flocks and herds and family and health, but by its relations to himself as a son of God and a believer in God. His fear centred in the possibility that God had forsaken his soul: and Job's patience appears in his holding fast by that thought, and in his steadily fighting his way toward God through all that agony, even though at times he raved at the Almighty. He clung to the hand that smote him, even while he struck at it, as the only hand which could unlock the mystery. He pressed his way through the darkness, groping after God. If he could but see God!

If he could but come into court with God and make his plea to His face! If God would only speak to him! And at last he prevailed. God did speak to him. Job's soul was calmed, though it was humbled to the dust. He won his soul in his patience.

So then, I repeat, the patience in which we shall win our souls is not mere passive submission to circumstances. It is not drifting at the mercy of circumstance and drifting uncomplainingly. A man does not win his soul by merely not complaining. The patience which Christ means is a productive force; a force which inspires a desperate and persistent fight for spiritual manhood; a force which makes a victorious man, and not a mere petrifaction insensible to "the slings and arrows of outrageous fortune."

For you and I are not victors if we do not bring something out of this struggle with adverse circumstance; and what we save out of it will finally determine the point whether we have all along been in right or wrong relations to the events of our life. A great battle is raging. There is a fort which is the key to the whole position. Whichever side can win and hold that, is victor. Here, then, the general masses his troops. Other parts of the field are carried by the enemy. The outposts are driven in. The batteries are captured. Troops cannot be spared for these. Everything is concentrated upon that fort, and at last it is taken. The dead and dying lie in heaps round it, but the flag waves over it. It has been taken at the sacrifice of minor positions, but these are of no account now. The enemy will abandon those of his own accord. He has nothing to gain by holding them any more. They are commanded by the superior post; and in the light of the fact that the general holds the point from which he can command the whole field and dictate terms, his former dealing with the inferior positions is explained and justified. He could afford to sacrifice them for the sake of holding the key to the field. The lesser thing was wisely given up for the greater. Well for us if we can carry that principle into our spiritual warfare. Well for us if we shall clearly recognize the soul as the key to the position. Well for us if we can wholly take in the meaning of the words, "What shall it profit a man if he shall gain the whole world and lose his own soul?" Get out of this struggle unscathed in fortune and in reputation; save for yourself the worldly advantage; let the soul take care of itself, and the great day of decision shall show forth your wisdom or your folly. You shall gain the world and its honors and comforts only to leave them behind. If you shall not have won your own soul, what will be left? Winning your soul, you will have won all. These minor positions you have let go. Well, you will have proved then that you could live and fight without them. You will have proved then that they are in no sense necessary to your real success: you will have proved yourself their master by being able to dispense with them: and meanwhile you will have proved yourself victor by having brought out of the fight that which puts you in eternal possession of heaven, and of the fellowship of God and of angels.

Perhaps life, this life, will have been yielded up. None

the less you will have saved your life in losing it. In your patience ye shall win your souls.

My brethren, if you shall keep this object before you in your daily fight with the world, it will greatly simplify your life. If our eyes are directed mainly upon the clashing elements around us we shall easily become confused. The multitude and the contradiction of the adjustments they require, will embarrass us hopelessly. But we have Christ's word for it, "But one thing is needful." We have the Psalmist's word for it, "One thing have I desired of the Lord, that will I seek after."

The day on which business-care or domestic trouble or social confusion calls off your thought from the purpose of winning your own soul, is the day on which the enemy gains, and you begin to go back from victory. This is not a mere dictate of selfishness. Christ commends to you no selfish principle when He bids you win your own soul. In such winning, in such making of Christlike manhood, you become a power to draw others into the circle of your influence. The more you become like Christ, the richer you make the world.

And note, once more, that these words have the character of a rich and consolatory promise. Patience here, hard, steady fighting, uncomplaining endurance, but, then, winning: the goal and the crown. The true measure of the things of this life is the life of eternity. Paul understood that when he said, "I count all things but loss if I may win Christ": when he called the afflictions of this present time light and momentary compared with the far more exceeding and eternal weight of glory.

Just here there comes to me a beautiful passage of Jeremy Taylor, and with this I will leave the subject with you. "Well, let the world have its course, I am content to bear it: God's will be done: let the sea be troubled; let the waves thereof roar; let the winds of affliction blow; let the waters of sorrows rush upon me; let the darkness of grief and heaviness compass me about; yet will I not be afraid; these storms will blow over; these winds will be laid; these waves will fall; this tempest cannot last long; and these clouds shall be dispelled: whatsoever I suffer here shall shortly have an end. I shall not suffer eternally; come the worst that can come, death will put an end to all my sorrows and miseries. Lord, grant me patience here and ease hereafter! I will suffer patiently whatsoever can happen, and shall endeavor to do nothing against my conscience and displeasing unto Thee; for all is safe and sure with him who is certain and sure of a blessed Eternity."

XIX.

THE CANKERED YEARS.

> *" And I will restore unto you the years that the locust hath eaten, the canker-worm and the caterpillar and the palmer-worm, my great army which I sent among you. And ye shall eat in plenty and be satisfied, and shall praise the name of the Lord your God that hath dealt wondrously with you; and my people shall never be ashamed."*—JOEL ii. 25, 26.

THE reign of Uzziah, King of Judah, was marked by a frightful visitation of locusts. You will find a most graphic description of this plague in the second chapter of the prophecy. The ground where they browse is scorched as with fire. The land which lay before them as the garden of Eden, lies behind them a desolate wilderness. The noise of their flight is as the noise of chariots on the tops of the mountains. The sound of their eating is as the crackling of fire amid stubble. They run upon the city walls, they climb upon the houses, they enter in at the latticed windows like a thief.

But it is the moral and not the picturesque aspect of this visitation which is uppermost in the prophet's mind. He plainly proclaims it as a punishment for the people's sins and as a call to repentance. If they shall repent, he promises a blessing which shall amply atone for past suffering. "The Lord will be jealous for His land and will pity His people. Yea, the Lord will answer and say unto His people, 'Behold, I will send you corn and wine and oil, and ye shall be satisfied therewith. And I will restore to you again the years that the locust hath eaten, the canker-worm and the caterpillar and the palmer-worm, my great army which I sent among you.'"

I am going to speak to you this morning about the canker-eaten years and the way in which God restores them. For wasted and blasted years are a fact in most human lives. Few of us, I take it, can look back, even from the stand-point of mid-age, without being startled and humbled at the number and size of the bare spots scattered over the area of his years. Some one has made a computation on the basis of a life of seventy years, according to which, deducting the first twenty years as a time of preparation, deducting the time consumed by sleep and by illness, and appropriated to recreation, eating, and the general care of the body, about eleven years of solid working-time are allotted to him who completes threescore and ten years. Possibly the computation may not be altogether fair; but suppose we allow twenty solid years instead of eleven, and patch them with the large areas of squandered time which mark the life of the average man, the solid margins are fearfully narrow.

And the appalling thing about this waste is not the large fragments which are struck out by sickness or by accident, without any responsibility of ours. It is the years which have been eaten up by little, scarcely appreciable agencies like a caterpillar or a canker-worm. Years which have gone, frittered away, we do not know how, and for which we have nothing whatever to show: years devoured in trifles, escaped, like subtle vapor, in musing and brooding over something we meant to do, but which we never did: years that fleeted, as on the wings of a hurricane, in the wild rush of dissipation, and out of which are left only the broken strains of old songs, and a few dry leaves of withered garlands. There they lie back in the past, in the sad light of a sinking sun, precious, golden spaces, teeming with possibilities of good, tracts of rich soil, on which we note the aimless traces of our idle feet, as we lounged with our eyes at the ends of the earth: lo, they are blighted and bare now, as though the army of locusts had swept over them. How late we are in learning that time slips through our fingers faster than pennies: in learning what grand harvests are to be reaped from husbanded minutes. We begin to economize time as the penitent spendthrift does money, only when he sees the bottom of the chest between the scanty pieces.

The exquisitely bitter thought in this vision of wasted years is that of our own share in the desolation; and when our eyes are once fairly opened to the waste, our first impulse is to cast about for some method of restoration. We see the man taxing body and brain to acquire the knowledge and the mental discipline which he ought to have acquired in youth. We see the pardoned criminal exerting every energy to regain the confidence forfeited by his crime. We see old age straining its failing strength to amass the competence which should have been won through the energy and economy of manhood; and the dying man in agony to compass, by a late repentance, the moral results which should have been the chief aim of his life.

Now no question can be of deeper interest to us than the question how God deals with such facts as these. Does His economy include any law of restoration, and if so, what is it?

It is evident at first sight, that any economy of restoration must not only be based on superhuman wisdom, but must include superhuman compassion. And yet our views of divine compassion must not lead us to imagine that God is going to be untrue to His own laws, or is going to reverse their action. "Whatsoever a man soweth that shall he also reap," is a law which God does not violate in morals any more than in the fields. Certain physical consequences of sin have to come. So do certain moral consequences. Viewed simply as a matter of law, the wasted years cannot be restored. God will not give back lost time by a miracle. The shadow on the dial of life will not go backward the smallest fraction of a degree. A man who has given 'forty years to the service of the world or of his own lusts, cannot exert in the ten years which he may penitently give to God, the moral power which would have attached to the consecration of the whole fifty years.

And the element of expiation only evades the difficulty. It does not meet it. Suffering is not a fair equivalent for the results of neglect or of wilful wrong. How contrition may affect one's moral relations to God is one thing : how it affects the results of his wrong-doing or idleness is quite another and a different thing. An ocean of tears will not give back life nor innocence. If you hand me money with which to relieve a woman who is dying of starvation, and I wilfully withhold it or forget to give it, though, in my future remorse, I impoverish myself and bestow all my goods to feed the poor, I cannot restore her to life. Repentance is a great power, but there are some things which repentance cannot do. Zacchæus, in his honest repentance, offered half his goods to the poor, and fourfold restoration to any man whom he had falsely wronged ; but no doubt there were men whom Zacchæus had wronged, who were in their graves, and beyond the reach of his reparation.

On this side the truth is awful in its inflexibility. I pity the materialist when he comes to the question of repairing moral waste. I pity the positivist before the frantic appeal of a remorseful soul. He is as dumb as the Sphinx. He has to deal with forces as remorseless as iron propelled by steam, or as Niagara under the power of gravity. And it becomes evident that if there is any such thing as restoration in the divine economy, the scheme must be far wider than this strict physical law of equivalents. If God does not ignore the action of the physical law, which is none the less His law, that law must at least be taken up and carried somehow in the sweep of a larger law.

And perhaps it is not possible to formulate that larger law. At any rate it is not necessary, however desirable it might be. All that we really want is to see, if we can, how and where it touches a man standing penitently in view of his eaten years.

Some things on this point we may rightfully assert: enough, I think, to give us consolation and hope.

First, we have the general, sweeping promise of God as voiced in our text: "I will restore the eaten years." We might fall confidently back on that alone. That tells us that restoration, according to a divine ideal,—quite possibly a different ideal from ours, certainly a higher ideal,—is a possibility and a fact in the divine economy. But we may go further. Some features of this process we know. For example, God turns the man entirely away from the thought and the work of literal restoration. In other words, He does not ask of him to make good, in the sense of a literal equivalent, the waste of the past. He is bidden to turn his back on the bare and wasted places. His concern is with the present and the future, not with the past. Look at David. There was one tract at least in his life which his own folly had made desolate; a tract scorched and blasted with the fires of lust, and drenched with the blood of deliberate and cruel murder. According to the natural law of compensation, there was no compensation possible. Uriah was dead. His household was polluted. These things could not be undone. David sees that; and hence his prayer in the fifty-first Psalm has no reference to this side of the matter, but is concerned with God's dealing with his own soul. "Wash me. Purge me. Create in me a clean heart." As for the matter of compensation, as for the problem of making good the ruin, he must leave that all with God. He says nothing about it, because there is absolutely nothing to be said.

Or Paul. So many years blasted by acts of violence and cruelty against the followers of Christ. How the transfigured face of Stephen, gazing upon the heavens through the shower of falling stones, must have haunted him as he recalled those days. And there was no calling Stephen back. There was no recalling the votes which had sent so many of God's own to an untimely grave or to cruel imprisonment. The marks of the scourge could not be washed out. I wonder if Paul did not think of that when the whip was laid upon his own back at Philippi. Paul mourned over all this, even in the full tide of his apostolic ministry. Even in the midst of one of the most wonderful of his inspired chapters, the old memory breaks up like a bitter spring in a fruitful garden. "I am the least of the apostles, that am not meet to be called an apostle because I persecuted the Church of God." But what then? Nothing but to let all that faultful past go. It has wrought its sorrow, and no restoration will take that away; but there is nothing for him now but to fix his eyes on the present and on the future; and so he does. "By the grace of God," he continues, "I am what I am." "This one thing I do, forgetting the things which are behind, and reaching forth unto those things which are before, I press toward the mark for the prize of the high calling of God in Christ Jesus."

Thus much, then, is clear. Whatever God may do with the faultful past, a penitent soul can only leave it in God's hands. His work now is not to make good the past, but to give himself to the development of his new life as a new creature in Christ Jesus. The self-scrutiny of a repentant and forgiven man ought to be directed not at what he has been, but at what he is. Christians often make a serious practical mistake here, in that they do not feel that they are permitted to drop the past, but suffer their past waste and neglect to cumber and hamper them in the effort to live their new life. You cannot live your new life and carry the old at the same time. Your life is in the present. That is your care to-day. You remember when Peter met the Lord by the lake-side after the resurrection. Peter had a dreadful past weighing on his heart. There was no taking back those three denials of his Lord. There was no denying that he had been a traitor and a coward. There was no blotting out the memory of that weary, care-worn face turned upon him from before the judgment-seat, of that brief look which burned into his weak, treacherous heart as fire into wax : and yet what is Christ's question to Peter? Not, " Have you loved me in these years past? Have you always been true to me?" But, "*Dost* thou love me? If so, take my commission. Thou who didst fail in thy love to me, thou who didst betray me, but who canst say this hour, 'Thou knowest that I love Thee,' feed my sheep. Feed my lambs."

Still, it may be said, this is not restoration, that a man should simply leave the past behind him. That is true. That is what I have been trying to show. But it is very important that the man should be in the right attitude toward the restorative work, however that may operate, and this he cannot be without giving over the impossibilities of restoration to God. Some things he may be able to make good. Those we are not now concerned with. Much he cannot make good. He must leave it. God does not say, " *Thou* shall restore the years which the locust has eaten," but "*I* will restore them."

We go on then to observe, as another feature of this restorative work, that God gives certain things which were forfeited in the wasted years of sin. Suppose that two ways lay before a traveller; the one a bright, open road, in the full sunlight, with singing birds and fair prospects; and the other, parallel to it, through a gloomy, subterranean tunnel, haunted with bats and serpents. Suppose he chooses the latter route for the time, and spends a day or two in the darkness, but thinks better of it, and makes his way out and up to the other road. He has lost time. That he cannot get back. Possibly he has gotten a fall or two of which he will carry the marks all the rest of his life. But when he gets into the brighter pathway, the sun is as bright for him as for the traveller who has never been in the tunnel. The birds sing as sweetly. Just so, when a man leaves behind him the waste of his years, he does not find God's love diminished. His own capacities for enjoying the tokens of divine love, and for making its gifts available may have been impaired. That is one of the sad results of the waste behind him; but God's love is given to him unimpaired. God does not let the darkness of a man's past come up like a cloud between the man and the outraying of His divine tenderness. The faultful past might, and often does, poison human affection. Human nature forgives hesitatingly, and there is a background of suspicion behind reinstated confidence.

"This world will not believe a man repents";

and the poet voices the feeling of the world when he adds:

> "Full seldom doth a man repent, or use
> Both grace and will to pluck the vicious quitch
> Of blood and custom wholly out of him,
> And make all clean, and plant himself afresh."

Whether that be true or not, God believes in the possibility of a genuine repentance, and frankly accepts it. Through such utterances as the parable of the Prodigal Son, and others of our Lord, we see repentance revealed as a factor of immense meaning in God's economy of restoration. That by which the world sets so little store and in which it is so slow to believe, is a thing which thrills heaven and the angels with joy. When God heals a man's backsliding, He loves him freely. There is not a promise of love, protection, sympathy, heaven, which is modified one jot for the penitent who returns after his years of waste. When the prodigal came home after having wasted his substance, the old house poured forth its best. The wardrobe was ransacked, not for a second-hand suit,.but for the best robe, and the table was spread with the best the larder could furnish. His entertainment was that of a king's son and not of a beggar. There is a mystery about all this which we cannot fathom because we cannot fathom the love of God. This giving a returned prodigal the best, this making kings and priests out of charred brands—if this be not restoration, I know not what to call it. It looks as if, while the world disbelieves and refuses the penitent, heaven has nothing too good for him. How the past waste and the eaten years are taken care of, I do not know, and God does not tell me. What God does with the sin I do not know, any more than the priest knew what became of the scape-goat when he turned him loose into the wilderness with the people's sins upon his head. I do know what God does with the repentant sinner, and that is the important thing after all. Restoration is included in restored sonship.

Yet there are certain incidents on the line of actual restoration which are noteworthy. God has a wonderful power of bringing good out of evil, and of getting interest even out of the evil of wasted years. You know that, in manufacturing communities, large fortunes are sometimes made out of what is technically called "waste." God discerns facts and possibilities in waste which we cannot see, and could not be trusted to see. You all know the story of that man whose eloquent lips were sealed by death a few weeks ago.* He had sacrificed genius, friendship, position, to appetite. He had drunk the cup of degradation to the dregs. But when, after all those blasted years, he threw off the yoke and became a new man, God took that old experience of his with

---

* John B. Gough.

all its woe and degradation, and turned it as a mighty engine against the sin which had so nearly unmade him. You know, many of you who have heard him, what a power in the interest of reform he made that sad story of his. Hundreds of drunkards whose blunted moral sense neither press nor pulpit nor wife nor child could reach, were moved by the appeal of a man who had been as low as the lowest of them, and yet had saved his manhood alive.

Some of you remember the crowd that filled these seats one Sabbath morning a dozen years ago, and that dusky, turbaned figure in the pulpit.* Behind him were long years of heathenism. So many years of his life canker-eaten and blasted by the blight of Brahminism: and yet those very years had given an added power to his Christian ministry among his own race, and clothed with moving energy his appeals to us in the interest of pagan India. Were not the locust-eaten years restored? So it often is that, in the years of absence from God, which must needs be desolate and barren years, a man is maturing and developing a line of power; developing it in the interest of evil, it is true, yet becoming deft in wielding it. God strikes at the evil, but He saves the power out of the wreck, and the man carries the matured power over to the side of God's kingdom, and makes it an instrument of spiritual victory and conquest. Saul of Tarsus was a persecutor. Years had been eaten by those belittling Rabbinical puerilities, yet, after all, that

---

* Narayan Sheshadri.

training was not wasted. The mental discipline, the knowledge of the deepest and subtlest Hebrew thought, stood him in good stead when he became a Christian apostle. God had made His enemies the schoolmasters of His chosen preacher, even as He made Egypt train Moses for Israel.

I repeat, we do not and cannot know what God does with the irrevocable and the irremediable in men's evil past; but we do know that He makes those barren and blasted heritages bloom again, and bring forth thirty, sixty, and an hundred fold. Both the Bible and Christian history are full of the grand, fruitful work of restored men, men with large tracts of blasted years behind them. Those lives have become recognized powers for good, fresh springs in desert places. We have the record of David's lust and murder, but we have David's Psalms, the comfort and inspiration of millions of souls. We have Saul's persecutions, his scourgings and imprisonments and murders; but we have Paul's history of self-devotion and Paul's Epistles. We have Moses in a heathen court, and Moses forty years keeping sheep among the rocks and thorn-bushes of Horeb; but we have Moses the leader of the Exile, the lawgiver of Israel, the man who stood in the cleft of the rock and saw God's glory. God's promise of restoration to His penitent people, given by His prophet in this chapter, is no stinted or modified promise. It is as full and generous as if the years had not been blighted. "Ye shall eat in plenty and be satisfied, and shall praise the name of the Lord your God that hath dealt wondrously with you: and my people shall never be ashamed. And ye shall know that I am in the midst of Israel."

Ah, that is the best of all. The worst thing in the blighted years is that God is away from them. They are years in the far country away from the Father's house. All blight and desolation are summed up in absence from God. Hence the best thing in the restoration is the getting back to God. Renewal, fruitfulness, peace are not in our new resolutions, not in our turning to new duties; they are in His presence, His touch upon us, His guidance.

And the promise of restoration shall have a higher fulfilment by and by. "In God," says one, "all lost things are found, and they who habitually plunge themselves in God and abide in Him, never become too rich. Nay, they find more things than they can lose." What thinks the traveller in the West, of the little, bare, scorched place where he has made his camp-fire for a night, as there stretches before him the illimitable expanse of the plains? This promise is for years eaten by other things than sin and neglect. Many of our years are cankered, or so we call it, by forces over which we have no control—by sickness, helplessness, poverty, failure. Those years are not lost. Surely if God blights or seems to blight, we may trust Him to restore. He who hath torn will heal, He who hath smitten will bind up. "After two days will He revive us: in the third day He will raise us up, and we shall live in His sight. Then shall we know, if we follow on to know the Lord, His going forth is prepared as the morning, and He shall come unto us as the rain, as the latter and former rain unto the earth." When a field of sugar-cane is cut, it is a bare and unsightly object enough. One who did not know the conditions of growth might say, "That will have to be all planted over again before it can yield anything." But the planter merely loosens the soil: he plants nothing, and soon the field is green again, and the tall stalks wave and rustle as aforetime. So God cuts His child's heritage sometimes, cuts it close to the ground, leaving nothing but stubble, or so we think, but we mistake. We know not what is under the stubble. We know not what secret forces are moving even now at the roots of the stubble. God knows. All we have to do is to tend the soil and to keep it loose and open to God's showers by prayer and fidelity. The former and the latter rain will come, and the field shall be green once more and rich with sweetness.

Only let us not presume upon all this to neglect our heritage. Let us not be tempted by this revelation of God's amazing goodness and restorative power, to think lightly of blight or bareness. God's promise of restoration is no encouragement to presumption. It does not make any less terrible the blight and canker which are due to our neglect or waste. You have already seen that, even with the utmost generosity in God's restoring, with the most wonderful power to redeem what is squandered, there are consequences of blighted and wasted years, painful consequences, which, reverently speaking, God himself cannot evade, and which must go with you into the redeemed harvest-fields of the future on earth. Remember the significance of every day. Your days are either the days of God's husbandman or the days of the locust and the canker. You have only so much time. You are making the area to-day, you were making it yesterday, you will be making it to-morrow, either a waste or a harvest-field. And remember one other thing. Every day you are away from God, every day you live in refusal of Christ's offer to save you, is a day given to the locust and to the canker.

God help us all! Who of us will not find the mark of the canker on his years—the corroding of idleness, the blight of sickness, the sad traces of weakness and indiscretion? These lives of ours have been so faulty, so fitful, so unproductive. But what shall we do? Surely we are not to sit down and mourn over the past; waste more time, and blight larger spaces with corroding tears; bestir heart and hand and brain with feverish activity to chase the receding past. To what purpose is this, when He says, "I will restore. As for thee, forget the things which are behind. Run with patience the race before thee. Look unto Jesus and not unto the past. Thou shalt eat in plenty and be satisfied, and shalt praise the name of the Lord thy God that hath dealt wondrously with thee, and my people shall never be ashamed."

XX.

THE GOODNESS OF GOD IN THE LAND OF THE LIVING.

> "*I had fainted unless I had believed to see the goodness of the Lord in the land of the living.*
> "*Wait on the Lord; be of good courage, and He shall strengthen thine heart: wait, I say, on the Lord.*"—PSALM xxvii. 13, 14.

THE words "I had fainted" are not in the original. The sentence is a broken one, such as one utters under strong emotion, suggesting possibilities, but leaving the hearer or reader to supply them for himself. "O had I not believed to see the goodness of Jehovah in the land of the living"—and then he breaks off, and we are left to imagine what dreadful thing would have happened.

Let us simply follow the suggestions of these verses in order.

"Unless I had *believed* to see the goodness of the Lord." God's goodness is often a matter of faith rather than of sight. We are prone to take it for granted that God's goodness must always come into our lives like ripened fruit; whereas, as a fact, it often comes into them like a seed which takes time to grow. "Light is *sown* for the righteous." And I think we shall find that the richest developments of God's goodness are of this character. A good purpose of His often takes time to ripen. Sometimes it is long before it even appears above ground. Meanwhile there is the bleak, dreary field and the dripping rain and the hot sun. God had a purpose of good, and a great purpose in allowing Joseph to be sold as a slave into Egypt; but the pit, and the sale to the Ishmaelites, and Pharaoh's dungeon did not look like good. As we look at those successive events, we are ready to say with Jacob, "All these things are against me"; and yet we can see now, and Jacob saw before he died, that the good purpose of God was ripening all the while, and that each succeeding calamity was really a stage in the growth.

We have gotten the goodness of God in nature reduced to a matter of comparative certainty, in some aspects of it at least, so that the harvest, for example, is hardly a matter of faith. But our Lord, you remember, uses the attitude of the farmer in the interval between sowing and harvest to illustrate the proper attitude of His disciples toward the development of the kingdom of God. The farmer casts his seed into the ground, and then, in the interval, while the clods are still untouched with a shade of green, he sleeps and rises night and day, in full assurance that nature will do her own work in her own time.

Faith in God involves and implies faith in good. The word "God" is "good." God is not God except He be good and do good. That we must assume in the very conception of God. And perhaps the stress of the doubt does not fall there. It is a good deal easier to believe a thing in the form of a statement or proposition or formula, or as an abstract fact, than it is to believe the same thing in its practical applications. Hundreds of people pray, ' Thy will be done," and would say, and sincerely, that it is the best of all possible things that God's will should be done; but when God's will puts itself into a thunderbolt which strikes straight down into their house or field, faith in the supreme excellence of God's will becomes quite another matter. We may believe, as I have said, in the goodness of God, as involved in His being. It is a commonplace to us that God is good. It seems as though we should as soon think of doubting the sun in heaven. And yet there come times to most of us when such a doubt becomes not only possible, but a fact: times when we cannot see the goodness of the Lord: when we cry out like Job, "O that I knew where I might find Him": when we open our arms to clasp some good, only to find them closing upon vacancy. The Psalmist has struck the real key-note here. It is not the goodness of the Lord as a matter of abstract faith at which we faint, it is the goodness of the Lord as a matter of sight. We faint because we do not see His goodness.

This fact is brought out more strongly by the next clause—" in the land of the living." That means the land which is the sphere of sight and touch; the land where the goodness of God or its withdrawal concerns us more immediately. It is the land where not only you live, trying to serve God in your living, and receiving the goodness of God with a thankful and humble heart, but where the wicked live in rebellion against

God; where sin, and its family of falsehoods, murders, cruelties, extortions, and oppressions live and thrive: where the purpose of God is working itself out through this complexity of factors known as life, slowly seeking an adjustment and a triumphant result out of the clashing of human wills, the conflict of selfish interests, the struggle between ignorance and knowledge, and between good and evil. It is this problem which troubles us. A good man is not usually disturbed about God's goodness beyond this world. He takes it for granted, indeed, that there every cloud will be dispelled and every hard question settled. It is God's goodness in the land of the living which sometimes puzzles him. The land of the living meant to the Psalmist, as we see by reading the rest of this Psalm, hosts that encamped against him; enemies and foes that pressed on to eat up his flesh; the being forsaken by his nearest of kin, and at the mercy of false witnesses and of such as breathe out cruelty. In such a land as this, if a man attempts to live by sight only, he will inevitably be discouraged and beaten. Life is a problem which sense cannot resolve. On its face it seems constantly to contradict the goodness of God. The goodness of God in the land of the living is the hard question which has persisted in coming to the surface from the time that men began to think about God. It might be comparatively easy, as I have said, to frame an abstract conception of a perfect being, and to write under it "Supremely Good," but goodness is not an abstract thing. Goodness takes shape and consistency only by contact with objects.

Goodness as a mere abstract quality might just as well attach to a statue of Jove as to the living God for any practical significance that it has. It acquires meaning only as the quality exerts itself. Men define it and conceive it only in its active relations. That goodness is essentially the contradiction of sin anybody will admit. The knotty point is, what can goodness do with sin? How are the existence and energy of sin compatible with goodness? Why sin at all where infinite goodness reigns? Once admit the existence of God, and the relation between God and life pushes at once to the front. The Epicurean got rid of the question (if he did get rid of it) by shutting God out of human life. Deity, according to him, dwelt in a remote region of the heavens, and did not concern itself with human affairs. The world and God had no connection any more than the new-born babe with the frosty peak of the Caucasus. Man was not linked to God by creation, for the world was created by the chance concourse of self-moving atoms. The Deist does little, if any, better. But to us who recognize the whole scheme of things as one, from the snail by the roadside and the stone on which he crawls, up to God upon His throne, the problem cannot be solved in that way. To us there cannot be a God and a world without links and relations between the two. The Pantheist does not escape the practical difficulty by refusing to recognize any God except the phenomena of matter and mind. That leaves him to solve the problem of this world practically by this world itself. Given this world as it is, and a personal God, and the existence and work of evil is not an easy matter to resolve. The question is summed up in a passage of that favorite book of our childhood, "Robinson Crusoe," where the poor heathen Friday, on receiving his elementary instruction in religion, and being told of God and the Evil One, asks in all simplicity why God, being all-powerful, did not kill the devil. Many of us have asked the same question—how the goodness of God is consistent with the existence and toleration of evil in the world, and have been tempted to faintness because we did not see the goodness of God in the land of the living.

And yet the fact of such goodness visible in the world and in human life is assumed by the Psalmist. He has faith in it. He believed to see it in the land of the living. Can we see as much?

In the first place, let it be observed that God does not throw us entirely upon faith for the testimony of His goodness in this present world. The goodness of God is seen in this land of the living. However hard we may find it to reconcile this fact with other facts, it is true that the world and human life furnish multiplied evidences of God's goodness which appeal to the ordinary sense. The provisions of nature, the herb for the service of man, the wonderful adaptations of animal and vegetable life to man's needs and uses in different climates, are illustrations of this. It was something more than mere ingenious artifice which made the bread-fruit grow in the tropics and not in the northern latitudes. In a tropical garden I noted one day a peculiar species of palm, the leaves of which radiated from thick, fleshy masses, and on striking a pointed instrument into one of these masses, a stream of water spouted forth, sufficient to quench the thirst of a tired traveller. That tree was not made for a land where the wayfarer could stoop down and refresh himself at wayside-springs or at mountain-brooks. The foot of the camel is made for the desert-sands, not for European highways, and the reindeer is not at home in the temperate or torrid zones.

Similarly this goodness is seen in a thousand things in the social and domestic life of men. There is the setting of the solitary in families, and the blessed ties which unite husband and wife and parent and child. There are the social sympathies which issue in organized charities. There too are the beneficent contact of minds, the evolution of thought, the provisions of the Gospel, and the institutions of religion. In the very constitution of society we may easily see infinite possibilities of good. The more we study natural social laws, the more clearly it appears that they have been ordained for man's well-being, with a purpose as definite and as beneficent as appears in the distribution of fruits and flowers and animals.

When it comes to the matter of personal experience, there is not one of us, however hard his lot, however large his share of sorrows, who has not seen the goodness of God in his life. Life has brought blows, but it has also brought balsams: calamities, but also mitigations. Labor has been offset with rest; tears with smiles. No life has been utterly bleak and barren. And for many of the worst sorrows and calamities of our lives we have ourselves to blame. They are not due to God. They have come through our refusing His goodness.

All these, I repeat, appeal to our sense. We have seen and been touched by the goodness of the Lord. These visible evidences of His goodness He has given in order to fortify and stimulate our faith at points where His dealing seems to contradict our ideas of goodness. He would make us all logicians to the extent of reasoning from the seen to the unseen. He would entrench us in the fundamental truth that He is good and means good and does good; so that when we sally out, as sometimes we must, into regions where we have to feel our way, we may always have this base of experience to fall back upon : so that there may always be roads cut by memory, and ever open behind us, leading back to the seen and felt goodness of God in the land of the living.

We must, I repeat, enter regions where we have to feel our way; where we cannot see anything that looks like the goodness of the Lord. In these we must believe to see, or be utterly confused and lost. If we once lose our hold on that first, fundamental, universal fact that God is good; if we consent to believe that fact only so long as it shall be a matter of sight and apprehension, there is nothing for us but faintness and despair; because a great many things in this world refuse to explain themselves : the contradictions and evils of society decline to furnish their own solution. If we are thrown simply upon facts as they stand for evidence of a beneficent will working among men, we must often say that they betoken a will the reverse of beneficent. A man starting out on a journey round the world, may look up to the blue sky with its sun and moon and stars, and say confidently to himself, "This sky spans the whole circumference which I am to traverse. These luminaries diffuse their light round the globe." Is he, then, the first time he sails into a mist, or the first time the blue above is hidden by black clouds, to say, "The sky and the light of the sun extend only so far as the edge of this fog or the skirts of this cloud-bank"? Does he not hold steadily by the fact that there is a sky over him with its great lights to rule the day and the night, whether he sees them or not?

Just in this steady hold lies the secret of escape from faintness and despair : just in this *believing* to see where we cannot see. According to the popular proverb, seeing is believing. Scripture reverses the proverb. Believing is seeing. Faith is the demonstration of things not seen ; and in those personal and social crises where everything seems going to ruin, if we have not faith we have nothing left. We shall faint if we do not believe. Because there is an earthquake shall I cease to believe in gravitation? I remember a land-locked bay, which, from some peculiarity or other, the tide used to leave two-thirds bare when it ebbed. It was one of the loveliest spots I ever saw at high water, but one of the most ghastly when the tide was out. I might stand by the shore and look out over the dismal expanse of mud, and say, "The place is ruined : it never will be beautiful any more." I look down into the stagnant pools, and they are glassy and motionless under the hot sun, and I say, "The tide is gone, the joy and life of the ocean come hither no more." Fool that I am. Out yonder in the ocean depths, even while I mourn, the sea is rallying, and gathering itself up to move upon the land. By and by the stagnant pools will begin to stir, and the little eddies to whirl, and pool to reach over to pool and to run into one, until soon the bay will be brimming again, and the mud-banks hidden and the fresh, living tide enfolding the rocks. There are periods of slack-water in the history of individuals, of churches, and of nations; periods of mud and stagnation; days and years without a ripple. And when the ripple begins to come, and the stagnation begins to be stirred, that which is the presage of better things often makes the prospect look uglier than before. It takes strong souls to go through such periods; believing souls, which have settled faith in the laws of God's tides, and which believe in the force when they do not see the ripple or the wave. Every time that the tide comes up, it washes away the forms of faint-hearted men who have lain down and died because they could not believe in a tide which they could not see; because they could not believe that God was in the ebb and in the slack-water, no less than in the grand inflowing. It is the men who stand by the bare shores, saying, "Hope thou in God, for I shall yet praise Him!" who are the hope and the trust of the Church and of the State in the days of weariness and desolation.

The goodness of God is a larger thing than human

goodness. It is capable of taking on a great many forms which human goodness cannot assume and which human minds find it hard if not impossible to understand. In our dictionaries we do not dare to write down opposite the word "goodness"—"wreck, sorrow, disaster, breaking-up." But you know how the skillful philologist, going below the popular meaning of words, finds their roots linked with those of other words lying far remote in the field of human speech, and will show you how a word carries in its bosom a thought of which you did not so much as dream. God's lexicon is a puzzle to the man who does not come to it with the key of faith. He assigns to words meanings which we think belong to other and contrary words: and He speaks out those words with His own meaning; utters them syllable by syllable; and every syllable is a crash of thunder to the man who interprets His speech only by his own dictionary and grammar. Faith hears a voice of love through the thunder. To faith the word which sounds "disaster," means "goodness."

Breaking-up is a not uncommon fact in the lives of good men and women. Occasionally they are thrown out of their tight, comfortable ships, and see the ships go to pieces, and have to cling to fragments or make rafts. It is hard to see goodness in such wreck as that; and yet when a ship goes down at sea, the man who has a life-preserver or a timber thinks himself happy. The question is whether we can bring ourselves to think that God is good when He transfers us from the ship to the timber: whether we can stretch the word goodness to cover timbers and rafts and life-preservers as well as ships. If we have taken it for granted that God's goodness means only a sound ship and a voyage compassed the whole way with its protections and comforts, then the wreck and the raft will come to us as terrible surprises. If, on the other hand, we believe in the fact of the goodness of the Lord, any way, ship or raft, storm or sunshine, sailing into port or washed ashore, we shall be strong-hearted and hopeful on the raft no less than on the ship. Only it is well that we take care how we build our ship to begin with. If it is to go to pieces, it is well that the pieces be strong; well that we provide something that will float when the wreck breaks up. If a man's life is put together with selfishness, greed, pride, vanity, he stands a poor chance when the structure is broken up. If he puts out to sea with only his money or his cunning or his social repute or his political or professional or business-standing under him, he will find that such timbers will not float him. They will break with the breaking of the ship. Gold sinks; political prosperity is worm-eaten; craft and cunning are knocked into splinters by the first wave. The man will go down. Faith, hope, love, are strong and buoyant. If a man has in his ship this single plank of faith, nothing can send him to the bottom. Life's currents will bear him to land alive. We freight our ships with a good many worthless things. It is none the less goodness because we do not see it as such, which compels us to throw a part of the cargo overboard. God does us the greatest of favors when He saves out of our lives only that which is worth saving; and sometimes He shipwrecks us for just this. Paul was heavily laden with rabbinical learning and with Jewish prejudices. All that was worth saving out of that mass of trash was such knowledge of his people's literature and thought as he could turn to account in winning them over to Christ. The rest went overboard and sank under that single bolt which struck him down on the way to Damascus. A notable Rabbi was wrecked and broken up then and there, but a Christian Apostle came strong and triumphant out of the wreck. It was a great change for Moses from the cool, dark halls of Egyptian temples and the society of cultured priests, to the barren solitudes of Horeb; but Israel's leader and lawgiver lives in history, while the temples are in ruins, and the literature of Egypt is a relic for learned curiosity, and the wisest of the priests and sages are forgotten.

In the light of all this we can understand the exhortations which follow in the next verse. In view of the truth that the goodness of God is an immutable, eternal, universal fact in this land of the living with all its confusion and contradiction, only one counsel is possible; and that the Psalmist gives us along with a promise: "Wait on the Lord! Be brave! He shall strengthen thine heart." To wait on the Lord is to serve Him, as we speak of a servant waiting upon us. In all the confusion and sorrow we are to be constant to duty. We are called to serve God under all circumstances whatsoever. We are to trust Him to adjust the circumstances to the service. Do you hold it as a mark of God's goodness that He calls and permits you to serve Him? Then believe that the service is good all through. You did not contract to serve God only in sunshine, any more than a sailor engages to do duty only in fair weather. You are serving God, and God will take care that service shall be a good and a wholesome thing, both in itself and in its fruits, whether it be service in the dark or in the light, in calm or in storm.

Waiting also includes tarrying. The servant waits *on* his Lord, but he also waits *for* his Lord. Remember, you and I are servants. It is not for us to say how fast God shall move, or when and in what way He shall do this or that for us or for society. God regulates His own movements. God moves at His own rate. It is for us to wait patiently when He delays. If He keeps us waiting in the dark, He knows why. If He keeps us standing still when we want to move, there is a sufficient reason for it. You and I have heard soldiers tell how, when a battle was raging, they were kept sometimes standing for hours, doing nothing except to pick up a wounded or dead comrade now and then, as a shot or a shell came over into their lines, until their impatience to charge grew almost into madness: but the general knew that the day would be won by holding that line in reserve. The hardest thing in the world is suspense, yet a servant must learn to wait as well as to labor.

He will strengthen thine heart. Not always your hands. "Even the youths shall faint and be weary, and the young men shall utterly fail." Not your position. That may be swept away from under you. But your heart. It is you God wants to save and bring through, not your position. "They that wait on the Lord shall renew their strength." The strength shall be given at the seat of the life. Under the yoke and the burden, ye shall find rest unto your souls. "Wait on the Lord and be of good courage."

> "Stand but your ground, your ghostly foes will fly.
> Hell trembles at a heaven-directed eye.
> Choose rather to defend than to assail:
> Self-confidence will in the conflict fail.
> When you are challenged you may danger meet:
> True courage is a fixed, not sudden heat:
> Is always humble, lives in self-distrust,
> And will itself into no danger thrust.
> Devote yourself to God, and you will find
> God fights the battles of a will resigned.
> Love Jesus! Love will no base fear endure:
> Love Jesus! and of conquest rest secure."

www.ingramcontent.com/pod-product-compliance
Lightning Source LLC
Chambersburg PA
CBHW022017240426
43667CB00042B/903